Snatched from Oblivion

Marian Cannon Schlesinger

❧❧❧

Snatched from Oblivion

A Cambridge Memoir

❧❧❧

Illustrated by the Author

Little, Brown and Company   Boston   Toronto

FIRST EDITION

Library of Congress Cataloging in Publication Data

Schlesinger, Marian Cannon.
  Snatched from oblivion.

  1. Schlesinger, Marion Cannon — Biography.
  2. Authors, American — 20th century — Biography.
  I. Title.
  PS2789.S53Z474   813'.5'4 [B]   78-31944
  ISBN   0-316-77348-4

MV

Designed by Susan Windheim

*Published simultaneously in Canada
by Little, Brown & Company (Canada) Limited*

Printed in the United States of America

Acknowledgments

For permission to quote from personal papers and letters, I am grateful to the heirs of members of my family no longer living: my great-grandmother, Harriet Williams Haynes; my great-grandfather, Francis Greenleaf Haynes; and my aunts, Miss Ida M. Cannon and Mrs. Margaret James Burt. I am also grateful to the heirs of Louisa May Alcott for permission to quote her letter to my mother; to Mrs. F. E. Fremont-Smith for permission to quote from Mrs. Samuel Eliot's "The Glory that was Cambridge," *The Atlantic Monthly*, September 1945; and to Mrs. Helen R. Pierce for permission to quote from Professor Pierce's letter. Thanks are due to my neighbors and friends, Sally M. Fitzgerald, Mary Nash, and Anne and Justin Kaplan, for helpful suggestions and especially to Elena Levin for her unfailing enthusiasm and encouragement.

To my sister, Wilma Cannon Fairbank, and her husband, John King Fairbank; to my sisters Linda Cannon Burgess and Helen Cannon Bond; and to my brother, Dr. Bradford Cannon, my deepest gratitude not only for their allowing me to quote their letters and writings but also for their good-natured willingness to put up with descriptions and memories of them in our childhood that I hope may bear some resemblance to the facts.

My father's autobiography, *The Way of an Investigator*, from which I quote liberally, was published by W. W. Norton and Co. in 1945 and was reprinted in 1965 by the Hafner Press, a division of the Macmillan Co.

MCS

Cambridge
October 1978

Cornelia James Cannon
Drawing by Wilma Cannon Fairbank

My mother, Cornelia James Cannon, was brought up in St. Paul, Minnesota, where her mother, Frances Haynes James, the daughter of early pioneers, lived all her life. When my mother married and went to live as a professor's wife in Cambridge, Massachusetts, she wrote to her mother every week as long as her mother lived, detailing the family doings, her letters newsy, sharp, and funny by turns.

From these letters, my grandmother, through the years, culled and copied out in her beautiful, flowing handwriting passages that she felt were most interesting and amusing, had them bound, and one Christmas sent them as a surprise present to all the family. The first volume was entitled "Snatched from Oblivion."

I have borrowed her delightful title, and am grateful to her not only for it, but for her labor of love in gathering and saving the fascinating collection of letters on which much of this chronicle is based.

Although this is a family memoir, the central figure and heroine is obviously my mother, the dynamic, humorous, tender, irresistible force that held her far-flung, idiosyncratic family together through her letters and through her vivid charm and wit.

This book is dedicated to my children, Andrew, Christina, Katharine, and Stephen, and all the rest of her grandchildren to quicken their memory of her and of the rest of her remarkable generation.

Snatched from Oblivion

~~~

chapter one

SOME TIME AGO, I HAPPENED TO RUN INTO THE EMINENT HARVARD psychologist B. F. Skinner at a gathering on Cape Cod and we fell to discussing my father, Dr. Walter B. Cannon, who had been for many years professor of physiology at the Harvard Medical School and whose student he had been. My father had been a friend of Ivan Pavlov, the great Russian physiologist, and there was some discussion as to whether there existed any photographs of the two men together. I recalled having seen in the family album a snapshot of the two men taken when Pavlov came to this country for the International Physiological Congress that was held in Boston in 1929. I promised to go back to Cambridge and look it up.

A few weeks later I was idly examining some framed photographs on the wall of my sister's house in New Hampshire and saw there an enlarged photograph of Pavlov and my father and the whole family taken against the hills of New Hampshire so many years ago. The thing that struck me was how Russian it looked. It might have been from an album from Yasnaya Polyana, Tolstoy's country estate, and used as an illustration in the biography of the famous writer. Even a clump of gray birches and the graininess of the print gave it a feeling of authenticity. Pavlov stood in the middle, his arms linked to those of my father and my ancient grandfather, who might have been an old retainer on the Tolstoy estate with his white, muttonchop whiskers and quaint air of nineteenth-century gentility, and who happened to be exactly the

2 Divinity Avenue, Cambridge

same age as Pavlov. My father, who had a wide, round face and
an expression of open simplicity and kindliness, seemed close kin
to Pavlov himself, who in turn radiated a feeling of gentleness and
high intelligence. They both had a fresh, almost childlike, "born
yesterday," air about them that is so often present in men of
imaginative genius. My oldest sister sat in front, very spiritual
and Chekhovian. As I remember, she was in love for the first time
with some forgettable young man, I suppose, and dreaming of the
world beyond the confines of rural New Hampshire and even
provincial Cambridge. The NKVD man, or whatever he was
called in those days, the official informer who accompanied distinguished Russians traveling abroad when they were allowed out at
all, lolled beside my lovesick sister, and Pavlov's son stood next
to his father. My brother, at that point a first-year medical student, in white plus fours, with his hair parted in the middle and
slicked down in an unwonted way, was obviously impressed with
the seriousness of the occasion. We three younger girls, in our
lumpish adolescence, looked as though we had just come out of
the hay fields with our sunburned faces and lank hair cut in
boyish bobs. We wore hopeless, shapeless, homemade shifts, run
up, no doubt, by our mother on the old pedal Singer sewing
machine with its lock stitch, which, should the thread snag, could
result in a complete parting of the seams. It might happen anywhere, and often did, much to our excruciating humiliation. My
mother, plump, vigorous, and pretty, with a black band around
her forehead, Indian style, her hair done in a no-nonsense bun at
the nape of her neck, and dressed in her cotton long-waisted shift,
completed the family picture. She believed in plain living and
high thinking and was of an iconoclastic turn of mind that would
have fitted in well with the teachings of Tolstoy (minus the mysti-
cism, since she was an implacable agnostic) and the mores of
Yasnaya Polyana; and from the looks of the photograph, so would
the rest of us.

Many interesting people passed through the family farmhouse
in Franklin, New Hampshire, over the years but no one more
lovable or distinguished than Pavlov. Had he stayed awhile he
would no doubt have recalled some simple dacha, surrounded by

woods and meadowlands, in his native Russia. Years later, when my mother and father traveled to Russia on the Trans-Siberian Railway from China in 1935 on the way to the International Physiological Congress in Leningrad, my mother wrote to comment on the scenery along the way that reminded her of the stands of birch and the rank fields of New Hampshire. Even the weathered wooden village houses were not unlike some of the tumbledown farm buildings falling into their cellar holes that dotted the back roads of our neighboring countryside.

It was here that we came every summer after we escaped from school in Cambridge, which as children we regarded as a place of temporary incarceration to which we were banished for nine long months of the year. Each June when we returned to our beloved hillside, it was as if life had begun again.

Our old, deserted farm had been bought by my parents in 1910 when my father was a young professor in the Harvard Medical School. They spent the vast sum of $1400 on sixty acres "more or less" (as the deeds always read) of rocky hillside and stony hay fields. The place fulfilled all the requirements they had set themselves; it had a view, a barn, and a stream, but most significant of all, it demanded enormous amounts of ingenuity and human labor to set the whole place to rights. The house and barn sat high up on a ridge commanding a sweeping view of the Pemigewasset valley with Mount Kearsarge in the distance to the west, and to the north, the silhouette of Cardigan mountain with its distinctive granite peak. There was a dilapidated orchard, a falling-down hen house, and some tottering out-buildings, and in late June fields were red with wild strawberries and bluebirds nested in the empty barnyard. The smell of the clover in the mowing fields was intoxicating and the steady hum of the bees in the hot early summer sun called up fantasies of pancakes running with honey and melted butter. At the foot of the lower field was the stream where random trout idled and, bordering it, granite ledges in whose crevices mayflowers sprouted in the early spring. The neighboring farmer's cows browsed in the boulder-strewn pasture at the bottom of the slope in front of the house and the jingle of their bells was one of the first sounds I remember as a child.

Alas, this is not where *real* life was led. That was reserved for the old house on Divinity Avenue in Cambridge. Here we lived in an extended family that would have met the requirements (or perhaps the misgivings) of modern psychiatrists lamenting the nuclear family. Nine permanent members — five children, two maiden aunts, my mother and father — and any number of transients — visiting physiologists, homeless students, neurasthenic relatives, old Radcliffe classmates of my mother, and hordes of "best friends" of my brother and sisters — made up the enormous household.

The ancient house, which belonged to the University, is still standing, still the sensible, muddy gray that was the prevailing color of all respectable arks in the old days. Like so many other Cambridge houses, it was uprooted in the late 1920s from its original site, winched on large wooden logs, and dragged by heavy draft horses across the street to a new location behind the Busch-Reisinger Museum. Some wit is said to have remarked on this peculiarly Cantabrigian habit of dislodging its domiciles, "One has to get up early in Cambridge before the houses begin to move."*

An ugly cinder-block office has been stuck on the back of the house off the kitchen and three or four generations of academic committees and bureaus have been housed there since the family moved out in the late thirties.

In a rush of nostalgia, I went to see it a few months ago, fearful that the old house might be torn down before I could once again explore it. The house looked much the same, though the presence of stark office furniture and steel filing cabinets in the downstairs rooms struck a mournful note. The dining room with its charming large bay window had been the scene of tumultuous talk and laughter in our youth. It had once held a generous dining table that had accommodated a basic family of nine and more often than

---

*Some wit was right! Since this was written, the house has again been moved to a new site, making it by all odds the most peripatetic house left in Cambridge.

not had been stretched out for the stream of extras dropping in for meals. A self-portrait of my portrait painter great-grandfather once hung over the black-painted onyx fireplace and under the bay window curved a window seat, with cushions upholstered in green velvet. There we children used to linger on Sunday mornings surreptitiously reading the funnies after my father had removed himself to sit by the living room fireplace and smoke his morning cigar. Funnies were anathema to him though as I look back it seems that nothing could have been more harmless than "The Katzenjammer Kids" or "Moon Mullins." My mother merely threw up her hands in resignation.

Beyond the dining room was the butler's pantry with its copper sink and deep, built-in drawers that used to contain geologic ages of linens: tablecloths that had not been seen, much less used, for decades; Irish linen napkins elaborately initialed in baroque script, ironed, folded, and forgotten. Topping them all was a yearly gross of embroidered runners and doilies that my mother always bought from the Armenian refugee woman, who, with the first breath of spring, arrived on our doorstep, two ratty suitcases of linens in her hands and the glint of a fanatic in her eye. She would tear her hair and wail, shedding copious tears over the fate of her countrymen, much to our fascination as children, for being little New Englanders, we were not often exposed to such emotional storms. More interesting still was the sight of my mother melting before the steamy tempest and each year piling up a new mound of *unwanted things*. *Unwanted things* were anathema to her, her philosophy being rather austere, not to say un-American; not "Do I want it?" but "Do I need it?"

To the left of the door was the long living room, which ran the width of the house. Four large windows reaching from the ceiling to the floor flooded the room with light and bookcases lined three sides. On the fourth side was the fireplace, its elaborate Victorian mantel embellished with a mirror, convenient for last-minute primping in our adolescent days. When my mother and father moved into the house in 1910, they were at a loss as to how to fill the yawning bookshelves and Dr. Crothers, the Unitarian minister, is reputed to have suggested that he lend them "a few bushels of theological texts." Whether they took him up on his offer, I don't know, but the bookcases were soon overflowing. One corner, seemingly the darkest, was given over to the children's books. On snowy or rainy afternoons, or on Sundays, when the adults were "taking their naps," we children used to repair to this cozy nook. It was often so dark on a really stormy day that we had to find our favorite books by feel. Electric lights were sparse, and at any rate, we knew where they were by heart. The Red and the Blue Fairy Books had a certain smell that identified them; the spine of the Howard Pyle Robin Hood was broken and the binding frayed; the Twin books were all in a row and it did not matter which volume one came away with, the plot and the illustrations being virtually interchangeable. The feast, though, was the volumes illustrated by Edmund Dulac or Arthur Rackham, whose *Ring of the Nibelungs*, which some indulgent uncle had given us one Christmas, fixed in my mind forever the brooding strangeness of the German myths.

At the far end of the front hall was the beautiful circular staircase curving up three stories to the top of the house, down whose mahogany banister we children slid for years from the third floor to the first in one mighty swish. No self-respecting child would have deigned to use the stairs, and I am surprised that no one was killed, or even toppled off, nor did the banister collapse under the strain. My mother, whose desk was under the stairs on the first floor, seemed to be hardened to flying bodies landing at her feet, though startled guests were often alarmed by small forms whizzing past them on the staircase. No habits were ever changed just because there were guests in the house.

My sisters and I used to occupy two rooms high up under the eaves, and when I saw them again, they seemed small and cramped. I remembered them as huge, with dark corners and hidden cubbyholes. How fearful we were of the shadows, cast on the slanting walls by the gas street lamp, of the leafless limbs of the elm tree towering outside our window and of the sound of its creaking and swaying in the wind! The floors were splintery under our bare feet and the walls were papered in a gruesome gray floral pattern left over from the previous tenants. These had been servants' rooms so naturally no provision for heat had been made. And it was bitterly cold in that great ill-heated house, when a northeaster swirled about and the snow sifted onto the floor through the window cracks, for no child could sleep with the window not open whatever the weather. Fresh air was *all*, in those days, taking the place of antibiotics, psychoanalysis, and health foods, so that the thought of denying one's child its benefits would have marked any parent as irresponsible if not criminal in his neglect. So we froze and were healthy.

When spring thaws came in late March and early April the windows would be thrown open, and if the wind blew from the west, the fetid odors of the abattoir in Brighton mingled with the delicious smell of damp earth; if it blew from the east, it carried a bizarre mix of other odors, the fat being rendered in East Cambridge at the Lever Brothers' soap factory and the tantalizing flavor of chocolate from the Necco factory in Cambridgeport. As spring progressed and the days became longer, when the six o'clock bells rang from the Divinity School's gothic tower at the end of the street, we children went to bed when it was still light outside. I used to think the lines from *A Child's Garden of Verses*, "In summer, quite the other way, I have to go to bed by day," had been written about me personally. I recall looking out from our third-floor aerie at the sun bursting through the clouds after a late afternoon shower, making the drops of rain sparkle on the purple blossoms of the lilac hedge, and hearing those bells and longing with all the keenness and poignancy of a child who has no sense of future time for the day when I should be grown up and the tolling of the bells would no longer fill me with such a sense of desolation. I don't think the bells still ring, but if they do, they could never carry for me such intimations of despair.

The varsity tennis courts were situated on the velvety green lawn that stretched away from the gothic pile of the Divinity School toward Norton's Woods, and I remember, as I grew older, sighing over the beautiful white-clad, long-limbed Apollos of the tennis team as they passed our house on sunny spring afternoons. I used to know their names, and follow their careers, and later in life, read of their deaths, respectable brokers and businessmen in old age, unaware of the swooning glances and unspoken passions that were expended on them in their youth.

From time to time President Lowell would take his solitary afternoon walk with his cocker spaniel past our house, swinging his cane as he surveyed his demesne with a proprietary air; but the traffic usually consisted of professors and graduate students, their book-filled green baize bags slung over their shoulders, walking to and fro from the science laboratories and the museums that lined the street.

Our house was surrounded by other Harvard buildings. On one side was the old Harvard University Printing Office, an elegant neo-Georgian edifice (long since demolished to make way for the William James behemoth), with its wooden platform at the back where heavy horse-drawn drays delivered enormous rolls of paper. It was, I think, the scene of my first childhood memory: a team of white fire-horses hitched to a flaming red fire wagon galloping into the staging area beyond our gray board fence. It is a memory as vivid as yesterday and perhaps foreshadowed a lifelong fascination with horses.

Just across the board fence that lined two sides of our yard was a three-story tenement housing a number of young Irish girls, fresh from the old country. They worked for a pittance cleaning the "young gentlemen's" rooms or waiting on tables in Memorial Hall where most of the undergraduates ate their meals. For some reason we children always referred to them as the "Dirty Dozens," an unattractive nomenclature bristling with childish hostility, and as I remember, we never exchanged a word with them. However, on warm spring days, we used to enjoy showing off to them as we climbed to the topmost limbs of the maple tree in the back yard. They would sit at their windows and register highly satisfactory wonder and fear at our daring but not a breath of recognition ever passed between us.

On this side, at least, there was a species of life and commerce markedly lacking in the Semitic Museum on our other side. It was a ponderous structure built of the depressing dark red brick popular with architects of the mid-nineteenth century, constructed with a variety of ledges and projecting masonry. We children used to compete fiercely with one another as to who could climb completely around the building clinging to the jutting brickwork of the ledges without falling the seeming killing distance to the ground. This was apt to be an autumn project, and if anyone slipped, there were piles of leaves to soften the fall. The museum was a place of mystery to us, its interior dark and somber as seen through the dusty windows as we clung perilously to the granite sills, our eyes peeping just over the tops. It seemed to be inhabited by enormous stone figures of animals and men with high ornaments or crowns on their heads, but it was so dim inside, with a single bulb hanging from the middle of each ceiling, that in our fleeting glances we never really got a good look. We must have been lamentably incurious children, for never in our wildest dreams would we ever have dared venture inside. It would have been as unimaginable as a trip to Persia itself. Not until I grew up did it occur to me to enter the museum, only to discover that it was just as gloomy and spooky as I remembered. The figures we had seen were indeed colossal plaster casts of Assyrian lions and Babylonian kings, and a few years ago, when I traveled to Iran and saw Persepolis, I realized that along with the others we had glimpsed through the streaked windows were huge replicas of the reliefs on the stairway of the Palace of Darius.

In recent years, the sleepiness of the erstwhile Semitic Museum was for a time rudely interrupted. The ancient building was refurbished and for some years served as the Center for International Affairs, once a realm of Henry Kissinger. During the late sixties and early seventies it became the scene of periodic bombings by anti–Vietnam War protesters, thus adding an exotic note heretofore lacking in this particularly dry and dusty corner of academia.

The Semitic Museum was just the beginning of our institutional entrapment. Across the street, the Germanic Museum, renamed the Busch-Reisinger, was peopled in its turn by a huge plaster cast of Barbarossa on horseback, an enormous stallion, with its back to the cathedral-like window, which became a fascinating bit of source material to us puritanically raised children. As if this were not enough, a compound of chemistry buildings stood opposite, and up the street the dour and forbidding Zoological Museums, whose occupants were, to be sure, genuine, if stuffed, completed the encirclement.

❧

Wedged between the Chemistry Laboratory and the Germanic Museum, however, was the only other habitation containing live, breathing householders; though it must be said that the Misses Peirce and their mother, a ramrod-backed, rosy-cheeked Scottish old lady, the widow of a professor of mathematics, were of such quaintness and such perfect specimens of nineteenth-century gentility as to be worthy themselves of being encapsulated and preserved for posterity. They lived in a clapboard house of the usual Cambridge gray full of antiques, old china, and cats. From time to time, all three would wait upon my mother, like characters out of *Cranford*, bearing gifts of calves'-foot jelly and broth in times of family illness. Whenever they came to call, there always seemed to be more noise and numbers around the house than usual, and I can remember having the feeling that Mrs. Peirce, a most gentle and proper lady, thought it rather vulgar of Mrs. Cannon to have so many children. The effect of their calls on my mother was remarkable. She, who was not particularly sensitive to atmosphere, would temper her verbal sallies with unusual constraint, sit almost as straight in her chair as Mrs. Peirce, and rather than direct the conversation, which was her wont, follow the bland lead of the unexceptionable Mrs. Peirce. I recall it was quite a strain for all of us, but of interest to see my mother cast in a role unusual for her.

Many years later, after their mother had died, the Misses Peirce, who had stayed on in the house, used to summon my father to "sniff the air for gas," which they were sure was poisoning not only themselves but their more than half-dozen cats. Although weary representatives of the gas company had already paid numberless visits, summoned from their beds, no doubt, in the middle of the night, they had found no leaks.

There was something reassuring to the old ladies about pronouncements based on evidence collected by my father's olfactory nerves. For, after all, he *was* a full professor and they were rather intellectual snobs. He was even asked to prescribe for their cats. The fact that he should be called on in the face of their knowledge that many of the experiments in his physiological laboratory were conducted on cats was discreetly overlooked, showing a touching faith in his forbearance and humanity. Even my father's reassurance that there was just as much oxygen in the air in our house as in theirs could not persuade them that it was safe for them to come to my sister's wedding. They feared that smoke from candles on the table would poison the air.

As time went on, they virtually withdrew from the world, barricading themselves and their cats from the exhaust fumes on nearby Kirkland Street, ahead of their times in recognizing the perils of pollution. But not before Miss Emily had one day rushed to my mother, wringing her hands in horror, to report that if she knelt down and peeked through one of the third-story dormer windows she could see a distinguished professor of chemistry kissing his female assistant in the laboratory across the way. It seemed to have been one of the few signs of life among our institutional neighbors and it was good to think that something besides flasks and retorts was bubbling in those austere buildings. My mother's advice to Miss Emily has not been recorded, though she was rather good at handling neurasthenic females. She understood the pleasure that both sisters took in Emily's "high-strung" and delicate constitution. It was one of the last times that Miss Emily was ever seen outside her house. As for the cats, they went on to a certain kind of fame. At one point, while canvassing for votes, I saw listed the name "Peirce, Oliver — Independent" on the voting list along with those of the Misses Peirce, all three of the same address. Oliver was indeed the old tiger cat saved from the nonexistent fumes by my father's sniffing and the first cat registered to vote in Cambridge.

❧

The Agassiz and Peabody museums were great resorts of our childhood, years before modern showcase designing had transformed museums into "educational experiences." On dreary Saturday afternoons we would troop off to look at the stuffed

giraffes and rhinoceroses in their dusty glass cases or delight in
the models of the Ute Indians' Great Hall or the undifferentiated
mélange of Indian artifacts that jammed the cases of the remote
third floor. I can still smell the pervasive odor of formaldehyde,
feel the gloom of the enormous, echoing dark rooms, and hear the
ring of our shoes on the iron stairways with the terrifying space
between each lift down which we feared to slip. They contained
(and still do) a unique jumble of treasures from priceless Mayan
gold ornaments to a stuffed dodo bird, but perhaps the greatest
prize of the Agassiz Museum was the collection of the Glass
Flowers. They were housed in ill-lit, grimy, glass cases with
unreadable Latin-German-English identifying legends, and were
visited sparingly in those days, being better known to visitors from
abroad than to local museum-goers.

My father was a research physiologist and teacher who had
many foreign students. It was often the fate of these scholars when
my father and mother would "have them around" for Sunday
dinner to be asked if they would like "to go and see the Glass
Flowers." This suggestion was always greeted by us children with
inward groans. We recognized it as a sign that conversation, apt
to be about the "exports or imports of Chile or Hungary" or
wherever the students came from, had run dry and we were about
to be drafted to conduct them through the midwinter slush and
snow whether they wished it or not.

My mother usually bore the brunt of such social intercourse, for
outside his laboratory my father was apt to be diffident and shy.
She was a woman of endless curiosity who liked a well-rounded,
concrete fact, and she genuinely wanted to know about imports
and exports and other solid statistics she could get her teeth into.
But it took me a long time to get over the idea that this was the
only form of "conversation." It was always such a relief to have
her "in charge"; no dreaded hiatuses ever yawned no matter how
boring the company. It seemed to me as a child no one could be
more skilled or gifted in the art of social intercourse than she,
though as I grew older I did think that subjects more soul-
searching, like art or music, or more worldly, like politics, might
be more edifying.

Opposite the Zoological Museums and behind the drab brick

16   dormitories where the theological students lived stood three
wooden gothic houses, their pointed gables festooned with
baroque scrollery, on sweeping lawns that were dotted with snow-
drops and daffodils in the spring. They belonged, like our house,
to the University, and therefore did not "count," in our minds, as
houses. The occupants, being academics, too, somehow lacked
validity. It was only over the back fence that the real world began,
where people lived in huge houses and had uniformed maids and
Irish gardeners; where fathers went to work downtown in Boston
and all the children were having their teeth straightened. It
seemed a no-man's-land of wealth and privilege and as remote
from our lives as the corridors of the Semitic Museum. In actual
fact, it was in this part of Cambridge that William James lived and
the families of E. E. Cummings and of the philosopher Josiah
Royce and other distinguished members of the Harvard faculty in
comfortable houses that had been built in the last decade of the
nineteenth century on land originally belonging to the Norton
estate. A scattering of lawyers and judges and a businessman or
two lived in this area, too, but as far as we children were concerned they were like creatures from another sphere and we kept
a wary eye out for their Irish maids when we climbed their fences
and sprinted through their gardens on mysterious errands that
took us through the neighborhood. It was an accepted fact that we
never walked on sidewalks ("step on a crack and break your
mother's back" was the couplet for cement sidewalks) but always
took shortcuts through other people's back yards. Once when my
nine-year-old sister Helen and a "best" friend were stopped by one
of the "college cops" on their way home from school, cross-country,
they expostulated in self-righteous indignation, "Our fathers are
Harvard professors and we can do anything we want!" This magnificent bit of priggishness was our shield against the world; it would
never do today! Nor would the remark reported by a neighbor of
another "college cop," a philosophical red-faced Irishman who used
to keep a solicitous eye on us as children: "It takes these Italians and
furriners a long time to learn that Cambridge is not a place but a
opportunity!"

Sledding on the Sachses' Hill

The only other house we knew was the beautiful nineteenth-century mansion that had been the home of the distinguished Harvard scholar Charles Eliot Norton, high on the top of Shady Hill, which Professor Paul Sachs of the Fine Arts Department occupied with his family. The Sachses were the neighborhood benefactors. Where other people seemed locked in their peculiarly reserved New Englandy lives, the Sachses brought a breath of the larger world. For they were from New York, they were *rich*, and they were generous. It was in their lovely long living room with its half-moon–shaped bow windows and its shelves and shelves of art books that we children first heard Mozart sonatas played by members of the Boston Symphony in concerts organized by the Sachses for young people. And later on, when we grew older and went to dances there, we saw hanging on the walls the drawings of Degas, Toulouse-Lautrec, and Matisse and many others long before many of us had ever heard of the French Impressionists. They are now part of the great Sachs collection of drawings at the Fogg Museum.

But when we were younger, it was much more important to go sledding on the Sachses' hill, the focal point in winter for all the children in the surrounding area, even for the "nameless creatures" from across Beacon Street, from "dread Somerville." We joyously dragged out sleds, pulling our younger sisters and brothers and joined the free-for-all.

The Sachses were the great ecumenicists of the community and it was probably only on that hill and at that time that the children from these sharply polarized groups ever had any connection with one another. I often think back to those days in these times of the ever crumbling away of prejudice and bias and remember with shame with what scorn, and even more, with what fear, we children talked about the "Somerville kids," as though they were some lower form of life. The profound division between neighborhoods and people that for so many decades seemed to be unbridgeable has lately changed. It is a question whether for better or worse. Somerville has been "discovered" by students and other young people seeking cheap housing, thus sending the rents sky-high, and I have no doubt that many of the older residents of Somerville wish that they could return to the comfortable obscurity of their leafy streets and pleasant wooden tenements free from the scourge of student intruders.

E. E. Cummings, the poet, who lived as a child in nearby Norton's Woods at the turn of the century, once wrote: "Only a butterfly's glide from my home began a mythical domain of semiwilderness; separating cerebral Cambridge and orchidaceous Somerville. Deep in this magical realm of Between stood a palace, containing Harvard University's far-famed Charles Eliot Norton: and lowly folk, who were neither professors nor professors' children, had nicknamed the district Norton's Woods."

The beautiful "palace" was torn down by the University long ago, in the name of progress, and the rolling lawns and secret fairy dells and glades that lured us as children are now choked with rank weeds and strewn with beer cans and broken bottles. A wash of blue scilla and white crocuses still pushes up through the tangle of briars beyond the tennis court where the hardy little flowers have been blooming continuously for more than fifty years under the giant honey locust trees. They were there when we took our first gingerly steps onto the court in early spring to test the clay surface, for along with their other generosities, the Sachses let us use their tennis court. I recall the short, well-tailored figure of Professor Sachs, on late sunny spring afternoons, clicking the gate to the tall white picket fence that surrounded the estate, and walking up the neatly raked gravel path to the house, swinging his cane and amiably tipping his bowler hat to us as he passed. I doubt that he knew who we were or who half the other children were who tried out their first forehands on his court, but he spread his benevolence over us all. Apple trees that once composed the orchard of the estate still bloom but they have been overtaken by a wilderness of trees and bushes. Those wild woods have no doubt been the site of many an adolescent experiment better left unexamined but they have also been a place of mystery and drama where generations of "Somerville kids" have played cops and robbers (*sic*) and hide and seek, and have "stalked game" through

20   the area in Cambridge and for many miles around, where nature
has been allowed to run rampant and where in the evening one
can still hear wood thrushes.

❧

Cambridge was full of sounds in our childhood. The seven
o'clock whistles of the factories in East Cambridge tumbled us out
of our beds on school days in the dark early mornings in winter
and the mournful moan of the foghorns of the boats in the Mystic
River channel haunted the freezing drizzle of a March afternoon.
There was a cacophony of bells and striking clocks: the old
Memorial Hall tower clock booming out the hours throughout the
day and night; the light metallic striking of the half and quarter
hours on the chimes of St. Paul's Catholic Church on Bow Street;
and other, distant, unknown bells, telling the hour at odd moments out of phase with the other timepieces in the city or summoning the faithful to mass or to vespers. The tinkle of the bells
on the harnesses of the horses dragging the ice pungs is a remote,
dreamlike memory. But the trampling sound of the hooves and the
lowing of the cattle as they were driven through the streets to the
old Brighton abattoir amidst the shouts and curses of the
herdsmen are still vivid recollections. At Christmas we sang
carols through the neighborhood in the time when windows were
aglow with wax candles and Christmas trees were often on fire
from the same source. In the spring, the groups of "Somerville
kids," two dressed up as King and Queen in gold paper crowns
and crepe-paper capes and followed by a retinue of small urchins
carrying a pole adorned with paper flowers and streamers, appeared, usually pushing a baby carriage festooned with bunting
and small American flags. In it reposed the youngest infant,
swaddled in pink crocheted jacket and bonnet, as well as the
picnic lunch, as the children made their way to a May Party on
the Cambridge Common, chanting "May Party, May Party, Rah!
Rah! Rah! Are we in it, well I guess we are! Somerville! Somerville! Somerville!" We would watch out for them each spring,
knowing that when May came, these gay little processions would
appear from their remote hinterland, celebrating some ancient

rite of spring and brightening the staid streets of our part of academia.

From my childhood, I always remember my mother best, standing over the hot-air register in the front hall of our Cambridge house, the short plump figure dressed in some shapeless, dark-colored, long sweater, her skirts ballooning out around her, an expression of sensual delight on her rosy, dimpled face as the concentrated heat poured from the furnace, which she had no doubt just finished stoking with coal and coke. Our house was always icy in winter and there was a good deal of competition for the favored spot. The hall register was the hottest, but the dining room one, depending on the crotchets of the heating system, sometimes overtook it, and I can recall the adults of the family perching like frozen birds over these delicious shafts of heat, discussing the subject of the moment from room to room, out of each other's sight but not each other's earshot.

My mother often lingered there after she had dispatched us off to school, enjoying the unusual quiet of the big, echoing house, perusing the pages of the morning *Boston Herald,* and humming slightly off-key to herself. It was the only time she was ever known to do "absolutely nothing," for she was a whirlwind of energy and for her to stand still for even a few minutes when she was up and doing would have been cause for anxiety about her health.

On one wall of the front hall, which extended straight through the house, hung a full-length rubbing of the brass of the Knight of Trumpington, his feet crossed and resting on the back of his faithful dog, showing that he had been a Crusader. My mother and father had made it on a trip to Europe in 1902 for some scientific meetings in Cambridge, England, and it represented for me something exotic, and wonderfully and inexplicably made. I can imagine now, my mother down on her knees, my father amiably following her lead, "trying out something new" as she energetically rubbed wax over the heavy paper laid out on the long brass slab of the tomb. Against the other wall, between the two doors that led into the living room, stood a low oak chest whose top had been carved by my mother in her personal style of "art nouveau"; she had romantically chiseled her and my father's initials, intertwined, in the very center of the lid, thereby assuring the imprint of the family brand on any luckless person who might sit down upon it.

A table stood by the front door, which was always left unlocked, on which the postman deposited the mail, at least twice a day in those years. My mother would leave her perch on the hot-air register to sort out the mound of mail; letters, circulars (as junk mail was called in those days), and packages for the adults; and for the children, *The Youth's Companion* and *St. Nicholas*, in which, as time went by, we would search the back pages feverishly to see whether our stories or drawings had gotten in. I think the most euphoric moment of my youth was the wonder of seeing one of my drawings actually reproduced on the Contributor's Page. Fame, at last!

After the arrival of the mail, the morning really began for my mother. She would bustle into the back hall, a black hole of Calcutta that ran from the front hall to the kitchen, in which the telephone rested on a small table, dimly lit by a forty-watt bulb overhead, the thrilling result of recently installed electricity. Needless to say, the light was turned on only when the telephone was in use, making any trip to the kitchen like running an obstacle course full of unseen booby traps, as all the paraphernalia of family living accumulated in the stygian hallway.

With a long list in hand and a stubby pencil that she often sharpened distractedly with her teeth, my mother would sit down at the phone and engage in her daily colloquy with the Manhattan Market. The Manhattan Market was a strictly plebeian establishment down in the wilds of Central Square. Whereas her decorous neighbors and friends dealt with more elegant purveyors in Harvard Square, such as Merrill's, and Conant and Stockwell, with their prime cuts of meat, hothouse fruits, and rare condiments, my mother believed that food was food; why spend money for frills? Besides, she had a large family to feed, not much money to spend, and rather despised people who fussed about their food. Among my mother's letters I found the dialogue of a skit that had been performed at one of the "Stunt Parties" which my parents and their friends used to have periodically, at which they did parodies and made good-natured fun of each other. With a bow to "Mr. Dooley," Rachel Perry, the wife of Professor Ralph Barton Perry, did a takeoff of my mother, much to my mother's delight. Cast as "Bridget" (the accommodator), she is asked, "Have you worked for Mrs. Cannon?"

"Dade 'n' I have! My, ain't she the smart woman! She has the world by the shcruff o' the neck 'n' she's busy shakin' it. 'Wat'll we be havin' for dinner?' I'd ax — 'Don't be annoyin' me with sich questions,' she'd say. 'You should have more respick fer the mishtress o' the house than be talkin' about food all the time. Lift yerself to a hoigher plane,' sez she. 'Inter more into the spirit o' this family. Ate to live, not live to ate,' sez she. 'Consult, if ye must, the Spicial Extra Edition of the Manhattan Market an' choose therefrom,' sez she, 'that food which weighs the most, and costs the least.' "

Having wound up the business of the day with the Manhattan Market after cross-examining the clerks as to the specials, she would make the beds, do the mopping and dusting of the second floor with lightning swishes, and then descend to her desk. From it she issued, every day, a flurry of letters; to her mother and sisters in St. Paul and miscellaneous other correspondents, and, depending on her most recent interest or outrage, commendatory or censorious epistles to the letter pages of the *Boston Transcript*, in its day, and the *Boston Herald*, the *Boston Globe*, and the *Cambridge Chronicle*, where for decades her peppery letters appeared almost until the day she died, at the age of ninety-three.

A long-suffering family of "colored" girls worked for us from the earliest years. When one sister fell by the wayside another would take her place, until finally the last sister, the adored Hortense of our youth, became incorporated into the family, the fixed lodestone of our daily life. Every morning, Hortense would arrive from some vague remote hinterland, Shawmut Avenue in the Boston South End. As far as our experience of life, she might have come straight from the Congo, so utterly remote was her world. We took for granted that she lived somewhere "out there," where people changed trains in the subway at Washington Street.

In fact, the Washington Street station was the farthest point of our travels; anything beyond it was alien territory, disturbing, foreign, trackless. From beyond came the dark Italian girls, their hair in outlandish beehives, the old women dressed all in black, their gnarled hands clutching wrinkled brown paper bags, talking impossible gibberish, the weary day laborers reeking of garlic and sweat, the bricklayers and plasterers dusted with white powder from head to foot, and the snarling drunks who sometimes lurched from the trains onto the subway platform.

Hortense brought with her more than a whiff of another world. Not only did she read the *Boston Advertiser* every day but she lent it to us to catch up on the latest rapes, murders, funnies, and doings of Daddy and Peaches Browning — the scandal of the moment. My mother might excite us with tales of the discovery of Tutankhamen's tomb, but we early learned where to glimpse the real meat of life — always, of course, at a safe distance. We would loll over the oilcloth-covered kitchen table perusing every scandalous word, with Hortense mildly scolding us, "Your mother wouldn't want you to read that!" as she did the family ironing with old-fashioned irons that had to be heated on the stove. She created for us a haven of fun and warmth on our returns from school each day, never complaining as we swept through her kitchen like marauding ants, eating any bread or cookies that were not carefully sequestered. On "No School" days she amiably played school with us, deserting the mounds of unironed clothes to preside over our arithmetic as we told her exactly how to behave "as teacher" in order to reproduce as faithfully as possible our daily regime. On gloomy winter afternoons, the single electric light bulb hanging from the middle of the kitchen ceiling hardly penetrated the dark corners of the room. The gas-stack hot-water heater would be lighted and rumbling next to the stove and we children and our friends would have gathered around Hortense as she got ready for dinner, teasing and bothering her to distraction, no doubt, though I never heard her complain.

At five o'clock sharp, there would be the sound of the determined footsteps and slamming doors, and through the swinging door leading from the butler's pantry to the kitchen onto this

scene of amiable chaos would debouch my mother, still bundled
against the cold, having no doubt just returned from setting some
municipal delinquency to rights. With a few well-chosen words
she would sweep all visiting children home and set us about our
appointed tasks: baths, homework, shredded wheat and
cornflakes for supper, and off to bed.

There was never any appeal in spite of loud complaints. I
marvel today over the discipline and authority she had, for there
was amazing order in a rather casual household. We never, for
instance, ever entered either of the rooms of our two maiden aunts
who lived with us unless we were invited and never used their
bathroom, which was much closer to our bedrooms and was one of
only two in the house. Besides, it had a tin tub, which as children
seemed to us deep enough to swim in, yet we would as soon have
used it as be sassy to our father.

The relationship between my mother and Hortense was as of
two equals; both were ladies. Hortense was always courteous and
meticulous with the elders and even with us. She had great respect for my mother, who in turn had great respect for her, and in
all their dealings with each other I never recall the slightest
suggestion of patronizing or harsh words. My mother never wanted
a live-in maid (there would hardly have been room), feeling that
people should have their own lives and not be forced to sacrifice
themselves to other people's lives. Perhaps she had seen too
much of it in her own childhood, the self-sacrificing maiden
aunts, the hardworking Swedish maidservants, and the homeless
hired man of her growing up, defrauded of life and gone to seed.

Newport, Minnesota

❧❧❧

chapter two

MY MOTHER WAS AN INTERESTING MIX OF NEW ENGLAND BLUE-
stocking and Middle-Western doer, with an irrepressible satiric
tongue and an intellect sharp and true, imaginative and unor-
thodox. She was not really an intellectual in the scholarly sense,
having little taste for abstraction, but she thought pragmatically
and sensibly about most of the important issues of her long
lifetime and was in the end proved remarkably prescient in many
of her conclusions. She was totally unafraid, either of ideas or of
situations, unimpressed by power or place, a free spirit, yet,
withal, a person of profound reserve.

Her roots were in fact deep in the austere rectitude of Puritan
New England, with at least four ancestors who "came over on the
Mayflower," all attested to in an elaborate family tree drawn by
some genealogically minded relative, the kind that used to appear
in families in America secure enough in the sense of their own
virtue and worth to dare to look back into the past. "We are all of
pretty royal blood," my mother wrote mockingly; "hardly an English king has been able to escape being an ancestor according to
the genealogy hound of the family." As for herself, she was com-
piling data about her "more humble recent ancestors who have no
glamor save that of hard work and honorable living, at least some
of one, some of the other."

Her grandmother had been born Harriet Williams in Augusta,
Maine, in 1827, the daughter of Seth Williams, the man who built
the first dam on the Androscoggin River. The dam, which was to

have made the family fortune, broke in a great flood and her father died at the age of forty-five of a "broken heart," leaving a destitute family, some of whom were brought up by uncles; Harriet by Reuel Williams, United States senator from Maine, who lived in a beautiful old house, standing until recently when it was torn down to make way for a gas station, with the original hand-painted French wallpaper of South Sea Island scenes in one of its octagonal rooms. His wife was unkind to his young niece, treating her like a servant, but she was unperturbed. "It takes two to achieve a snub," she used to say, and went cheerfully about her life. She had an eager mind and listened with fascination to the discussion of great affairs while she waited on her uncle's table, and read and educated herself to become a teacher.

In 1852 she married Francis Greenleaf Haynes, a portrait painter, born in East Livermore, Maine, on the farm that had been originally settled by his grandfather, Peter Haynes, who had bought a square mile of land in 1790 on the Androscoggin River. He lived the life of an itinerant portrait painter, going wherever a portrait was to be "taken," staying in the home of his patron, and often being separated for months at a time from his wife and family. It was said that while painting the portrait of a dead child in the family vault, often the mournful duty of these traveling painters, he caught a chill and became ill, an illness that turned into consumption, from which he died at the age of thirty-five. An infant son, "a noble little boy," had died of the same disease the year before. He was a man of great sweetness, who wrote poetry and played the violin and the flute and overflowed with gaiety and fun and was apparently beloved by all who knew him. Something of the sense of his untrammeled spirit is caught in his witty statement about conventions: "Well, all strange circumstances and vicissitudes arise more or less from living in a world filled with conventionalities. They compel us to do as others do, and be as tame in all our flights, and whatsoever we would do, the yarded fowls must have their time to cackle at us."

He seems to have been irresistible to women and rather a high-minded flirt, his flirtations reflected in various letters in which sentiments were couched in such lofty and spiritual terms that it would take a trot to translate them into their more earthy synonyms. There are a few portraits by him still in the family and no doubt many unrecognized ones in antique shops and auction rooms, for like so many workaday painters of the period, he never signed his portraits. One wonders whether he felt that being a portrait painter was like being any other kind of artisan, and thus did not attach importance to identifying his work by putting his name to it.

He was obviously a sensitive and remarkably accomplished artist, self-taught except for ten lessons, whatever they were, with a marked gift for likeness and in no way a "primitive" painter. In a letter to his future wife he describes his passion for his art: "Since I have resolved to learn painting, my skill as well as my painting, has been mounting up. I have had the slow fever of the intellect in the department that favors *ART*. And under its excitement have thrown off much better paintings than heretofore. Charles Weston thinks that I have equalled Badger in some of my late likenesses. . . . What if my manifest destiny should be after all to paint and paint? . . . I promise you not to persevere with *ART* unless I am far, far above mediocrity. I aspire always to the highest, and if I fail, it must be with *clipped wings*."

His last days were spent in Manchester, New Hampshire, and when he died in 1858, the Unitarian minister, a Reverend W. L. Gale, wrote in memorializing him: "In Manchester, among a population of nearly 20,000 he was, in our opinion, the leading man in all that relates to subtle insight, wit, appreciation of mind and art, and in that union of common sense with genius, which is so rare." There is a self-portrait, the face delicate and already drawn with disease, which my mother resembled in the fine line of the nose and the elegance of the nostril, and the high small bones of the cheek.

The distraught widow, with no means of support for her young daughters and herself and little help from her Maine relations, went out to St. Paul, Minnesota, where a relative who had just begun publication of the first daily newspaper, the *St. Paul Pioneer Press*, offered her work. Besides, she feared for the lives of her two surviving children, and in the 1860s, for some mad reason, Minnesota's subzero winter weather was thought to be therapeutic for a weak chest.

The New England sense of duty and hard work and the atmosphere of high-minded rectitude as well as concern for things of the mind were transported intact in my great-grandmother's baggage. But set against this rather rigorous heritage was a warm and deep sense of family, a devotion to various cousins, aunts, and uncles, an interest in the minutiae of their lives, and an extraordinary willingness to take in any stray that happened along.

Those were pioneer days in Minnesota. There were pigs in the muddy streets as my great-grandmother landed in 1860 from the Mississippi steamer that plied between Dubuque, Iowa, the nearest railway stop, and St. Paul, at that time the head of the navigation on the great river. She became the first teacher in the newly established St. Paul High School and, later, its principal, and she and a maiden sister, a seeming fixture of nineteenth-century families, rented a house and eked out their living taking in boarders. It must have been a household of real quality, for everyone who lived there became a friend of the family. There the two daughters grew up and married, my grandmother, a young lawyer, Henry James, and her sister, a successful Unitarian minister.

The family artistic gift was handed on to my grandmother, who, in her turn, helped out the family fortunes by painting and selling cards and little boxes when her husband's speculation in land, something all self-respecting pioneers apparently indulged in, went "bust" in the depression of the 1890s. A series of her charming sketches of early St. Paul, scenes of the Mississippi and of Lake Minnetonka where the family spent many summers, accurate, detailed, very much in the genre of the genteel watercolorists of the period, are now in the collection of the Minnesota Historical Society.

Part of the land speculation involved the buying of a large tract in 1887 in Newport on a bluff above the Mississippi east of St. Paul, where my grandfather built a many-turreted late-Victorian mansion, with porte cochere, barns, and stables. He hoped to made a fortune selling house lots to like-minded people who wanted to move out to the country around St. Paul and would be attracted by the elegance and class of his own establishment.

The fortune never materialized (apparently a family failing) and the family eventually fell on hard times, but the rich years of country life formed a glorious chapter in the growing up of my mother and her five sisters and brother that read like a passage out of some idyllic Victorian novel.

Transplantation to the Middle West for many New Englanders like my grandfather, who left Haverhill, Massachusetts, as a young man to practice law in his uncle's office in St. Paul, had a galvanic effect. The fact of being uprooted seemed to reawaken latent expansiveness, energy, and willingness to take risks. All things seemed possible, life was to be lived, and taking economic plunges was the order of the day. He had the optimism of a Micawber as well as his open-handedness, but for a time at least, more worldly success. He rather looked like Micawber too, being somewhat stout, with bushy side-whiskers and a habit of whistling between his teeth in a genial way as he went about his acres, conferring with the hired man, planning the vegetable garden, inspecting the horses, and playing the role of country squire and welcoming host that became him so well.

He was the head of a largely female-dominated household, most of whom would be considered today to have been premature women's libbers; his wife, a gifted New England bluestocking and born executive with a will of iron; her mother, another strong individual, intellectually vital and a great reader like her daughter, but in her old age a bedridden, frustrated invalid who lived with the family until she died and to whom her son-in-law was infinitely kind; five daughters, all potent characters; Swedish maids, the seamstress, Grandmother's nurse, the baby's nurse (there was always one in attendance for the unending stream of babies that appeared for years), visiting cousins, aunts, friends, ladies of the village, members of his wife's Discussion Club, the children's teachers, and many more. Only his son, Henry, and a Mr. Fitzpatrick seemed to be steady male familiars of the house, but even Mr. Fitzpatrick would come down on the late afternoon train from St. Paul to read Spenser and discuss Carlyle's *History of the French Revolution* with my grandmother and two other like-minded ladies. No wonder my grandfather used to spend evenings with his male relations, friends, and law partners in St. Paul playing euchre and whist (drawing rather tart comment from his mother-in-law in letters to her sister in the East: "Our friends are full of society. Well, is there not something better than this whirl? I believe in friction of mind with mind. I want 'Folks' but Society, especially fashionable society, I do not want."), or go fishing or duck hunting in the fall, sometimes taking my mother along for a treat. Being rather a scornful child, she reported on one occasion, "We had eight guns to shoot with and got only one old chicken!"

He apparently loved the atmosphere of the riotous open house in which he lived (and incidentally supported), where seldom fewer than fourteen or fifteen people sat down for dinner, and seemed to have invariably cast a benevolent eye on the hoards of relatives and friends who often came to stay for weeks and even months under the family's hospitable roof. Even my mother's invitation to "95 children to our lawn party" was taken in stride and to many of her high school contemporaries in St. Paul, the high point of their adolescent memories was the fun of going to spend a weekend with the Jameses in Newport. According to his children, their father was the kindest and most even-tempered of men, always full of projects, always ready to harness up the team to the three-seated buckboard for a picnic, sometimes driving as far afield as the St. Croix River or just taking a spin in the carriage to give Grandmother a little air.

The whole family's adoration of horses amounted almost to a mania. My grandmother, writing about her portrait-painter father, says, "he was a fine horseman, his dashing steed 'Black Hawk' [which he rode with passionate recklessness even in the last stages of tuberculosis] filled a large place in the memory of happy days; and the many horselovers in the family, of later years, may well find here, a kindred spirit!" They were always exchanging and selling (amid copious tears on the part of the children) — but mostly buying — a "spanking pair" or ponies or some colt to break to harness. The accidents that befell the various carriages and pony carts and their passengers as a result of runaway horses were terrifying and it was a miracle that no member of the family was ever killed or even badly hurt. But the upkeep of the broken spanners, torn harnesses, wrecked wheels, must have been greater than that of any modern car.

Harvard Place, as my grandfather named his "estate," out of sentiment for his alma mater, had a lovely site. In a letter to her aunt in Massachusetts, my mother described the view: "looking across the fields where the colts are grazing we can see St. Paul beautifully in the distance across the river [the Mississippi]. The clear blue sky, the misty distant hills, the quiet little village, the soft green of the fields and the darker green of the trees, the sweet clover on the front lawn, the warm winds fanning the woodbine and swinging the hammock to and fro, the sweet little birds singing in the trees, and the quiet peacefulness of the scene. I wouldn't change this place for a king's palace." This was indeed quite a concession, as there was much reading of Scott, especially *Ivanhoe*, and a good deal of swooning over knights and their ladies. In the plays, usually written and produced by my mother and her younger sister and presented in the drawing room with its convenient sliding doors, the emphasis on kings and their consorts, their offspring and their courts, was noteworthy.

The guiding hand of this multitudinous household was that of my grandmother, who in spite of her small-boned, delicate appearance, was a woman of tremendous drive and energy. She bore seven children, ran an establishment overflowing with family, connections, and friends, cared for an invalid mother and sick children (children were *always* sick in those days) — one of whom died, a death that she really never recovered from — established the library at Newport and the Woman's Club (one of the earliest in the United States), at which such subjects as "The Women's Sphere," "The Slipper in Education," and "Should the Truth Always be Spoken?" were discussed. She read voraciously, made clothes, covered furniture, saw to the planting of the flower garden and the trees around the place, guided her children's education with ideas that were way ahead of her time (learning through doing), encouraged them in writing and acting plays (she

often made the costumes for them); soothed adolescent moods,
rode horseback with a passion, carried on a huge correspondence
with relatives in the East, painted delightful portraits of her children, laid out the dead, comforted the afflicted, and generally
performed the role of Renaissance woman in the early expanding
days of Minnesota. Her description of herself is full of insight.
Writing to her sister about their bedridden mother, she says,
"Mother grows desperate every little while at being an invalid
with her tendency to extreme activity and controlling the affairs of
men. . . . It is a terrible thing — I feel for her because I think I
am growing more like her in some ways as I grow older. I am
irresistibly pressed by powerful forces to *do* and impress the world
around me with the same motive that governs me. It is heredity
and I shall try to respond as best I can while strength and vigor
are mine."

My mother was the second oldest and more like her mother
than any of the other children. As a perceptive and relentless
adolescent, she wrote of her mother: "I am beginning to study
Mama. We are very much alike in a good many ways and yet
unlike enough to lend a little spice to our intercourse and I find
her a very interesting study. She is an extremely aristocratic
woman and yet her life here is taking that out of her and giving her
the humanity of man to man that she has lacked greatly."

Her mother describes her in turn as "bubbling over with life
and spirit, she is not bad, but jubilant with perfect health and
tantalizing power, and a tongue of the keenest sarcasm." It would
appear that both had each other's measure, for this last attribute
(or curse), the cutting tongue, could be very wounding, and my
mother learned to save its edge only for fools or knaves who
crossed her path in later years.

Her aunt, who lived with the family, promised a silver watch if
"Cornelia could go through three months without teasing anyone
in this house," but, alas, there seems to have been no record that
she ever qualified for her reward. When she went to visit her
relatives in Massachusetts, a sardonic cousin sent a telegram
announcing the time of her arrival: "Cornelia will be with you on
Sunday evening at six o'clock. The Lord be with you!" But as she

was seen off on the train, there was much weeping and wailing on the part of the other children, for as their mother wrote, "They seemed to realize that all the fun of the house would go with Cornelia."

She once sent a "tidy," crocheted by her lightning though not always precise fingers, to Louisa May Alcott in Concord, the favorite authoress of the day, in whose *Little Women* and *Jo's Boys* the James girls felt themselves depicted to the life. Miss Alcott replied: "Dear Cornelia, I am an invalid and cannot write many letters, but when a pretty gift comes, I feel I must exert myself to thank the sender. The pretty tidy hangs on my chair and I lean my tired head on the roses your skillful little fingers worked so patiently for me. It was better than a 'grand speech' and it always pleases me very much when boys and girls all over the world send me letters saying they are enjoying my stories, or feel better for reading them. I have a big box full of such messages and some are very funny. One little girl wrote me, 'Miss Alcott, if you don't have Laurie marry Jo in the second volume I won't read it and none of the other girls in my school won't neither, and we will *never, never, forgive you.*' . . . Please give my respects to your grandmamma who reads to you. . . . Your friend, L. M. Alcott."

For a highly religious period of American history, the James family, who were Unitarians, took their religion rather casually. On unspecified Sundays they would take the train to St. Paul to hear the Reverend Samuel McChord Crothers preach, more for the intellectual stimulus, one gathers, than for the spiritual uplift. Dogma was anathema to the ladies of the family and the children were encouraged to read the Bible as literature rather than as scripture. They were apt to sandwich it in between lighter reading. "I read a book in the Bible whenever I finish a novel," wrote one of the girls, thereby expiating the sin of pleasure with a good stiff dose of moral uplift. For though the attitude to formal religion may have been lighthearted — "We astonished the natives last Sunday by going to the Methodist Church" — there were high moral standards exacted and a broad streak of morbidity prevailed among the older adolescent girls. One, as Senior Class Orator at her high school graduation, addressed her classmates on the

"Delights of Martyrdom." Another sister wrote to Dr. Crothers asking him if he would not preach on Death sometime.

There was much death, sickness, and tragedy on which to dwell, since diseases like typhoid fever and diphtheria carried off small children and adults in alarming numbers and with terrifying speed. But in part, one surmises, these were considered respectable and desirable emotions and showed a depth of spiritual character that was much esteemed. When it came to boys and the more carnal passions, the usual Victorian taboos were invoked. Sex was a word that never passed the lips of anyone in the family, it would seem. My grandmother wrote, "The introduction of Boys in the Christmas Week made quite a change. They [the girls] enjoyed it very much and after a little talk which I gave them on the best deportment when in the society of the boys, they organized themselves into a Band of Social Purity and are snubbing the familiarity of the Boys right and left."

The depression of the early nineties put an end to the idyllic country life of the family and for a while to the ambition of my mother to go to Radcliffe College. "You don't know how I can't bear to give up Radcliffe when I have passed the examinations — to have to stop for such a small thing as money! But it seems to be the way of the world. We shall have to teach school and be old maids before our time. To settle down as so many girls do and just wait until a husband turns up is too disgusting." She and her sisters were very definite about scorning love and such weaknesses and were all for the world of the intellect. They "pined for careers," whether as actresses, musicians, or sculptresses, and were enthusiastically supported in their ambitions not only by their powerful female relations but equally by their doting father. When my mother finally went off to college, one of her sisters wrote about their father, "Papa is so funny. He has such an exalted opinion of all his children. He thinks you must create a sensation in Cambridge. We just laugh at him."

A maiden aunt at last saw to it that my mother went to Radcliffe. Aunt Lucy, terribly crippled with arthritis and living on a small income, came out from Massachusetts to live with the

Jameses and in exchange provided the money for her tuition. She took enormous interest in her niece's intellectual progress and when she died midway through my mother's college course, my grandmother wrote to my mother, "Don't feel for a moment that you did not show Aunt Lucy all the gratitude you felt. . . . She took pleasure in all you wrote, always reading your letters first and then handing them to us. In speaking of your going to college once when I spoke doubtfully about the next year for you she said, 'Oh, I guess there is no doubt about Cornelia finishing her course,' and said it in a rather bristling manner, too, as though she wasn't to be beaten in that; a little pugnacious, if such a thought would be connected with her."

My mother's years at Radcliffe were apparently passed in a state of continual euphoria. She was one of the two or three girls from west of the Berkshires in her class of 1899 and was considered rather an exotic by her classmates because of her Middle-Western background, which she loved to describe in exaggerated detail, implying that a fresh Indian scalp was hung over the fireplace every week or so. Her enthusiasm and energy appeared to be overwhelming, for she held every office in the class, acted the ingenue in the Idler plays (the theatrical society of the college), played basketball in serge bloomers, and went with her classmates on picnics and canoe trips on the Charles River. She threw herself into her courses with the same zest, taking a wide sampling of everything that was offered, which must have suited her inquisitive and darting intelligence. She "chose the man and not the subject and in that way I became remarkably inspired!"

In the early days, Radcliffe must have been something like a superior female boarding school full of highly motivated girls eager for knowledge. They lived in carefully chaperoned boardinghouses and were not allowed to go to Harvard Square without hats and gloves. The camaraderie and loyalty of my mother's classmates were intense; even in their very old age they would come together for Class Reunions, leaning on their canes and often still wearing hats left over, it would seem, from those lighthearted undergraduate days.

The founding of Radcliffe College (originally called the Harvard Annex) in 1879 was an act in keeping with the humane and high-minded tradition of the Cambridge intellectual community.

As early as 1849 the Reverend William Stearns, after speaking of "our noble University, with its professional and scientific schools towering in our midst," wrote, "if private munificence would endow one additional school, in which our daughters could obtain advantages for improvement approximating those which our sons enjoy in the University, the opportunities for education would unquestionably be superior in Cambridge to what can be found in any other spot in the globe." But the Reverend Stearns's prophetic words seem to have fallen on heedless ears. Not until parental solicitude showed the way did the movement to found a women's annex to Harvard College become a fact.

In 1878, Arthur Gilman, a prominent citizen of Cambridge who was concerned for the higher education of his daughter, wrote a momentous letter to President Charles W. Eliot outlining his plan "to obtain the services of certain professors at Harvard to give instruction . . . to women able to pass the same examination for admission as the men," and "to offer them a course of instruction which shall be a counterpart to that pursued by the men." President Eliot's response was apparently immediate and enthusiastic. "The President called at my home," wrote Mr. Gilman, ". . . and expressed willingness that the experiment should be tried, for all felt that it WAS an experiment to graft the education of women upon the stock of a university nearly two centuries and a half of age." He was told that it was to be tried by a few ladies who were quite unorganized, so that if failure should be the result, Harvard would not be responsible, though "if success should crown the effort, Harvard should have the glory."

The seven ladies of Cambridge who formed the "Committee" to oversee the running of the new institution seem to have been far from "unorganized." All were ladies with impeccable credentials, among them Mrs. Gilman, Miss Alice Longfellow, and Elizabeth Cary Agassiz, wife of Louis Agassiz, the distinguished scientist.

The academic community in those days was comparatively small and homogeneous, and the ladies' connections with many members of the Harvard faculty intimate enough so that they seemed to have felt no compunction in going to some of them and soliciting their collaboration in their project. President Eliot made the College Library available, and the first classes were held in borrowed rooms in a little gray clapboard house on Appian Way. "Seldom if ever has a collegiate institution been carried on at such an economical rate," wrote Mr. Gilman. "It was a college without endowment and with borrowed professors. There were no official salaries, there was no heavy outlay for buildings and their care. The money was paid almost exclusively for teaching and the teachers would have been obliged to cultivate literature 'on a little oatmeal' if they had not had other means of support."

There were seven graduates in the first graduating class, and "the feeble start that . . . some doubted might not last long enough to carry its first class through its four years" had been accomplished. Commencements for the first few years were held in the parlors of the ladies of the "Corporation." By the time my mother came to Radcliffe it had been incorporated into a college named for the Englishwoman Ann Radcliffe, who had been one of the first benefactors of Harvard College; it had acquired buildings and endowments, its diplomas bore the signature of the President of Harvard College and its seal, as well as that of Radcliffe College itself. It was well on its way to "making serviceable to women the most thoroughly organized body of professors that any college for women can boast and the largest college library in America."

On her graduation from Radcliffe in 1899, my mother returned to St. Paul, inevitably, to teach; for teaching was one of the few respectable professions open to educated women in those days. With her usual spirit, she threw herself into the role. "The first day I taught, I decided teaching was my forte; the children were interested and behaved like angels. The second day I was not so enthusiastic, and on the third day, I decided to go to Montana and work on a ranch. There have been the same barometric variations since then but now I am resigned for I earn three dollars a day and

40   have lots of time to make clothes, to make the home beautiful for mother and do other sweetly womanly [*sic*] duties that fall my way." Her dressmaking was of a piece with her other lightning activities, and her younger sister Helen, at one point, announced in a tone of quiet determination, "I am going to have *one* new dress and I am *not* going to have it made by Cornelia." My mother, who seemed to have no pride of seamstressness, remarked with some mirth, "What a vista of ill fitting, misshapen garments that opens up."

She apparently caused a furor by applying for membership in the Harvard Club of Minnesota. "I thought I might as well make a test of myself so I applied for membership and the poor things have called a special meeting of the Club to consider the question." She must have presented too much of a hazard to the gentlemen, for there is no mention of her being admitted; but she must certainly have been one of the first Radcliffe women to make such an assault on the sacred precincts, a trailblazer in her own typical way.

During my mother's years in Cambridge she began to see something of Walter Cannon, then a student at the Harvard Medical School. He had been a brilliant upperclassman at the St. Paul High School when my mother was a freshman and was looked upon with some awe by the James sisters, who felt that he thought them too flighty and frivolous for his notice. Apparently they underestimated him; at least, one of them did, for my mother and he were married in June 1901, two years after her graduation from Radcliffe. My mother, after much to-ing and fro-ing, is said to have written him a note of rejection on a piece of brown paper that had wrapped up the fish, a gesture of offhandedness that she often ruefully referred to in later years. But my father, who was one of the pioneers working with the newly discovered X rays, seemed unperturbed; he offered an X-ray picture of his hand, presumably taken while it was pressed to his heart, as an avowal of his devotion, and won the day.

ॐ

In my father's autobiography, *The Way of an Investigator*, in describing his forebears, he writes as usual, the analytic, scientific observer. "Besides biological inheritance there is tradition to be recognized as a potent agency in affecting behavior. The tradition on both my father's and my mother's side was not favorable to a fixed, sessile existence. Both lines were composed of a restless folk, the men and the women ever moving into new ventures. A brief account . . . will make clear their pioneering habits."

He goes on to write that about 1700,

there appeared in the small frontier village of Deerfield, Massachusetts, a French Canadian *coureuer de bois* named Jacques de Noyon. He was a handy man about the village and in the course of this services he became acquainted with the Stebbins family. The bushranger and one of the Stebbins' daughters, Abigail, fell in love with each other and were married on February 3, 1704. Only a few weeks later French and Indian raiders descended on the village, set fire to its dwellings, killed forty-seven of its inhabitants, and made captives of one hundred and twelve others. The next day the marauders and their prisoners started on the long journey to Montreal through the winter's snow and cold. Jacques de Noyon's acquaintance with the French and the Indians had enabled him to save from the slaughter Abigail's parents and their six children; his knowledge of woodcraft made the hazardous and exhausting trip easier for them.

Many of the Deerfield captives remained in Canada; de Noyon and his wife settled in Boucherville, a village on the south bank of the St. Lawrence River, not far from Montreal. Of their many children the first, René, when about ten years old, was sent with a party of French and Indian traders to visit his grandparents who were back in Deerfield. His grandfather Stebbins persuaded him to stay and when the traders were ready to return, René could not be found. The name René de Noyon had an outlandish sound. Furthermore, the grandfather had gone to scriptural sources in naming his own children. He selected Aaron for the little boy, and René de Noyon grew up in Deerfield as Aaron Denio. Such was the origin of the Denio family in the United States.

The original name has come down through generations. One of my father's uncles was an Aaron Denio, a Colorado pioneer, and his mother's name was Sarah Wilma Denio.

As generation followed generation the Denios went north through Vermont and then scattered. The line to which my father belonged moved into the state of New York in the nineteenth century and thence west to Minnesota and on to Colorado and Wyoming. Always they were settlers.

My father's paternal ancestors arrived in Boston in 1718, as Scotch-Irish immigrants from County Ulster. Samuel Carnahan, the spelling of whose name was soon simplified to Cannon, settled in western Massachusetts and became a farmer. They were apparently "the bluest of blue Presbyterians," my father writes; "one of my ancestors was fined four dollars for swimming on Sunday!"

Early in the nineteenth century, the Cannons left the little town of Blandford, in the Berkshire hills, and headed west, migrating to the Western Reserve in Ohio, and later some of them went on to Wisconsin and Iowa.

My father writes about one of his great-grandparents, Laura Cochran Cannon, who when a girl walked much of the way from Blandford to Aurora, Ohio, beside a covered wagon:

Many stories have been told of her pioneer pluck, her good nature, and her unselfish services to the whole community. She once rode alone at night, on horseback, through miles of winter wilderness to secure needed medical aid. It is reported that the extra work done by her in one year included weaving six hundred yards of woolen cloth, one hundred yards of yarn carpet, five blankets and five plaid shawls. She bore eight children and lived to be nearly ninety years old. It is at least pleasant to think that bodily energy is heritable, as has been claimed, and that the group of genes responsible for it have had their way in some of Laura Cochran's descendants.

My father was born in Prairie du Chien, Wisconsin, a sleepy little river town on the upper Mississippi. His mother was a schoolteacher and his father, Colbert Hanchett Cannon, a railway employee. It always intrigued him that it was in this small town of his birth, the site of old Fort Crawford, that in the 1820s the American army surgeon William Beaumont, the "backwoods physiologist," as Osler called him, made his classic observations on digestion; some seventy-five years later my father was in turn to make *his* classic observation of digestion. Using a primitive apparatus of the newly discovered X ray to watch a pearl button pass down the esophagus of a goose, he was able for the first time in history to study the motor activity of the alimentary canal under conditions uncomplicated by anesthesia or operating procedure.

His mother, a highly sensitive, perceptive, and unselfish woman, died tragically when my father was ten years old, leaving a motherless family of my father and his three younger sisters to be raised by a moody, difficult father. Before she died, my grandmother called the broken-hearted ten-year-old boy to her bedside and said tenderly, "Walter, be good to the world." My father writes: "That wish was most natural for her; it fixed deeply in her son a sacred and haunting memory."

His father soon married again, and the children were brought up by a kindly stepmother. Colbert Cannon was throughout most of his life connected with western railroads and finally became superintendent of transportation on James J. Hill's Great Northern system. He "was ingenious. He invented new ways of keeping records of the movements of cars belonging to the railroad and was instrumental in developing the use of heavy engines to pull long freight trains economically, with little increase in train crews." But he was a frustrated man, having wanted all his life to be a doctor. He encouraged his son to go into medicine and his eldest daughter, Ida, to become a nurse. And at the age of sixty he threw over his job with the railroad, entered the Chicago School of Homeopathy, and like his ancestors before him moved west, to Oregon, where he finally achieved his lifelong dream, becoming a homeopathic physician, rather to the dismay of his son, who looked upon homeopathy as a form of witch-doctoring.

There seems always to have been financial stress in the home and a pervasive anxiety about money and debts, in spite of which the father spent freely on medical books, sets of the classics, and other books like those by Huxley and Darwin, which he never read but had heard were considered good reading. And the children were able to travel a good deal in their youth on passes to which their father was entitled as an employee of the railroad.

They would get on the train in St. Paul and sit up in the sooty day coaches and watch the great wheat plains of the Dakotas and Montana unfold before them, dotted with remote huts of home-steaders. They would go as far as Kalispell, Montana, the entrance to present-day Glacier National Park, where Blackfoot Indians in full regalia would lounge on the station platform. It established in my father an abiding passion for the West, which he assuaged the rest of his life by reading books on western history.

My father was an indifferent student and at the age of fourteen, his father removed him and put him in the railroad office where he worked for two years as a timekeeper. This experience at a youthful age seems to have had two effects. For one thing, it made him fanatical about time so that for the rest of his life he was compulsively "on time," consulting his watch in an access of anxiety should he be even moments late. For another, he returned to school and never looked back. He was valedictorian of his high school class and at the urging of his English teacher, Miss May Newson, he applied for and was admitted to Harvard College, from which he graduated in 1896. Miss Newson had rather a record of sending able students to Harvard and President Eliot told the admitting office to "accept anyone that May Newson recommends." His father gave him his railroad passage and $100 and other than that he worked his way through college with scholarships, tutoring, or waiting on tables at some long-forgotten club called the Fox Gold Club.

He always came home to Minnesota for summer vacations and visited his mother's relatives in the little town of Elba on the family farm. He would get off the stage at the top of the hill and run down to the old homestead lying by the White Water River. He mingled so easily with the simple folk of the village, was so friendly and genuine, that one neighbor is reported to have said, in obvious approval, "You'd think he ain't had no education."

While still in high school, he passed through a fundamental intellectual crisis, a falling away from the strict Calvinism of his upbringing as the result of interest in reading of the controversy between Huxley, the Bishop of Peterborough, and Gladstone as to the foundations of Christian doctrine. His inner turmoil finally drove him to the confession that he no longer held the views accepted by members of the Congregational church, which he had joined, and he withdrew. When the clergyman in the church, to whom he went for counsel, wanted to know what right he had, as a mere youth, to set up his opinion against great scholars supporting the church's doctrines, his response was typical. As he said, "This appeal to authority did not impress me at all, because I knew that there were great scholars in the opposition. Furthermore, I had the feeling that I was entitled to my independent judgment." Independent judgment was his hallmark; judgment based on a meticulous, thoughtful investigation of the facts, no matter where they led, which typified his long and fruitful life as an investigative scientist.

Harvard College was a new experience: listening to lectures and having to take notes. My father tells a funny story about sitting next to a battered football player in one of his first classes and turning to him for advice as to what to put down in his notebook. "He growled back *sotto voce*, 'Wait till he says something loud. Put that down.' " His college career, after a slow start, ended successfully, as he graduated summa cum laude and went on to the Harvard Medical School, where, when he received his M.D. degree in 1900, he was offered an instructorship in physiology at the Medical School. In 1906 he succeeded Henry P. Bowditch as George Higginson Professor of Physiology, an appointment that continued until he became professor emeritus in August 1942.

His student years were a period of great intellectual excitement, during which he was attracted by various intellectual disciplines. He describes some of his most influential teachers, among them William James, whom he found fascinating in the freshness and constant unexpectedness of his ideas and the phrasing of them. "In my eagerness," he writes, "to take much of knowledge as my province I was attracted at one time toward philosophy. I recall walking home with Professor James after one of his lectures and at the end of our talk confessing my inclination toward philosophic studies. He turned on me seriously and remarked, 'Don't do it. You will be filling your belly with east wind.' The remark probably sprang from his quick recognition of my lack of fitness rather than from his disdain of philosophy. What ever the reason for his advice, I followed it."

There is a studio photograph taken of my mother and father on their wedding trip, supposed to be in imitation of a bucolic bride and groom. As my mother said, "Too successful to be wholly imitation!" It must have been posed for toward the end of their strenuous honeymoon, after a canoe trip down the St. Croix River to the Mississippi. In their birchbark canoe and with their "fiery sunburn and general dilapidation" they were often taken for Indians by the clam-diggers looking for pearls, the lumberjacks, and the peaceful fishermen along the way. "I am taken everywhere for a squaw," my mother writes. "Walter says it is because I do all the work, but I ascribe it to my looks." At one point when my father went ashore at a tiny hamlet to get some information at the local store, an old German sitting there took the pipe out of his mouth and asked, "Dot your woman?" My mother reports, "When Walter admitted the fond impeachment, he asked, 'Goin' back harvestin?' "

On the ubiquitous railroad passes supplied by Grandfather Cannon, they finished their honeymoon by traveling west to Montana, to the present site of Glacier National Park. There they climbed the previously unclimbed 10,000-foot Goat Mountain at the head of Lake MacDonald, my father galvanized into action by the manic energy of his irrepressible bride, who was determined to be first up. Neither of them had ever climbed a mountain before, but with the aid of a French Canadian guide named Comeau, they overcame various vicissitudes such as rock slides, snowslides, and sheer rock walls, and by following mountain-goat trails and seeking narrow ledges along which they could creep, they reached the summit. My mother preceded the two men and announced on their arrival at the top, "This is Cannon Mountain!"

On their way down they crossed the path of the U.S. Geological Survey team that had been laying elaborate plans to climb and map the mountain. Some years later they learned that word of their ascent had been reported back to Washington and that the stunning peak had been rechristened Cannon Mountain.

So imbued with the tale of this mountaineering feat were we as children that it proved to be something of a psychological hazard in my adolescence. I too must climb a mountain on my honeymoon. It was an axiom, a prescription for a happy marriage. But how to fulfill this destiny? Decadence had set in. The next generation was lazy and self-indulgent; potential fiancés preferred sedentary pursuits: card games, movies, reading, sitting around, an idle game of tennis from time to time, anything but reckless adventuring. Besides, all the mountain peaks worthy of the name were long since climbed, the quarry of those physical types that I snootily considered "less highly evolved" than we "intellectuals" (I speak for myself, for my sisters were more generous-minded). It was a great relief to figure out a whole new set of criteria for marriage based on more worldly if less worthy principles.

First Church, Unitarian, Cambridge

chapter three

THERE WAS NOTHING NUCLEAR ABOUT OUR FAMILY. TWO remarkable maiden aunts, my father's sisters, lived with us through our growing-up years so that we were that rare occurrence in nature, children with *three* mothers! Mothers have come in for a lot of criticism of late; either smothering their children with concern or possessiveness, or neglecting them for a career, but, having had three "mothers," I can report that one cannot have too much of a good thing. There was always someone to bind up our wounds; the baby-sitting problem never existed; and if one of them was preoccupied, there was always another to read aloud, play Parcheesi, or just "be interested."

There was good reason that the aunts might be tired or preoccupied. My Aunt Ida was chief of the Social Service Department of the Massachusetts General Hospital for thirty-seven years and founder, with Dr. Richard Cabot, of medical social service in this country. My Aunt Bernice was head of personnel training at Filene's store for many years until she opened her own children's shop in Harvard Square in the late twenties, which became a Cambridge institution. But to us children, they were Dada and Beecie, childlike names by which we called them throughout their lifetimes. To the uninitiated, those pet names must have sounded queer from our middle-aged lips.

My Aunt Ida had been trained as a nurse in Minnesota, after graduating from St. Paul High School in 1896. My sisters and I remember her vivid stories of her days as a student nurse when

50   she had to care for a ward of twenty patients during a typhoid epidemic and her tender memories of the pathetic feebleminded children that she worked with, the year after she graduated, at the State School for the Feeble Minded at Faribault, Minnesota. She was a natural "taker-carer" and when we were sick as children, to have Dada present, usually after a hard day's work, with her cool gentle hands and total attention, was a tonic in itself.

As a visiting nurse for the St. Paul Associated Charities in the river slums of St. Paul, on the flats where the poor Swedes and Germans lived herded together in "Swede Hollow," not only did she become acutely aware of the evil effects of illness when added to poverty, but also she recognized that medical care was not meeting the needs of the poor. She saw how little was known about the patients outside the wards when they were dismissed from the hospital, often to return to overwhelming family problems, drunken husbands, senile, helpless parents, children to care for, not to speak of unheated houses and insufficient food and clothing. She realized that medicine and nursing required better understanding of the social problems of illness and her experience had shown her the often mechanical nature of care in large hospitals and the rigidity of nursing training. She also realized that social workers, being closer to the patients over a longer period of time, were in a better position to bring a kind of understanding and help that neither nursing nor medicine could supply. The working together of these three elements was the basis on which medical social work was founded.

At one point after my aunt had suffered an unhappy love affair, my mother, who always "wanted to do something about an impossible situation," prevailed on her to come east to attend the newly opened School for Social Workers in Boston, inviting her to live with the family. It was in the first year of her stay that her path crossed that of Dr. Cabot. She had gone with my father to Professor Royce's home one autumn evening where "a small group of young people met occasionally for discussion of philosophical subjects, among them our friends Ralph Barton Perry, Ernest Southard and Robert N. Yerkes." She goes on to recall:

Directly in front of Prof. Royce was a fair-haired young man, sitting on the edge of his chair and taking vigorous part in the discussion, head tilted to one side and very positive and alert. A few days later, I saw him again, at the opening of the then new buildings of the Harvard Medical School; he was leading the chorus of young medical men, with great energy and enthusiasm. Not long after, while attending a Massachusetts State Conference of Social Work in Worcester, I was a bit surprised to see this same young man on the platform, and to hear him tell of his first year's demonstration of social work at the Massachusetts General Hospital. The program told me that he was Dr. Richard C. Cabot. Coming so recently from the Middle West, I was too unsophisticated to appreciate the name Cabot! But I did recognize that here within my experience was a new kind of doctor and that he was expounding an idea that seemed to me the answer to my vague misgivings and desires. He was presenting the idea of social service *within* the hospital, where sick patients, although separated from their home and families, nevertheless cannot separate themselves from their personal problems.

Dr. Cabot was apparently the most approachable of men and after the meeting my aunt spoke to him with appreciation of his talk about his new work. His swift response was, "Why don't you come and work for us?" She murmured something about being a full-time student at the School for Social Work, but Dr. Cabot brushed such remarks aside and turning to his assistant, Miss Farmer, said: "Miss Cannon is coming to see us on Saturday." As my aunt recalled, "And on that Saturday I did just that! And I stayed for thirty-nine years."

It was an eminently workable collaboration. Richard Cabot was exuberant, confident, and creative; also somewhat quixotic and forever off on tangents. My aunt was wise and steady, full of humor and warmth, and with a delicate grasp of the intricacies of administering medical social work as a new service in an extremely conservative hospital. She was willing to go slowly in order to achieve her long-range goals, steering her way through the complexities of a medical institution peopled by egotistic, hidebound physicians and a nursing staff equally tied to traditional ways of doing things.

But we children knew nothing of all this. It was a great treat on a spring vacation day to visit Dada in her tiny office to the right of the entrance door to the hospital. It was always strange for us children to see our aunts "at work." We habitually thought of them as belonging to us, our own private fairy godmothers, so that seeing them transformed into executive figures presiding over offices and staffs was a queer experience. We would find our Aunt Ida, looking much the same as she did at home, her thick brown hair coiled in a braided halo around her head, her pince-nez glasses pinned to her dress, and around her neck, suspended on a gold chain, a tawny piece of amber that she had bought in Sicily on a trip to her beloved Italy. It was her talisman and ours, a source of unending curiosity to us children, for when she let us rub it briskly it became electrified like a magnet and would pick up small pieces of paper or bits of straw.

Her modest desk would be heaped with books and pamphlets and overflowing with letters and reports and yet there was a kind of basic order about it. Nothing seemed to be "scheduled" about my aunt's office, her staff coming and going informally, exchanging ideas, and discussing problems in the easy atmosphere she created. The walls of her office were covered with photographs; of physicians that she worked with, of social worker colleagues, and an especially poignant picture of an immigrant mother standing on the grass outside the hospital peering up at the windows of the ward where her child lay quarantined for infantile paralysis. There was a reproduction of the Giotto fresco *St. Francis Feeding the Birds* and directly over her desk a reproduction of the drawing of the dodo bird from the original illustration for *Alice's Adventures in Wonderland,* with a quotation under it, "The best way to explain it is to do it." My aunt loved to refer to it as symbolizing the pioneer days of the Social Service Department. "We had to work our way into our thinking," she wryly remarked.

For a child, a visit to the Massachusetts General Hospital was an overwhelming experience. It was a kaleidoscope of visual and sensory impressions: the pervasive smell of ether and carbolic; the sweepers and cleaners, worn old men and women with their mops and brooms, creeping along the corridors in their dreary, shapeless dusky apparel; the patients stoically waiting their turns on the hard wooden benches lining the mournful red brick hallways — a poor Italian mother with a sick baby in her arms, old men in depressing gray hospital wrappers drooping in their wheelchairs, a senile old grandmother, speaking no English, tenderly watched over by a distracted son, the anxious and the resigned, wordlessly huddled together. There were the student nurses, so purposefully rushing through the halls, in their black stockings and starched white pinafores over their blue uniforms; the registered nurses in gleaming white, their elaborately starched and fluted cupcake caps with black velvet ribbons placed upside down squarely on top of their heads; and the lordly doctors, in long white laboratory coats, with stethoscopes draped around their necks, exuding an air of confident superiority. I remember my aunt introducing us to the Head Nurse, who had an office next to hers. She was a formidable major general of a woman, her MGH nursing pin firmly placed in the middle of her ample bosom, with a ramrod stance and eyes as cold and sharp as an eagle's. I thought her a terrifying figure but I did not learn until many years later that she had been a thorn in the side of my aunt, feeling that the Social Service Department was poaching on her territory and had no business being in the hospital at all. The hostility of the nursing staff and the antagonism of the doctors were formidable problems in the early days of my aunt's stewardship but with her usual tact, confidence, and humor she guided the evolution of the department until after fourteen years, in 1919, it finally became an integral part of the hospital, on the wards as well as in the Outpatient Department. It was typical of the bigness of her spirit and her intelligence that she used to say, "I have always maintained that some skepticism was good for us. . . . Out of acute awareness of our critics we evolved some of our soundest principles."

Visiting my Aunt Bernice's office in Filene's was quite another matter. Dressed in our so-called best, usually going two at a time as that seemed to be all the traffic would bear, we would take the subway to Washington Street, get off and run up the steps to the main store, where we would rather proudly ask the elevator man for the seventh floor. We would walk through a congeries of small offices to my aunt's, behind that of her secretary, looking out on Washington Street. To have a secretary at all seemed extraordinary and being ushered in by her to my aunt's office was intoxicating. My Aunt Bernice's office was in marked contrast to my Aunt Ida's. A large executive mahogany desk shone with a great sheet of glass on top, with no messy papers or unanswered letters lying about. The wall was lined with filing cabinets, the books in the bookshelves were all concerned with "Management" and "Retailing"; and a single *executive* photograph of *Her Boss* (by Bachrach), conventionally framed, hung on the wall. Sitting in the middle was a most unexecutive-looking aunt. She was plump and round-faced, with pinch glasses over the kindest brown eyes, her hair parted in the middle and coiled on the top of her head. Her voice was soft and low with a slight touch of anxiety in it, as though she was worried as to whether her plans for our visit would work out.

She was a planner and liked to have things orderly and neat, but if they were not, her impulse was not to repine but do the best to tidy up the situation. It was characteristic of her that in the summer, when the family was away in the country, it was she that gave the house an old-fashioned "spring cleaning," causing my mother to reflect on her own housekeeping. "The house is spotless. Nothing very definite has been said, Beecie fears my wrath at her nobility but I gather she has washed all the woodwork herself. She feebly protests that it was good exercise for her and that she needed it but I cannot help ascribing it to the ideals of housekeeping which she finds an unknown matter to her careless sister-in-law." In fact, my Aunt Bernice used to say that when she was depressed she liked to "get down on her knees and wash the kitchen floor." It always made her feel better!

A sense of decorum prevailed about her office and her person in her job. It was "Miss Cannon" this, and "Miss Cannon" that, by her assistants, who were, incidentally, devoted to her, for she was meticulously fair and even-handed in her dealings with people. After much ooh-ing and ah-ing by the same assistants over the ragamuffin nieces, with perhaps the slightest note of sycophancy to please their beaming boss, we would take the elevator to the eighth floor and the restaurant. Going to a restaurant was a heady experience. There was no McDonald's in those days; children had their cornmeal mush and were sent to bed. The idea of eating out and choosing *anything on the menu* was a once-a-year-experience and it invariably took place in the Filene's lunchroom. When we were faced with the menu, however, our natural timidity and fear of impoverishing our kindly aunt reasserted themselves, and instead of ordering the "De Luxe" luncheon that had our eyes popping out of our heads, we would settle for a sandwich and a chocolate milk shake. Then, having worked our way through some indescribably rich dessert, we would take the elevator to the children's department, amid the usual "How do you do, Miss Cannon, and these are your nieces!" There we were allowed to pick out one garment, usually a sweater, which was charged to my aunt. For years I used to think that she merely had to wave her hand and anything she wanted was hers for the taking. Innocent child! But it was pretty exciting to have a piece of clothing *not* bought by my mother, who never got above the Filene's Basement level.

My Aunt Bernice had also come east from St. Paul, at the suggestion of my mother, who felt that people should get out of their ruts and "have new experiences." She went to the Prince School for Merchandising and for many years after that carried the heavy responsibility of her personnel training job at Filene's.

When my father and mother decided to move into the big house on Divinity Avenue in 1910, the two aunts joined them, helping to pay the rent, $100 a month for all the twenty-seven years they lived in the house.

❧

Two large square rooms on the second floor belonged to my aunts and each resembled its owner in much the same way that their offices did. My Aunt Ida's room poured with sunshine. Her bookcases overflowed with books until some had to be stacked on the floor: poetry, plays, memoirs, secondhand volumes picked up in her pokings through Charles Street as she went back and forth to the MGH; a majolica plate, Florentine boxes from Carbone's, a bit of Italian brocade tacked to the wall with a della Robbia angel hung against it, a print of Leonardo da Vinci's drawing *Mother and Child*, and a foamy shetland shawl across the back of her worn chaise longue. Letters, old photographs, papers, crammed every pigeonhole in her antique desk and a framed poem by Edna St. Vincent Millay hung over it, bracketed on each side by children's drawings. Sundays were often given over to cleaning her room, a futile gesture, since after shuffling through the piles of correspondence and snapshots she could not bring herself to throw anything away and merely transferred them all from one box to another and pushed them under the bed for some future confrontation.

For some reason or other, the furniture in my Aunt Bernice's room always seemed too high for her. She was a passionate collector of American antiques with a good eye for quality and line, not necessarily for size. Since she was rather short and plump her high four-poster bed with its elaborate canopy required a two-step stool for her to climb into it at night; it was as hard as a rock, a good solid horsehair mattress being de rigueur. (No one ever suffered from back ailments in our family. All the beds were like granite.) Her pretty Sheraton desk was too tall so she had to pile two cushions on her straight Chippendale chair. Even her bureau, with its curved front and always shiny brasses, seemed uncomfortably high, and the glass in the mirror, equally antique and rare, was so wavy as to give out a bizarre reflection. She could scarcely read by the light of the whale-oil lamp, to be sure wired for electricity as a bow to modernity, because the charming parchment lampshade let hardly any light through. But all was authentic, which is what mattered to her; comfort was secondary. Even her room, which was north-facing and dark, was apt to be uncomfortably cold in winter, because of the quixotic behavior of the hot-air furnace.

Whatever her room may have lacked in bodily ease was compensated for by the warmth and sweetness of her person. Whenever the household became particularly overwrought or ennui overcame us children, she used to ask my younger sister

and me to come to her room where she would read aloud "Doctor
Dolittle" by the hour, in her soft, gentle voice. She seemed to
embody the very lineaments of the dear Doctor or of Prince
Bumpo or any of the retinue of animals. That she should have
gone on to run her own store for children in Harvard Square
seemed the appropriate fulfillment of the role of universal aunt to
all children that she filled for us.

❧

My Aunt Ida was eclectic in her friendships, rather "fancy" in
her tastes, according to us children. We took our cue from our
mother, who believed, in an inverse kind of snobbery, that the
common people were somehow worthier and more interesting than
people of fashionable society. Yet her use of the word "common"
could carry with it the most scathing derogation; it was an
aesthetic pleasure to hear her fling out this ultimate denunciation
in her analysis of some hapless though probably deserving victim.
In fact, she found it hard to make up her mind, on the one hand
writing, "It is lovely to have a home which can be the refuge of
outcasts, isn't it?" and on the other expressing boredom at "worthy
but ordinary" relatives that turned up on her doorstep. At any
rate, worldliness was to be despised and she somewhat scorned
my Aunt Ida's liking for the aristocratic "Lady Visitors" with
whom she worked at Massachusetts General Hospital and her
other grand friends.

My aunt seemed to attract overwrought hysterics of a certain
age who must have recognized her strength and her appreciative
enthusiasms. I remember two arty, "highborn" sisters who became her protégées. They were very a la mode for the twenties,
swathed in the fashion of Isadora Duncan in purplish hand-dyed
chiffon and ropes of beads, with a faintly unwashed, musky air
about them. It was a period in which patriotic anniversaries were
celebrated by grandiose outdoor fetes and the sisters would
periodically dream up ethereal and unproduceable pageants to
memorialize some historical event, involving cavalcades of
horses, hundreds of extras, and scenery on the scale of the Baths
of Caracalla. However, they were not so rarefied in their thinking

that they did not recognize a good thing when they saw it: the exploitable child labor of the Cannon family. We were amazingly meek and were forever being drafted for their wacky schemes, which never seemed to come to anything. We finally saw the light and struck when they suggested what "fun" it would be in preparation for one of their impossible productions to clip a large field of grass with hand scissors.

Because there were so many of us and we were comparatively "poor," we were the objects of charity (or the dumping ground) in the way of hand-me-downs from my Aunt Ida's friends. It turned out to be quite a bonanza. Once a year, Mrs. January, a vivid and spirited gentlewoman from St. Louis with glorious Titian red hair piled like plumage on her head and with the manners of a duchess, would swoop down upon my Aunt Ida, bearing in her baggage three or four French dresses with the labels of Patou or Molyneux still sewn in the seams. My mother may have despised the worldly but I can recall dressing up in these overlarge gowns and feeling like some kind of tsaritsa; the exquisite feel of the pure silk chiffon, the detail of the hand-lashed seams and the hand-rolled hems, the sensation of style and elegance, did not escape my burgeoning adolescent senses; after a diet of Filene's Basement, it was like tasting caviar for the first time.

Mrs. January's visit would electrify the whole household. My aunt would move out of her room and sleep in the sewing room; there would be much tiptoeing and loud, penetrating "shushing," as breakfast trays would fly up and down with fresh orange juice and toast wrapped in napkins, an unusual occurrence except in times of dire sickness; and we would be allowed to watch Mrs. January ironing her stockings, which seemed somehow the height of class.

My Aunt Ida had many foreign visitors, for social workers from Europe and the Far East came to see what was being done in their field at the MGH. Many of them became her close friends — among them two charming Englishwomen, Miss Ann Cummins and Miss Cherry Morris, Head Almoners (social workers) at St. Thomas's Hospital in London. "Almoners" seemed to us children a very strange title for them to bear, suggesting some form of rich bonbon. It somehow did not fit their tweedy, rosy-cheeked, sensible-shoed, fluty-voiced personas. They would often visit Aunt Ida in her "Little House" on a hill near ours in Franklin where, as my mother observed rather disapprovingly, "they were waited on by inches," after which my aunt would return from her vacation "only a little more tired than when she went away. I fear that she is a slave to her friends as well as to her family and nothing can be done about it."

The strain put on good manners and family meals by my Aunt Ida's guests was formidable: conversation at table proceeded at a moderate pace, with children waiting to be spoken to by their elders rather than the other way around, which too often occurred; the quality of the food was upped, though my mother thought it an unworthy gesture "since our simple food should be good enough for anyone." But she knew it would please her rather nervous sister-in-law and did her best. Even her verbal sallies were suppressed lest she discomfort genteel sensibilities. Even so, on her guests' departure, my aunt would take to her bed with a sick headache, and the rest of us would return to our bad habits with relief. But it was always a good exercise in what has come to be called "consciousness-raising," that the possibility for exemplary behavior lies in all of us.

When my Aunt Bernice had her friends "from Filene's" come for dinner it was a different story. Life was comported in the everyday way; they were treated like family, and had to take pot luck and the usual confusion. It must be said her colleagues were not of the attenuated ilk that we expected from our Aunt Ida. Some of them were buyers or saleswomen for the store; some, managerial types with whom there were earnest discussions of "sales techniques" and "personnel policy." They were comfortable guests. No big effort had to be made to entertain them as they laughed excessively at the mildest jokes. Even my mother's outrageous broadsides, which she often exploded in order to enliven the dinner table, were not embarrassing because no one reacted one way or the other.

There wasthe dour, jowly, bushy-browed Mr. Thomas, who was a buyer of men's gloves and socks (dark and depressing objects that seemed to suit him) for Gilchrist's; he used to come to dinner from time to time when he was advising my aunt on "inventory" and "cash return" after she owned her own store in Cambridge. He would sit in utter silence while the talk boiled around him, looking neither left nor right, eating his food dutifully, and never cracking a smile. I often wondered what he made of the household and couldn't imagine what this cipher could tell my aunt that she did not already know. They would withdraw to the music room after dinner where he would tot up figures, do averages, list outlays, and "advise" my aunt, who for some reason or other was always modest and deferential before men whom she considered to be "experts," though she was smarter by far than most of them. Considering the fact that my mother supposedly had a penchant for the common people, she always rather sniffily put Mr. Thomas down as "ordinary."

Every spring my Aunt Bernice would have a party in the back yard for "the girls" in her department, where they would disport themselves in the rustic "Summer House" in the corner of the garden, play baseball, or swing on our swings. Only lemonade and cookies were served in our strictly nonalcoholic household (incidentally, Prohibition was in force), but nothing stronger was apparently needed to send the ladies into an ecstasy of laughter and song. The walls of the Semitic Museum would ring with the sound of "Yes, We Have No Bananas"; not the usual fare of Divinity Avenue or of the passing Divinity students who viewed our household with some alarm and perplexity. My Aunt Ida once met a former Divinity student who had lived in the dormitory at the end of the street, who when he heard that she lived at 2 Divinity Avenue said, "Oh, but I thought that was an orphan asylum."

Neither aunt ever married. Whatever their private emotions may have been, and they no doubt were deep and often troubling, there were never any references made to past romances or current possibilities. Not only would this have been a gross invasion of privacy, but, in fact, the honorable role of the career woman was taken for granted.

My mother, who admired and loved her sisters-in-law and who must have sensed a certain deep undercurrent of frustration and sensitivity on the subject, once wrote about the pros and cons of marriage with the picture of my two aunts obviously clearly in mind:

I have no sympathy at all with people who look upon it [marriage] as a social "duty." The whole theory of women existing to people the universe is absurd. What is the use of the world anyway and what possible obligation is there to keep it going? Instinct pushes us so that we *do* people the world and the whole scheme of things keeps going, but I see no place for obligation. To make the world as pleasant a place as we can for those in our midst is only decency, and to those women to whom family life presents itself as desirable, well and good, but it is not the only way of happiness nor of the upbuilding of character [the New Englander speaks!]. Some of the noblest women I have ever known never were married. It seems to me evidence of our advance from savagery that this implies not the slightest slur on their womanhood. I should like to ask in turn why is the unmarried woman so often more interesting than her married sister? So many bright girls who become wives and mothers settle down to being brooding hens of no interest and of use only to their ugly ducklings. All the sparkle gone and the primitive passion of the female absorbing the person . . .

This sounds like the 1970s but was actually written in 1909.

For my Aunt Bernice, whose nature was placid and utterly giving, adjustment to the life of spinsterhood seemed equable and serene. She did not ask for things for herself and had the capacity to pour out her affection and warmth without demanding emotional response in return. She knew who she was and in her loving way achieved a fulfillment that brought happiness to herself and to all who touched her life. I never remember her saying a mean or cutting remark about anyone. But if anyone were dishonest or unfair with her or in circumstances in which she was involved, she was unbending in her principles. Dishonesty and unfairness made her literally sick.

My Aunt Ida was a more complex and passionate person who I think felt throughout her long life that she had been cheated by never having married and had children. But she took us as her children and we were in luck. All the imagination and generosity of her nature she lavished on us or on the "little people" she befriended. She drew around her the halt, the lame, and the blind like iron filings to a magnet; the Italian shoemaker at the corner of Blossom Street near the hospital whose wife was dying of cancer on the ward of the MGH; or crippled Mary, who sat in her wheelchair in the crumbling family home in Medford making enchanting miniature "fairy gardens," and whom Aunt Ida supplied with moss and butterfly wings and dead dragonflies from Franklin for her tiny fairy figures.

There was a positive pleasure in being sick, for she could not resist "stopping in" at Amees' to pick up a puzzle or decalcomanias on her way home from work, or bringing a bunch of spring flowers from Becker's greenhouse on Cambridge Street; "just a little present" to make the sore throat feel better. She was so extravagant in her generosity that my mother, who was prudent and not given to gestures, always worried about her finances for her sake, especially since she was miserably paid all her working life. "You'll send yourself to the poorhouse, Ida, with your dear generosity," she used to say, even though she knew it would make no difference.

And so we were reinforced to a fare-thee-well by three "mothers." However, the burdens of being an aunt seemed to have made a strong impression on me as a child, for I am quoted as having remarked, "I want to hurry up and get married before someone gets me for an aunt."

It was an amazingly harmonious household. I do not remember a cross word spoken or an unseemly argument among the adults as we were growing up. It seems incredible today as I look back on it, but my sisters confirm the accuracy of my memory. It is considered undesirable in certain psychiatric circles and among theorists concerned with child-raising (they change their theories so often that it is hard to keep up) that expressions of aggression, anger, and hostility should be repressed. But I do not think that these emotions underlay our elders' relationships with one another. There were, to be sure, hurt feelings sometimes, especially as the result of my mother's slapdash approach and sometimes thoughtless disparagement of things that mattered to my aunts or to my father. But she was always quick and generous in her apologies, promising "to do better next time" — which sometimes she did and sometimes she didn't. My Aunt Ida's boss, Dr. Washburn, Superintendent of the Massachusetts General Hospital, was horrified to think that she lived in a house with five children and a sister-in-law!

Not that there weren't some neurotic manifestations flying around. My father was given to sick headaches on Sundays, as was my Aunt Bernice, and there were deep tendencies toward melancholy on his side of the family. My Aunt Bernice once wrote a sweet letter to my mother when she was on shipboard on her way to Europe: "What would we have ever done without you, dear Cornelia, I tremble to think. I know the Cannons needed you if anyone was ever needed."

My mother's response was to make light of these expressions of gloom, minimizing the weight of my father's depressions in such a way as to make us children feel that they were phenomena of nature, like rain or winter storms, about which nothing could be done. We merely sighed or tiptoed around the house on Sundays but otherwise went about our busy, heedless lives, unperturbed.

I have often wondered how a complicated household like ours survived with such an atmosphere of peace about it. Perhaps in some sense it rested on the old-fashioned virtue of good manners among adults and a built-in reserve on the part of each, an emotional distance maintained instinctively, which was something distinct from the obvious warmth and humor that they shared.

Needless to say, we children could not be accused of being such paragons, though my brother Bradford, when not engaged in open warfare with his four strong-minded sisters, could be a veritable Pied Piper. My mother, much to the dismay of many of her conservative friends who did not let their children stray far from home, used to let him take his sisters on "expeditions" on Saturday mornings when he was barely twelve, knowing that given responsibility for us, no one could be more benign. Our usual outings were to the Audubon Lectures at Tremont Temple, where we would sit in the balcony transfixed by the dim, wobbly movies of birds nesting and feeding and some gifted representative of the Audubon Society whistling bird calls. My brother, although so-licitous up to a point, always ran about ten paces ahead of us, so that we streamed out in a breathless row, running after him up the steps of Park Street Under, fearful that we would lose him in the Saturday crowd. Once or twice he took us on the ferry from Rowe's Wharf down in the market district on Atlantic Avenue across to East Boston. There we caught the narrow-gauge railway to Revere Beach and blissfully spent our hard-earned pennies on "rides" and pink spun-sugar candy.

But once we were back under the family roof, the oppression of too many females overwhelmed my brother, and warfare would be resumed. Besides, although he was his father's pride and joy, he was also the thorn in his flesh, as in high school he flunked Latin, did badly in his English, and insisted on studying with the radio receiver clamped over his ears. My father's anxiety about his academic achievement and general adolescent fecklessness was such that my mother observed, "Walter is inclined to think that if the children don't get A's they are lost souls. But I tell him they are lovely human beings, unselfish and dear, but his gloom does not lighten. He gets a lot of emotion over artificial standards of measurement. . . . What is the matter with fathers. They will not let the plant grow quietly but are always jerking it up to see if the roots are secure."

In spite of my father's pessimism, my brother grew up to be a distinguished surgeon and the comfort of his old age. And when my brother married he proceeded to have four sons and a daugh-ter, thereby restoring the balance of nature!

chapter four

THE CAMBRIDGE TO WHICH MY PARENTS RETURNED TO LIVE WAS in many ways a divided city, its neighborhoods isolated from one another not only because of economic and ethnic factors that cut deeply into the fabric of the community but also for historical reasons that long preceded the influx of immigrants into the city in the mid-nineteenth century. Cambridge at the beginning of that century was composed of three distinct villages: Old Cambridge, the site of the original settlement and of Harvard College, Yankee to the bone, its citizens living along the streets fanning out from present-day Harvard Square and farther, toward Tory Row (Brattle Street); East Cambridge, the area around the present Lechmere Square, a small hamlet situated at the edge of the swampy shores of the Charles, a tidal river then and until 1912, when a tidal dam was finally built; and Cambridgeport, another small village approximately in the area between Central Square and the river. Communication between the three settlements in the eighteenth century was difficult, with indifferent dirt roads and no public transportation.

In the early nineteenth century things began to change. Two important bridges were built across the Charles, turning Cambridge from a virtually isolated peninsula separated from the metropolis by water to the main thoroughfare for the transportation of goods between outlying towns and farms to the west and north of Boston. The construction in 1809 of the Canal bridge from East Cambridge to Boston resulted in a boom in the growth of East

Soldiers' Monument, Cambridge Common

Cambridge. From a comparatively bucolic place where farmers used still to harvest salt hay in the adjoining swampy salt marshes, it became the site of the industrial expansion that made Cambridge the second most important producing area in the state in the latter part of the century. A similar growth took place in Cambridgeport with the building of the West Boston (Longfellow) Bridge a few years earlier. In 1853, horsecar tracks were laid along the main thoroughfares, Cambridge Street and Main Street (Massachusetts Avenue), leading to the bridges and joining the disparate sections of the city together. In the 1890s the horsecars gave way to the electric trolleys and between 1909 and 1912 the present subway system was finished. The expansion of transportation in the nineteenth century had another effect on Cambridge. It became for many people a suburb. Businessmen, bankers, and lawyers who enjoyed the edifying, genteel atmosphere of Cambridge could take the "electrics" every morning to their offices in Boston and easily return to their comfortable houses in the evening, thereby living a more spacious if less fashionable existence than their Boston counterparts in their row houses and mansions along the streets of the Back Bay and Beacon Hill.

Cambridge at the turn of the century was still a leafy, tree-girt town. The chestnut trees that had shaded its streets for a century were being destroyed by blight, but some still remained, heavy with their conelike, pale pink blossoms in the spring. The honey locusts dropped their long black pods into the gutters in the fall and huge elms towered over the comfortable houses set back on their pleasant lawns in the streets around Harvard Square. The delivery wagons were still horse-drawn and the clatter of the hooves on the pavement made an agreeable staccato sound; the riotous fighting of the English sparrows over the horse droppings was an accompanying counterpoint. Apartment houses were being erected, but on the whole, Cambridge was still a community of individual houses of a variety of architectural styles. The beautiful eighteenth-century mansions of Tory Row and later the columned Greek Revival houses set the tone. The ubiquitous Victorian mansard-roofed mansions were succeeded by the more flamboyant experiments of the Edwardian period: turrets, fancy porches and porticoes, wooden Romanesque arches, elaborate shingling, and domestic stained-glass windows. It was a time of architectural ebullience in which various themes mingled to produce a lively conglomeration of styles in the space of one street or neighborhood. Since for three hundred years Cambridge has been a city of homes, it is today one of the treasure houses of American domestic architecture.

At the other end of town, in East Cambridge, the Irish and Italian immigrants, crowding into the late eighteenth-century houses that had once been the fine abodes of prosperous merchants, were turning them into tenements and everywhere the "three-deckers" were being thrown up by developers for cheap housing for the poor. North Cambridge was again an area of separate two-family houses, with yards and fruit trees, with the usual sprinkling of three-decker tenements. For people coming up in the world in places like East Cambridge or Cambridgeport, the move would be to North Cambridge, so that by the first decades of the twentieth century, North Cambridge had become, on the whole, middle-class, French and Irish and Catholic. To most people whose lives centered on Harvard University or the environs of what was originally Old Cambridge, North Cambridge, East Cambridge, and Cambridgeport were as remote as Timbuctoo, passed through on the streetcar or on the subway, but seldom penetrated.

My mother and father decided that Cambridge was the place for them, even though it was far removed from the Harvard Medical School whose new buildings were being erected along Huntington Avenue in Boston. Most of his colleagues on the Medical School faculty lived in Brookline or Boston, but my father preferred the long commute, first by streetcar and then for many decades in his beloved Fords, for which he had an unswerving devotion. Indeed, his life virtually could be measured out in Ford models; from the Model T's to the Model A's to the various specimens of other models until he died in 1945. I think his devotion to the Ford stemmed from an early admiration for the uncluttered simplicity and ingenuity of the Model T, which appealed to his own native ingenuity. He liked the fact that a piece of haywire or a hairpin could often restore a failing engine. He was forever experimenting as to how far up the steep hill in Franklin, on which our summer house was perched, he could go, "getting a good running start" before he had finally to press the left-hand pedal to the floor. No one who has never driven a Model T Ford will know what I am talking about, but driving one was one of the big thrills of our youth.

Like the immigrants from Ireland and Italy, my father and mother came into the long-established, closely knit, family-oriented Cambridge of the turn of the century as virtual aliens. My father was one of the first professors from "away" to breach the sacred precincts of the Harvard Medical School, long considered a private fiefdom of the Boston medical world.

His appointment was an example of the "new broom," the "breath of fresh air" with which President Eliot was transforming Harvard into a great university. The classical tradition of Harvard was still strong. Distinguished professors of Greek and Sanskrit lived in our professorial part of Cambridge, but a faculty that was largely composed of New Englanders was being infiltrated by foreigners: Professor Josiah Royce, the philosopher, from California; Professor George W. Pierce, the physicist, from Texas; and many others besides my own father from Minnesota. It was the beginning of the wave of brilliant interlopers who through the next decades turned Harvard into a university of international renown.

Both my parents carried with them all their lives a strong pride in their Middle-Western roots and my mother was not to be intimidated by what she considered New England stiffness and reserve. Her breezy ways and uninhibited outspokenness were, she used to say, often "unduly stimulated" by many of her more proper acquaintances, one of whom was reported to have said, "Why, I did not know you were nice enough to know the Crothers" (the Unitarian minister in Cambridge and his family, old friends of the Jameses in St. Paul). She had no desire to "belong" and rather preferred the role of the outsider and gadfly, which better suited her independent nature.

Actually, my mother fitted into a tradition of freewheeling, independent-minded ladies of Cambridge. It has long been a city with a record of hospitality to originals, male or female, native or adopted, and I believe that it has been the women of Cambridge who have set the tone. To a much greater extent than their more conservative and conventional male counterparts, they have been responsible for the atmosphere of openness and tolerance that has characterized it as a community.

It goes without saying that "doing your own thing" has for years been an established practice among these free-spirited ladies of Cambridge. In the past, they often looked upon males as frail creatures who had to be handled and propitiated like small children. Having dealt with them by placing them on their pedestals (their accustomed perches where they happily sat), the ladies went ahead with the serious business of their lives: their own self-improvement, whether it lay in intellectual pursuits, in social reform, in educational innovation, or in the arts or literature.

In fact, through the years, a typical query remorselessly addressed to newcomers to Cambridge (especially in the case of academic wives), though they might have five children, no help, a demanding husband and a house to run, was, "But what do you *do?*" The truth is that long ago in this community the contemporary term "Women's Liberation" became a phrase of supererogation.

There was Margaret Fuller, the transcendentalist and friend of Emerson, who is remembered as the woman who told Thomas Carlyle in England in 1846, "I accept the Universe!" Carlyle's supposed retort was, "By Gad, she better!" which was supposed to be the ultimate put-down. However, Professor Perry Miller, writing of her in 1963, said, "Margaret's affirmation, if she made it, was fully in character; she fought hard and valiantly for a liberalism so positive as immediately to excite Carlyle's ire." This redoubtable woman was born in Cambridgeport in 1810 and spent the first fourteen years of her life there, being educated by a domineering father to be a true bluestocking. "Her learning," as Professor Miller wrote, went "far beyond that possessed by the young men of her circle who were moving towards Harvard where they acquired at best a modicum of the erudition she so painfully mastered." Needless to say, there was no place for her in that institution. In spite of such exigencies, she became in truth the precursor of many women intellectuals and activists of the city who, determinedly and often against great odds, have pursued their goals.

There was Elizabeth Cary Agassiz, the wife of the Swiss scientist and Harvard professor Louis Agassiz. She traveled with him in the 1850s on many of his scientific expeditions, acting as his amanuensis, taking notes for his lectures and books. On one trip to South America she wrote in her diary that "she feared that her concern for the 'picturesque' might *weaken* Agassiz's thought," a delightfully unwitting recognition of the tacit ascendency of the New England female over the male, even in matters of the intellect.

It was she, of all the ladies on the "Committee" that founded the Harvard Annex, who was able, through her wide connections among the Harvard faculty and the authoritativeness of her personality, to co-opt her professorial friends to teach in the Annex. It was she above all who was determined that there should be no "ladies' degree" allowed to be created for Radcliffe, and finally it was she who became its first President in 1882.

Mrs. Thorp, one of Longfellow's daughters, epitomized another type of selfless, public-spirited woman so characteristic of the Cambridge of her time. Mrs. Crothers, the wife of the Unitarian minister and herself a rare spirit, wrote of Mrs. Thorp, "She had what Mr. Crothers used to call 'a reticent soul' that threw a certain dignity about the big things of life. . . . She was one of those to 'be counted on' in movements for the public good. Her life was 'given' to others but she never got that 'good' look that is so deadening, nor acquired that professional philanthropic air that gives one a sudden distaste for 'causes.' "

There were the glorious Cambridge eccentrics, contemporaries of Mrs. Agassiz, on whom the community smiled in amusement and appreciation. Mrs. Samuel Eliot, a daughter-in-law of President Eliot, recalled some of those colorful originals. "I remember coming home on a trolley one afternoon from a concert. When the car stopped to let Miss Kitty and Miss Carrie Parsons alight, Miss Kitty was still talking to her neighbor. She made no move to rise.

The impatient conductor shouted, 'Get a move on, lady!' I remember with what dignity Miss Carrie drew herself up and said, 'Cambridge has come to a pretty pass when Miss Kitty Parsons is not allowed to finish her conversation.' And one evening I met Miss Carrie, who was rather an elderly lady, walking to her sewing club dressed as Little Bo-Peep, crook and all."

There were the Misses Palfry, middle-aged maiden sisters, who lived in a big house that still stands at the end of Divinity Avenue, again, like so many other Cambridge houses, plucked up and moved from its original site. One of them rode a tricycle, a machine fashionable in those days, which she modestly draped with a concealing fringe threaded on a circular bar to hide her ankles from the rude gaze of the public.

When the Harvard Summer School was started after the Spanish-American War, Cuban students were invited to attend. The Misses Palfry, living near the college, hastened "in some perturbation to see their old friend and adviser, Dr. Henry Walcott. They asked him earnestly if it was quite safe for them to remain in their home — 'Because,' they said, 'we hear the Cubans are very passionate people.' " It was one of the Palfry sisters who made the famous criticism of matrimony, that "it broke down the natural barrier between the sexes."

It is no news in this day and age that New England spinsters were "hung up" on sex, but I doubt if such indecent reflections disturbed the thought of the Misses Palfry's contemporaries who looked upon them with affectionate indulgence. After all, the influence of Freud was some decades off and almost every family had one or two loony relatives secreted in the attic or in McLean, the mental hospital where one's genteel, if mad, relations were put away.

One of the Misses Palfry, who survived into old age, struck a final note, appropriate to intellectual Cambridge; when approaching her end, she took in hand the study of Hebrew, defending her action by her anticipation of her early departure of this life and her desire to address her heavenly father "in his own language."

My mother recalled another "resolute old lady of Cambridge

accosting a policeman during the First World War when barracks for soldiers were being built on the Cambridge Common and waving her cane at the offending buildings. 'What does this mean? I do not approve of this *at all!*' 'You must not talk that way, Miss H,' said the guardian of our national life," according to my mother; " 'You know it ain't allowed.' He wasn't going to have any enemy 'propoganders' on his beat."

In recent years, Miss Jessie Whitehead, the daughter of Alfred North Whitehead, used to thread her way through Harvard Square traffic on her ancient bicycle, a rear-view mirror on her handlebars and a green parakeet on her shoulder. But the eccentrics are now indistinguishable from the regular run, with long hair and beards proliferating and oddity of dress become a la mode. No one would turn a hair if the Misses Palfry rode their tricycles through the streets of Cambridge today. Anyway, today they would probably be in some crackpot cult or "consciousness-raising" group "dealing with their problems," thereby robbing their contemporaries of a good deal of pleasure.

There was another category of earnest women, the passionate lady lecture-goer. My mother and grandmother belonged in this group. When my grandmother came to visit from St. Paul there would be a perfect orgy of lecture-going. Within the space of a few days they would run the gamut from "Variable Stars" at the Observatory, to "Ice Patrol" at the Geology Museum, Professor Kirsopp Lake on "Catholicism," and finally a lecture on "Electrons" — "incomprehensible but interesting." As my mother once remarked after attending a lecture by Professor Stetson on Einstein's new doctrine of relativity, "One of its chief charms to me is that I can understand practically nothing of it but I get the sense of dealing with mental immensity." No wonder that when my sister Helen, aged ten and ill in bed, declared, "I'm only going to be sick this morning, for I want to go to the Star lecture at the Museum this afternoon," my father commented philosophically, "It's three generations of lecture-goers, heart palpitations and nose bleeds, it makes no difference. To lectures they will go."

I remember one indefatigable lady lecture-goer, the widow of a professor of music, who was a fixture, and a vocal one, at all

74 public lectures at Harvard. She lived in an old house on Ellery Street, which resembled the establishment of the New York Collier brothers, with tunnels running from room to room between mountains of newspaper and trash that she refused to part with. Each morning she must have addressed herself to the *Harvard Gazette*, in which the events of the week were listed. Then, invariably wrapped in a paisley shawl, mission bonnet on her head, dressed in skirts and petticoats that swept the ground in a time of strictly short skirts, she would sally forth to do battle, for she seemed to have looked upon the public lecture as a call to arms.

She would seat herself squarely in the front row where she was the terror of the New Lecture Hall. She would harangue the lecturer with sharp questions, interrupting the flow of words, or wave peremptorily (there seemed to be a good deal of cane-waving by the old ladies of Cambridge) and demand that he "speak up" as she "could not hear." In fact, Cambridge audiences, especially those peopled by such dragons, could often be unnerving experiences for the uninitiated speaker, no matter whether he were the Norton lecturer or a less exalted figure.

In another sphere, there was Maria Baldwin, a remarkable black woman, highly educated and cultivated, who up to the present time was the only black principal that ever headed a Cambridge public school. She presided over the Agassiz School, the neighborhood school that we attended as children, a woman respected and loved by her all-white staff of teachers. She made an inerasable impression on me as a small child in the first grade: her ample figure as she came to visit "our room," the low, quiet timbre of her voice, and her seemingly effortless control. I cannot remember that we thought anything of her being black. She and my mother were great friends and she came often to our house for dinner. My mother recalls a discussion of W. E. B. Du Bois's book *Darkwater:* "Miss Baldwin was so big and tolerant about the whole subject — it seems to me remarkable that she has been able to preserve so generous an attitude." When she died in 1922, my mother wrote, "I went up the next day and spent the morning at the school — the weeping heartbroken teachers could hardly control themselves enough to carry on the school and the children were full of awe and sadness. It was a wonderful achievement to leave so much affection behind. I did so depend on her tenderness and wisdom in the training of the children and when we think of what we *may* get next, our hearts sink." She was buried from the Arlington Street Church in Boston, with President Eliot among the throng of white and black people attending her funeral.

Perhaps the most vivid figure among the galaxy of Cambridge originals was Mrs. Agnes Hocking, the founder of the Shady Hill School, one of the first progressive schools in the country. It was her spirit and imagination that had inspired the establishment of the school in its collection of one-story wooden huts under the willow trees at the foot of Shady Hill, part of the original Charles Eliot Norton estate.

May Sarton, herself a distinguished author and native of Cambridge, in her delightful book *I Knew a Phoenix* describes Mrs. Hocking: "the wife of the philosopher, William Ernest Hocking, and the daughter of the poet, John Boyle O'Reilly; revolutionary blood flowed in her veins. The school was born of this marriage of poetry and philosophy, and though philosophy was worshiped, poetry ruled. Mrs. Hocking never referred to her husband otherwise than as 'Ernest Hocking,' and always with the same intonation, which suggested that she considered him a deity." (There seems to have been a good deal of deification of husbands in those days, from Mrs. Agassiz on down!) "Once, discovering in the subway station at Harvard Square that she had forgotten her purse, she walked right past the collector, uttering the magic words 'Ernest Hocking will give you five cents tomorrow' and sailed through the wicket."

May Sarton goes on to describe her extraordinary quality in this charming evocation: "We were set down in the center of a primal force at work. . . . Mrs. Hocking was poetry incarnate. Her very person, glorious in red velvet on a special occasion, but more often resembling the old woman who lived in the shoe, was exhilarating. . . . She did not administer, she created, and part of the creation was, of course, to find teachers who would go their own way, unadministered." She talks of Mrs. Hocking teaching poetry: "She did not tell us about poetry; she made us live its life. . . . We were not given a poem to read or study; we learned each one through hearing it repeated by Mrs. Hocking until we knew it by heart. . . . We had become whatever it was long before we guessed we were learning it."

At some point in her life, Mrs. Hocking discovered Filene's Basement, long a haunt of my economy-minded mother. She was enchanted; it must have appealed to her gypsylike spirit, for she would sweep into this wonderland of bargains to buy dresses for her long-suffering adolescent daughters, and if one caught her fancy she would buy eight or nine with scant attention to size or color. She must have been an irresistible force to her children, for they meekly wore what she provided although the garments almost invariably were too long or a size or two too big.

In later life, Mrs. Hocking became a passionate follower of Gandhi, and I can remember her coming to my wedding in a sari-like costume made out of an old velvet curtain, ropes of beads around her neck, and navy blue sneakers on her feet. She was accompanied by a swami, conventionally and elegantly dressed in a well-cut Western-style suit. As she confided in my mother, dashing at her with arms outflung in extravagant greeting, "Cornelia, I'm wearing my sari to make *him* feel at home!" It was all perhaps a portent of things to come decades later in Harvard Square where saris, dhotis, dashikis, and Sikhs, Hare Krishnas, African chiefs, Arab sheiks, had become commonplace.

At another time, Ernest Hocking took up painting, and Agnes Hocking, ever the worshiper at his shrine, used to startle the philosophy graduate students when Professor Hocking addressed one of their monthly meetings. She would creep silently across the platform in front of the lectern where he stood speaking, doubled over in order not to interfere with his flow of words, with one of his paintings clasped to her bosom. Having reached the other side, she would snatch up another painting in exchange, and noiselessly repeat the exhibition. No reference was made to this unusual phenomenon by Professor Hocking, who imperturbably carried on the discussion of the evening as though it were the most natural happening in the world. One has heard of "action paint-

ing," but this seems to have been an example of "action showing."

My mother remembered one Christmas Agnes Hocking giving
her a jar of canned food marked, "Merry Christmas to Cornelia, I
love you! From our farm!" As she observed with some bemusement: "And I looked at the label pasted on the glass jar: 'Candied
Pineapple.' It was so like her; snatched up the first jar she saw,
despatched it with exuberant affection and probably thought it
blueberries but anyway a product of her New Hampshire farm!"

I can still recall her spirited Irish face, her blooming red
cheeks, and vivid gray eyes that fixed one like the Ancient
Mariner, the tumble of her words, and the intensity with which
she clasped one's hands in her two hands in lavish welcome.

Then there were the Cambridge hostesses. Boston may have
had her hostesses like Mrs. Jack Gardner, but Cambridge in later
years had her exemplars, too. No one would have referred to Mrs.
Kingsley Porter's Sunday evenings as a "salon"; that would have
been much too vulgar for Cambridge, though there were those who
often irreverently referred to her as Mrs. Queensley Porter because of the general hauteur of her manner. She rather
specialized in the fine arts — the aesthetes and the art historians — and was known for the excellence of her table, with her
Italian cook and butler, when she presided over Elmwood, the
beautiful house on Elmwood Avenue originally belonging to
James Russell Lowell that is now the residence of the President of
Harvard. And there was Mrs. William James (the daughter-in-law
of the elder William James), a less forbidding person; faintly
malapropian, she was a grande dame, a ship under full sail,
rather an opéra bouffe character. A friend of mine was once called
up on the day of one of her parties by Alice James (all James
females seemed to have been named Alice), who explained,
"We were going to have a small party, a very small party, for
Isaiah Berlin. But the list kept getting bigger and bigger. So we
decided to have everybody, just *everybody!* Won't you come!" My
friend was too enchanted to refuse.

She and her husband, the portrait painter, lived in Professor
James's old house on Irving Street, and she gave her parties in the

beautiful long room that had been his study, and was still lined with his magnificent library. Her husband, a charming, diffident man, suffered all his life from having his sentences finished by his wife. He was a slow starter, finding the enunciation of his ideas a painful process, and Alice James would swoop down upon him in mid-sentence, telling him in no uncertain terms what it was he wished to say. He sweetly deferred to her, never raising any protest. When he married again, after Alice's death, he was apparently allowed to finish his sentences but was forced into a diet of health foods, which was the crotchet of his second wife.

A salient point about these two Cambridge hostesses was that they both came from Chicago, which might explain their somewhat un-Cantabrigian dash. Although they were both lion-hunters, their hunting was on a rather exalted level and they performed a certain function in their day. They brought together interesting people from academia and the "haut monde," if such a phrase could be applied to Cambridge and environs, who would not normally cross one another's path. But those days are long since gone; with the disappearance of the cooks and the maids, the Cambridge hostess is no more.

Brilliant women in academia and in the professions have found Cambridge a hospitable place to live; in my mother's day there were Dr. Alice Hamilton of the Harvard School of Public Health and Miss Annie Jump Cannon (no relation), astronomer at the Harvard Observatory, each that rare phenomenon, a woman member of Harvard University. The presence of women doctors, social workers, teachers, headmistresses, and many other professionals in the community reinforced an atmosphere of tacit female ascendancy rooted in a strong feminist past.

It is interesting that distinguished women psychoanalysts like Helena Deutsch and Greta Bebring found a haven in Cambridge after their flight from Hitler and the Nazis during the thirties and that they were instrumental in making Cambridge and Boston one of the most significant centers for psychoanalysis in the western hemisphere.

Again, during the thirties, prominent Cambridge women organized the Window Shop, on the site of the Old Village

Blacksmith's Shop, a unique institution formed to give employment and financial aid to the streams of German Jews and other displaced intellectuals escaping from Nazi Germany. It became a fixture in Harvard Square, a store selling Viennese pastries and dresses, that forever transformed the diet of Cantabrigians by a rich flow of apfelstrudels and linzertortes, and turned out two or three generations of dirndl-garbed girls and, rather disastrously, two or three generations of dirndl-garbed middle-aged ladies as well.

Of course, women always did the dirty work at election time, canvassing, doorbell-ringing, checking at the polls, standing in the rain handing out candidates' cards. But of late, they have stepped out and taken their place in the elective process. In recent years, we have had a woman mayor, women members of the School Committee, a woman member in the State House, and women public servants of all kinds. They have been in the vanguard of political uplift and reform in a city that would have long since expired under the weight of corruption without their watchful and active reforming zeal.

Such, then, is the almost overwhelming reputation of Cambridge ladies as forces for intellectual attainment as well as forces for the higher good. A son of a friend of mine, a grown man now working in a Boston law firm who was brought up in Cambridge, was at a party recently with a group of friends. A colleague, also a native son, turned to him in the middle of the party, looked pityingly at the gathered guests and said, "You know, John, you and I have something that none of the rest of these people has — we each have a Cambridge mother!"

chapter five

ON STORMY, FRIGID DAYS, MY MOTHER WOULD SOMETIMES compromise her New England conscience by building up the fire in the living room and sitting down and reading a book *before* midday. It was a luxury normally reserved for the sickbed and I think she rather enjoyed her moments of poor health, which were rare, because they gave free rein to her passionate love of reading.

It was often in this position, toasting her feet before the fire, that we found her on "No School" days. We children, having streamed out only a little earlier, would stream back through the front door, triumphantly crying, "No school! No school!" and strewing caps, mittens, and overshoes in a sodden pile, having trudged through the blinding snow to find the school doors closed. I recall the look of incredulity and horror on her face and her inevitable remark, "How perfectly ridiculous! What is the *matter* with the Cambridge schools!" and if it was rain that sent us home, "You would think that children were soluble in water."

In all probability, we had crossed the path of the Shady Hill School "kids" in Norton's Woods, shooshing through the tempest, to their open-air schoolrooms at the foot of Shady Hill. They exuded for us "public school kids" an intolerable sense of their own purity and high-mindedness, not to say "specialness." Besides, it apparently would not have occurred to them, being pious children of nature, or to those in charge to close down the classes, wherein a merit was made of windows thrown open to the foulest weather, just because a howling northeaster was blowing.

Mother reading in warmth

With that philosophy my mother agreed, for she was rather in favor of physical hardship as efficacious in developing character. Beyond that she would not go, for she was an ardent believer in public education. Many of my mother's more conventional and timid academic friends were shocked at her sending us to public school as though she were committing us to some sort of custodial institution. But she was a person who hated elitism or special privilege and once said in later years, "The one and only thing we did for our children was to *live* with them, hoping that that would take the place of the elaboration of culture, governesses, and privileges other and richer parents lavished on their offspring. I believe it is a sound principle and much of the fuss of modern parenthood is to find substitutes for this old-fashioned way of giving the children a touch with life."

She was one of those unusual people who acted on principle and felt if you were going to do special things it should be for "all the children" and not for just a select and pampered few. Her theory and practice was, send your children to public schools and work to make them better, and she gave the public school system of Cambridge a whirl that was not soon forgotten in the span of our educational life. As she wrote in 1923, "In such a heterogeneous democracy as ours, we must face association with all kinds. They are here, we are committed, and, as Tom Perry [Ralph Barton Perry] says in his sardonic way, 'We must pray for strength to bear democracy when we get it!' "

And so the old battle between the partisans of public and of private schools, which has become one of the greatest bores of social intercourse of the age, was even then off to a fiery start. And nowhere was it hotter than in academic Cambridge.

A number of my parents' friends and contemporaries had banded together and under the spirited leadership of Agnes Hocking had established the Co-operative Fresh Air School, later rechristened the Shady Hill School. Fresh air in those days (when it was still available), besides being considered a panacea for all ills, was thought to clear the brain, brighten the eye, quicken the imagination, and endow the most laggard scholar with a zest for learning. A falling mercury seemed only to increase its virtue. In preparation for this invigorating experience these children wore what seemed to us the most outlandish clothes: long gray wool sweaters reaching below the knees, four sizes too big (bought large on purpose), lumbermen's boots and "woodchoppers' socks" from Sears, Roebuck, long woolen underwear and oversized mittens at the ends of strings, and the first parkas we had ever seen outside the Peabody Museum where they adorned realistic models of Eskimos. Once in their classrooms, each child sat in a kind of gray woolen bag called a "sitting bag," which must have been absolutely essential in the zero weather and, according to May Sarton, was eminently adaptable, when the children, acting out a poem of the sea, rolled on the floor as seals. Actually theirs were sensible getups and elements of their costuming have become standard winter dress for modern children and adults.

These youthful denizens were in many ways forerunners of modern "hippies." All Shady Hill girls seemed to possess prodigious heads of hair, worn either lank and loose to the waist, or in aggressively fat braids. The boys were practically indistinguishable, and since they all dressed alike they appeared to us like a band of little gray trolls as we caught glimpses of them on our way to school. Their freshly scrubbed, rosy-cheeked faces radiated exaltation and "wholesomeness," a bad word to us "worldlings," and there was a purposefulness and smugness in their walk that did not allow of any idling along the way, no hopscotch or feckless dawdling. They seemed to inhabit a world apart, dedicated to self-expression and naturalism, with a combination of innocence and arrogance as of rarefied creatures partaking of some secret essence. In short, all little Shady Hill children were geniuses. And how we despised them!

And yet, we secretly wondered whether we were missing something. Perhaps they knew something we did not know. They did Morris dances and sang English folk songs and acted their own plays based on Greek myths. To be sure, we sang English folk songs and danced Virginia reels, and every summer for many years, my brisk mother would put on plays on the pine-needle–strewn stage in Franklin. She even rewrote *Iphigenia in Tauris* for the under-ten set, with the Greek chorus composed of two six-year-olds cheerfully intoning "O Agony! O Agony!" But summer plays did not by any means stack up beside dramas acted "in school." It was just "Mother being energetic" and therefore did not count.

However, skepticism would not be downed, and a final broadside was said to have been delivered by me. When there was a discussion of the so-called genius children of my parents' circle (which I may say did not include any of us), I was said to have burst out passionately, "I'd rather be dumb and coordinated!"

And so we were full of contempt and secret yearnings, like sinners left out of paradise, though we felt in our heart of hearts that "they" did not know anything about "life" and we did, and everyone knew that it was that "that mattered."

Since no one else seemed to be "enriching the curriculum" in our neighborhood school, my mother went ahead in her irrepressible way and did it herself. In the 1920s she would work up talks on any topic that was current, from the treasures of Tutankhamen's tomb to the total eclipse of the sun, borrowing slides from appropriate departments of the University, whose directors seem to have cooperated meekly. After a series of talks on asteroids, Jupiter, comets, and Saturn at the Agassiz School, my mother wrote, "I gave the last of the astronomy talks to the children today, and tomorrow night I give one to the parents covering the field of astronomy in one hour! As Ida says [who incidentally was a student of astronomy and spent many evenings at the Harvard Observatory], 'If only I had your gall!' " She goes on to say that her astronomy talks "may lead me into conflict with the authorities. It is a dangerous subject for it tends to make people think. How can one study astronomy and still stick with the orthodox faith!" The School Committee apparently felt they were losing control, for they advised the superintendent "not to allow Amateurs to lecture without consent of the board on account of Mrs. Cannon's lectures on Astronomy."

The pupils and teachers used to look forward to Mrs. Cannon's lectures, but, such is the perversity of children, all we wanted was a mother like other mothers, who *didn't* come to school and give lectures.

She was once called upon by boys in my brother Bradford's grammar-school class to act as a sponsor for a school paper they wanted to start. She reported with a good deal of amusement, "The boys at school decided to have a boy, who expects a printing press for Christmas, for their printer. But Bolshevism has reared its head in their midst. The printer has struck, and refuses to do the work unless he is made editor, the proletariat wants to take over the function of the intelligentsia and on the refusal of the editorial staff decided to start a rival paper of his own. The strike of a printer, based on a hypothetical printing outfit which in turn depends on a mythical Santa Claus, for the printing of a school paper, which as yet exists in the minds of a few ardent boys, and the setting up of a phantasmagoric rival paper, seems to me of the figment of dreams!" She seems to have been readily accessible to the classmates of us children and recalled a would-be youthful poet who brought one of his creations for her to look over. "I advised him not to use 'you bet' and 'we ain't fools' in the poem. He sighed profoundly and said, 'It's awful hard to get words to rhyme.' "

She was full of sensible ideas about what should be taught in schools. In 1918, during the First World War, she wrote, "I have just made out a course in household physics for the High School. I had an appointment with the principal to talk it over but at the last minute he could not come. There is no escape for him, however. He will have to hear my ideas whether he acts on them or not. The whole question of fuel conservation is so important that the need of instruction in the use of fuel may serve as a fulcrum to get some kind of fuel instruction in and at the same time some ideas about light, hot water, and ventilation. Just to have children know the principles of plumbing, and the entrances and exits of pipes into homes would be a gain. I have just about come to the place where I should like to be on the School Committee and although I am ignorant about education I can with all modesty say that I know more than the honorable present members." She was always as ready with a barb for the "honorable members" as they were for her!

In 1925, she wrote to suggest to President Lowell that there should be a resident artist at the Fogg Museum "but no one listens to me. Some other college will see the light and Harvard will realize how stupid she has been." Such was the flow of suggestions and ideas and the power of her reforming instincts that it became a family joke. When my brother was ready for college he is said to have remarked, "I should think that President Lowell would shudder when he heard I was coming to Harvard, with my mother getting interested."

❧

She had a zestful approach to the reforming of corruption in city government, of which there was a goodly amount, and took on such doughty figures as the perennial Mayor Quinn, who was long on charm, but also on cronyism, patronage, and graft. In one of her more resigned moments she admitted, "Our grafting Mayor Quinn had been re-elected, so weak and shifty and so charming. The Irish make the political villains too attractive for defeat." The "boys" did not appreciate my mother's attentions and she was long referred to around City Hall as "that woman." She cheerfully answered in kind, describing a mayor of Cambridge as an "ex-superintendent of sewers and not above his profession!" Once, reporting on a School Committee meeting after having excoriated the members in a letter to the local newspapers about the constant closing of schools at the least suggestion of stormy weather, she wrote: "Mr. Hurley [later Governor Hurley] had his chance, roaring and bellowing at me as a cold blooded, heartless creature, asking me whether I would compel a child to go to school without shoes or stockings or rubbers. It was all very well for the *rich* to want school open in bad weather, but how about the *poor?* You can imagine what rot it was. After the meeting Mr. Cassidy said if Mr. Hurley had spoken about his wife that way he would have punched him in the nose. The implication was that poor innocent Walter was not doing his duty as a loyal husband." My mother, however, could take care of herself. It is reported that "with the spirit that is part of Mrs. Cannon's character, she resented Mr. Hurley's hectoring manner as insulting and arose and left the chamber saying, 'My hair may be gray, but my hearing is good, don't yell at me, Mr. Hurley.' "

In moments of despondency, she could only reflect, "The children of Cambridge, though sanctified like the Virgin Mary by a catch in the throat, have none the less been the instrument of the Irish politicians of this city for the last fifty years. Generations of children have grown to manhood and womanhood in the intervening years, no better or worse for the pols who have used them as footballs through the decades."

No matter how despondent, she rose year after year like the phoenix from the ashes to take up her civic duties like so many other Cambridge women before and since, remarking with some acerbity, "I have taken up my civic responsibilities once again. I have been busy, getting signatures to nomination papers, women out to register, and all the rest of the labor to get a democracy to run *your* way — and how entirely it runs the *other* way!"

A notice that was printed in the *Cambridge Chronicle* at the time that my father received an honorary degree from Yale in 1923 sums her up in her role as citizen rather charmingly. "Among those receiving an honorary degree from Yale University was Prof. Walter Bradford Cannon, of Harvard, as a physiologist. To most people in public life, Prof. Cannon is perhaps best known as the husband of Mrs. Cornelia James Cannon, secretary of the Cambridge Public School Association, whom everyone not only loves and admires for her engaging personality but for her constructive and sympathetic work for public schools and in other civic lines."

Although the scourge of City Hall, she was by no means a Mrs. Grundy. She wryly observed on the subject of her flow of words and advice: "Well, if words would save the world, this old Globe would be in Heaven, thanks to my outpourings alone!" And as for my father, his rueful comment from the sidelines was, "A woman's first duty is to her ward!"

❧

My father was the most undemanding of men, almost to a fault.

Perhaps the sheer numbers of strong-minded females that made up the household discouraged any impulse to domination or the heavy hand. He would not have known how to go about it anyway, I suspect, and no doubt he was relieved to be off and away to the peace and order of his laboratory, leaving the discipline of us children to my mother. She was on the whole easygoing and permissive although she sometimes resorted to the repulsive wash-ing-out-of-the-mouth-with-soap mode of punishment much in vogue in those days after some bit of reprehensible language. Words that were supposedly washed away with numberless cakes of Ivory soap in my childhood now enrich the vocabularies of all well-brought-up progressive school children (*sic*). As to the general question of discipline, she once observed after having been away on a visit: "I find the will to compel obedience is contained in the abdominal muscles, and mine are flabby after two weeks of disuse."

My mother at one point remarked apropos the numerous guests that gathered for Sunday dinner, "When the initial family is nine, entertaining becomes major surgery on the part of the carver!" My father, the carver, in fact carved like the meticulous surgeon that he was, and since my mother was all for speed and my father was all for standards, Sunday dinner and the weekly roast became the amiable battleground on which the contrast between their two natures was revealed.

His carefulness, his intellectual sobriety, the necessity of proof that he scrupulously demanded of himself and required of us children from an early age, had a profound effect on our mental processes. He would bring us down to earth good-naturedly with, "What are the facts?" after some extreme pronouncement. His scorn for sloppy reasoning and hasty, unverified conclusions was a potent force turning us into a tribe of unregenerate rationalists. My mother's mind was almost the exact opposite; speedy, emotional, full of ad hoc opinions and conclusions, and usually directly on target on a myriad of different subjects and problems. She once mournfully reported a comment on an article of hers printed in *The Atlantic Monthly*, "Can Our Public Officials Be Our Leaders?": "I have already had my first comeback from a grieved admirer, Professor Frankfurter. [Professor Frankfurter objected to an apparent endorsement of Coolidge, whom he despised. I cannot seem to find the reference so I do not know whether the endorsement was apparent or nonexistent.] Why do not they let a poor lady have her ideas without being so severe about it? If I had to *prove* every statement I make, I should be stricken dumb for life! I might as well devote myself to the encyclopedia as the essence of literature!"

My father had a profound commitment to the pursuit of truth in scientific experimentation (as well as in all other facets of his life); the working out of hypothesis by scrupulous verification under laboratory conditions and under the most exacting standards of proof. For that reason, I presume, although intrigued, he was ambivalent in his attitude to Freud and to psychoanalysis. Yet his basic work on the effects of the emotions on the body, summed up in his classic book *Bodily Changes in Pain, Hunger, Fear and Rage*, on which is based much of the modern theory of psychosomatic medicine, dealt with many of the same phenomena that he passionately believed were subject to the rules of cause and effect to be discovered and proved by scientific method and the human intellect. He would often good-humoredly quote Huxley: "The tragedy of scientific inquiry is the slaying of a beautiful hypothesis by an ugly fact."

He was a constant experimenter throughout his life, inside and outside his laboratory. Early in their marriage my mother wrote, "We are trying vegetarianism this month. Walter wants to see its effects on sleep, activity, metabolism etc. It is strenuous on the cook." In his study of the effects of the emotions on the body he became interested in voodoo death, writing a paper about it in 1942. Although he planned at one time to go to Haiti to look into the phenomenon at first hand, his final illness intervened before he could carry out his project. In his old age he used himself as an experimental animal in an informal inquiry into the problems of aging. He was always interested in how things worked and was ingenious and imaginative in creating his own apparatus for experiments in his laboratory. As a medical student in 1897 he fed bismuth to the aforementioned goose, so that he could watch the progress of the pearl button down its long neck by the means of the newly discovered X ray. The Canada goose was enclosed in a cardboard box with its head and neck protruding through the cover. A long collar made of cardboard firmly fixed to the box further surrounded and immobilized the goose's neck. "Thus," my father wrote, "the goose with the appearance of using the most stylish neckwear presented to the fluorescent screen a very satisfactory extent of the esophagus," and became the first subject in which the peristaltic waves of the stomach were observed. This first bismuth meal was the basis for millions of other bismuth and, later, barium meals downed with loathing by human patients submitting their stomachs and intestines to be X-rayed.

As one of the pioneers in the use of X rays, my father prudently protected himself with a lead apron when performing his experiments, but many of his colleagues who were not shielded from the rays died young from their devastating effects. Even my father did not escape; his hands were badly burned in a few places and his death from leukemia in 1945 was no doubt the direct result of his early exposure to X rays.

❧

My father's career as an experimental physiologist was extremely fruitful throughout the thirty-six years of his professorship at the Harvard Medical School, with over four hundred graduate students and colleagues working and collaborating in the physiological laboratory during that span.

As a medical student my father had found medical textbooks hard going and sleep-inducing and had observed with some envy the enthusiasm of his roommate, a student at the Harvard Law School, where the case system of study was being used. Recognizing the similarity between medical and legal case histories, as a Medical School senior in 1900 he wrote an article suggesting that hospital records should be used to teach medicine. In the years that followed, his suggestion was acted upon and the case system of teaching became an integral feature of medical education.

His early studies of the mechanics of digestion and the gastrointestinal tract led eventually to his studies of the effects of the emotions on the body. As he wrote in his autobiography, *The Way of an Investigator:* "The whole purpose of my effort . . . was to see the [peristaltic] waves and to learn their effects. . . . Only after some time did I note that the absence of activity was accompanied by signs of perturbation and when serenity was restored the waves promptly reappeared. This observation, a gift for my troubles, led to a long series of studies on the effects of strong emotions on the body." And, "The idea flashed through my mind that [these changes] could be nicely integrated if conceived of as bodily preparations for supreme effort in flight or in fighting. . . . The inhibition of digestive activity by emotional excitement . . . was an interruption of a process which is not essential in a life-or-death emergency and which uses a supply of blood urgently needed elsewhere." On the basis of these experiments carried on over a period of years, he wrote *Bodily Changes in Pain, Hunger, Fear and Rage.* Over the years a large body of research was carried on in his laboratory on the emergency function of the sympathetic-adrenal mechanism and finally on the eventual chemical mediation of nerve impulses.

In the early thirties, as the result of his conviction that "it is important that science be understood in a democracy," he wrote *The Wisdom of the Body,* a fascinating description of the factors involved in the preservation of the internal equilibrium of the body, which he called "homeostasis." The book often reads like a book of wonders as it describes the extraordinarily complex internal world of the human animal and the mechanisms by which the body acts to maintain the balance essential for continuing existence. How, for example, the water, sugar, and salt content of the blood is kept constant; how the body temperature, exposed to great fluctuations from within and without, maintains constancy; how in case of an emergency in many organs, the margin of safety to draw on is often fifteen times that necessary for rectification. He describes how the processes of repair and adjustment go on independently of conscious thought, triggered by an incredibly

In the laboratory

sensitive system of automatic indicators, which set the corrective process in operation.*

❧

Like many other creative people, my father had periods of depression, in part resulting from a sense of creative aridity when nothing seemed to be coming out the way he had hoped and his ideas had seemed to dry up. My mother was philosophical in the face of such melancholy, writing, "Walter thinks his career is over because he is getting no results from his researches, a sure preliminary to another meteoric jump." No doubt her buoyant optimism may have been irritating at times to one steeped in gloom, but it was the agent that maintained my father's life on an even keel and kept the household spinning along unperturbed by the periods of his despair.

When one of his experiments became exciting or some new idea formed in his mind that promised a fresh insight, he would often confide it to my mother, who, much to his dismay, would soon have it turned into a fait accompli. As she ruefully remarked about this tendency of hers, "An idea to be tested becomes established fact as soon as it enters my brain."

My father's laboratory was his castle and I think in the thirty-six years during which he presided over it I visited it only two or three times and then when I was well into adulthood.

We may have called on our two aunts at the Massachusetts General Hospital or Filene's but my father's office was sacrosanct. But if it was sacrosanct and off limits to us, there was plenty of traffic in the other direction. A steady stream of visiting physiologists and foreign graduate students from the Philippines, from Chile and the Argentine, from England and France, from Hungary and Spain, came to dinner or tea or were put up for a few nights by a judicious rearrangement of beds and bodies in our already overcrowded house.

*My father's book provided the springboard for Stanley Burnshaw's fascinating article, "The Body Makes the Minde," in *The American Scholar,* Winter, 1968–69, upon which some of this paragraph is based.

My father was always a bit nervous about the impact my mother's rather unconventional approach to entertaining might have on his foreign visitors. She was not unaware of his discomfiture, writing, "Walter seems a bit nervous, and would like to have an elaborate meal served by a maid with cap and apron, but I call that panicky servility to fashion and shall put on my 'Bridget' unblushingly." Her "Bridget," a piece of furniture of her own invention, was an open-sided box on wheels with shelves, which she put beside her place at the table and on which she deposited the dirty dishes so that no one need rise from the table and interrupt the conversation, which she considered paramount; perhaps because she was invariably at the center of it. This was an invention rather ahead of its time, and she wrote about it in her usual exuberant style in the June 1902 issue of *The American Kitchen Magazine*, whatever that was. "I think they [young housekeepers] would find the graces of life augmented and the stress of mind and body much lessened if they could summon to their aid this domestic Ariel to do such gentle spiriting albeit with the stolidity of a Caliban." It was typical that after this literary flight of fancy she should christen this utilitarian object "Bridget." Later she reported that the dinner was a success, "Bridget" having broken the ice (or so she says) with the stiff British physiologists, and added in her usual insouciant manner, "though they could not see our jokes, they looked pleasant all the time." One can only imagine that the visiting physiologists took away a sprightly if unconventional impression of American domestic life.

My father was also somewhat uneasy about my mother as linguist, especially in the face of nonnegotiable languages like Finnish or Hungarian. A visiting Finnish physiologist and his wife came to dinner one evening after my mother had called on the wife "and held a fluent talk with her in German as her German is almost as bad as mine and gave me courage. I hate to think of Walter's look of pain when I try the same tactic tonight. Fortunately we can eat in any language. I am feverishly conning the dictionary so that I can have nouns on tap. Genders, case endings, and construction hold no terrors for me but I *do* like to have nouns handy." She also believed in jumping in quickly and starting the conversation so that she would know what the talk was about and preferred to keep it abstract in subject matter as involving fewer concrete, unknown, incomprehensible words.

Every two years a domestic crisis of formidable proportions occurred when my father took his turn entertaining his shop club at a formal dinner. My father's club, the Cambridge Scientific Club, was (and is today) typical of such institutions, permanent fixtures of the intellectual life of Boston and Cambridge: a gathering of serious men, academics, doctors, scientists, lawyers, and literary men who came together once a month through the winter at one another's houses for dinner, after which the host usually gave a paper on work in progress.

Formality was a note seldom struck in our household, but everyone fell to to see that all went well. The child that was to answer the door was slicked to a shiny pitch and dressed in *The Dress,* a pretty yellow one lovingly smocked by my Aunt Bernice and handed down through the ages. I can remember when my turn came almost fainting with fright and shyness at having to usher President Eliot through the door, a most benign but, to me, terrifying old gentleman.

The silver was polished and glistening, the glasses sparkled, the huge linen napkins with their elaborate monograms, freshly washed and ironed, fairly shone with opulence and grandeur. The accommodator, one of many who shuttled from one academic house to another, was invariably recognized with amiable nods by guests as having performed the same function at their tables. Ours was usually a patronizing and rather ghoulish black lady from the Barbados, who ruled the kitchen, cooking up a storm, ordering our dear Hortense around like a slave, and pinching our cheeks and tweaking our hair as we sat around the kitchen table transfixed by her witchy tales of spider pies and fried beetles, which she claimed to be her specialties. A stream of exotic foods flowed through the swinging doors of the pantry, food that seldom passed our childish lips except at these biennial events when we were allowed to lick the bowls and finish up the leftovers. The steady murmur of masculine voices, which could be heard through the dining room door, was reassuring to us that all was going well and Father was content. For we all felt his anxiety and wished him to be happy.

There was a basic simplicity and unworldliness about my father combined with a wry sense of humor about himself. Early in their married life my mother reported, "Walter went to dinner a few days ago with some wealthy Boston doctors. They were talking about what they would do if they had all the money they wanted. Dr. B asked Walter what he would do and he answered, 'I have all the money I want. Mrs. Cannon gives me ten dollars a month and that is enough to buy my lunches, pay my carfare and get my hair cut.'" My mother goes on: "I would like to know what the other doctors thought in their heart of hearts," no doubt reflecting on the picture they might have of her as a domestic virago.

When my father's academic title was advanced to full professor, a sensitive Cambridge lady who had learned somehow that he was working on the activities of the digestive tract was heard to remark, "I hope that he will now give up those disgusting researches on the stomach." He observed with some amusement that he was not aware of becoming "more refined" as his interests turned from concern with the alimentary canal to studies on the influence of the emotions on the body.

My father was known as "Doc" to the neighboring farmers in New Hampshire, who consulted him not only about their ills but those of their cows and horses. Their faith in him was touching and as Mrs. Patten, the wife of a farmer "up the hill," who had been ailing all one winter, said, "I told Mason, didn't I, that if I could see Dr. Cannon I would be well." He was much given to punning when in good spirits (a type of humor that typified his generation, I think) and could be a wicked mimic, having a good ear for the New Hampshire dialect as well as the Swedish, which he had heard all about him in his youth in Minnesota. When Magnus Johnson, a Swedish farmer, was elected senator from Minnesota, my mother wrote, "The papers are ringing with Magnus Johnson's election, and Walter is in his element, putting all his comments on the election in the dialect. I can see a happy life for Walter the next few years following this humble apprentice in the language!" And so absurd was my father's takeoff of Harding in a skit given at one of my parents' and their friends' Stunt Parties that Professor Perry's young son turned anxiously to his father and asked whether Harding actually was such a fool.

As in so many doctor's families, especially a doctor who believed in the wisdom of the body, sickness got short shrift. As children, no pills, not even aspirin, ever touched our lips; it was just bed, water, and milk toast, and if we were lucky, and my Aunt Ida were in attendance, cambric tea on a tray. My mother, who was brought up in a homeopathic household and rather liked the comfort of pink pills, which used to be dispensed freely, once described my father's technique with a cold. "He comes into the room with a dark frown on his face and attacks the victim's failure to keep warm. He insists on a safety pin at the throat, suffocating heat in the room, while continuing to reproach the invalid for previously disregarding his warnings. He visited his physiological disapproval on Marian the other day until with a cheerful laugh she observed, 'You believe in curing by invective, don't you, Father?' "

He showed his rather deflating, self-deprecatory sense of humor on receiving the Companion of the Bath from Great Britain, honoring his research work on traumatic shock in the First World War, by asking, "Companion of whose bath?" My mother remarked, "We had a Debrett Peerage given us when we were in England and hastily looked up our place in the order of preference. I ran my eye down through the Dukes, etc. and found 'Master in Lunacy' and then 'Companion of the Bath' so I didn't feel too dazzled."

❧

The concentration of professors living in the Norton's Woods section was such that the whole area acquired the sobriquet "Professor's Row," rather a genteel social and intellectual ghetto tucked away in its corner of Cambridge. The college, although always the pride of Old Cambridge, was an institution somewhat apart; a community of intellectuals, especially one increasingly peopled by "men from away" whose names were not *familiar,* did not make for social ease. The naturally diffident, family-oriented society of the Brattle Street area kept its distance, in the face of "scholarship" and "learning," which they respected as an admirable social good but which seemed to have produced certain feelings of uneasiness and insecurity.

Life in general was certainly lived at a more leisurely pace in those days. And this was true of the academic world as well, when even the most underpaid professor could afford domestic help, and there was a good deal of dropping in and good talk, which went on in a casual way that was altogether delightful. It seemed to me that my father and mother were always going to gatherings with their friends or having Discussion Clubs or, less seriously, the Stunt Parties. Any excuse would do for a Stunt Party: birthdays, housewarmings, departures (faculty people seemed to be periodically "called" to another "chair" in another university), or non-departures (my father was "called" several different times to other jobs that he invariably turned down). He was apparently untemptable even though on one occasion Harvard refused to add to his salary on the theory that the honor of serving on the Harvard faculty was sufficient although the pay was pitiful even for those days. When an unknown admirer added a thousand dollars a year to his salary for five years after he had turned down a bid to go to the Mayo Clinic, my mother in her staunch and humorous way said, on thinking about what worthy way they could spend it, "the situation now revealed is that of a 'beer taste' and a 'champagne income' " and went on to raise the maid's pay as feeling it the only fair way to "divide the melon."

Theirs was a witty and delightful circle of friends, among them Professor Ralph Barton Perry, the philosopher and biographer of William James, and his brilliant wife, Rachel, the sister of Bernard Berenson; and Professor George W. Pierce, the physicist, a droll Texan who used to brag that he had to hide his outlaw uncle under the bed in the tiny town of Webberville, Texas, when the sheriff was after him. He also liked to "touch up on his past life," as my mother commented, when in the presence of stuffed shirts or bigots: how he was a butcher boy, ran errands for the saloon keeper, weighed cotton for a year and liked it, "but a man came along and handed him fifty dollars and said, 'Now go and borrow fifty more and get an education.' He did not want to do it, but they made him, wouldn't let him weigh any more cotton and pushed him out." So the story went and no doubt it was true. When he gave the prestigious Lowell Lectures one year, he said he planned to wear a dress suit but have a screwdriver behind his ear so that "people would know that if anything happened to the plumbing he could fix it." Also, "he was not going to have people think that just because he was dressed up that he was without weapons!" He and his wife were the beloved Uncle George and Aunt Florence of our youth. There were Judge Franklin Hammond of the Massachusetts Superior Court, a mirthful man, who observed the shenanigans and outrages of generations of peculating politicians with a sharp and philosophical eye; the architect Allen Jackson, a gifted versifier, an actor, and a master impersonator of the pompous blowhard (in my childish eyes, however, his chief attribute was the fact that he had a stuffed peacock on a mahogany stand in his front hall); Dr. Crothers, the Unitarian minister, whimsical and wise, and his sprightly wife and daughters; and many others who came and went through the years.

It was on the occasion of the Perrys' housewarming in December 1913 that my mother inadvertently launched a lively career as a monologuist. When it came to acting, she was a real ham. In her costume trimmed with tin wear, soap shakers, paste earrings, soap dishes, tin pans for stomachers, and a tiara of utilitarian objects on her head, she read her "Apostrophe to Woolworth," repeated by popular request on many other occasions in the ensuing years.

> *Oh, the 5 and 10 cent store,*
> *With its flaming sign board, its youthful salesgirls,*
> *Its cash registers*
> *To you I sing*
> *You are mine and I am yours*
> *We are the great democracy*

You, with your dollar purchases and free delivery
   to the suburbs [sic]
I and mine elbow over your counters, in velvets,
   or in rags, one common blend.
And you welcome us all alike.

Oh, the joy of every five cents, with the exception
   of what is ten,
I come with my nickel, I come with my dime,
Oh, the counters heaped high with seconds!
Oh, the joy of seconds, the little nick, the tiny hole,
   the subtle blotch
All that makes you scorned by the rest of the world,
Makes you dearer to me.

And so forth!

She wrote a series of poems "taking off" Amy Lowell, who was then at the height of her notoriety. When her mother wrote to ask whether Amy Lowell was the sister of President Lowell, my mother answered, "Amy Lowell certainly is the sister of President Lowell. He is understood to think his sister a bit 'risque'; she is so strong on the nude!"

With her plump figure bestrewn with chains and necklaces, a pince-nez on her nose, and a bejeweled band around her throat, my mother would read her poems to delighted audiences. As my mother wrote, "She, Amy Lowell, is very fat and ordinary looking, like me, and steps heavily, and makes a good deal of use of spectacles, so there were all the elements of a stunt to begin with." My mother had no false pride and was perfectly willing to make a fool of herself in the service of "art" or fun.

As For Me

She has nothing on
But what of that?
The daffodils look at her unashamed,
The sun does not hide his face from her bareness,
Who am I that I should put on my derby and walk away?

Rich, pink flesh, shall I spurn you?
The cannibals love you.
Am I so old a poet that I cannot sing afresh the glory of
nakedness?
No, I am new and unabashed.
I rejoice in the fat coating of the bones and the absence
of feathers and wool,
I am the poet of the tropics and the toute ensemble.

When she was to give a reading in the conservative town of
Milton, she was urged by her rather anxious and conventional
friends as well as by her mother in St. Paul not to be too specific
about whom it was she was satirizing as "being in questionable
taste," and in order to soothe these doubters she agreed to call
herself "An Imagist Poet." Not that she really cared a fig.

What Then?

A dark wood
Through it comes the haunting odor of the skunk,
A red cardinal flower nearby would show if it were
daylight
But it is night.
The flower is invisible in the dim rays of the moon.
A low rustle
Perhaps it is the fairies getting ready the ring for
the dance.
Or is it a skunk?
No, it is his step, for whom I wait.
Oh, at last I am enfolded in his passionate embrace.
His buttons make dents in my cheek.
What of it?
Love is the eternal dent.

At another reading in Cambridge before a large gathering of
social workers and colleagues of my Aunt Ida's, Dr. and Mrs.
Richard Cabot happened to be present. Afterward, one woman

spoke about how she had enjoyed the performance and my mother rather ruefully said, "I hope you are not a relative of hers."

"*I* am," said Mrs. Cabot, who stood nearby.

My mother reported: "Then she started to speak disparagingly of Miss Lowell, but I was too canny to be caught in *that* trap, so I defended Amy vigorously to her cousin. The Bostonians like to run down their relatives themselves, but they would not relish anyone else doing it. Dr. Cabot never said a word to me. I suppose he thought, 'What is this upstart from the West making fun of our culture for! It shows her crudity and bad taste!' "

We were a family of public speakers, my two aunts often addressing professional groups, my father in constant demand as a speaker, and my mother covering a multitude of subjects from birth control to bringing up children, as well as pursuing her role as a monologuist. There was always a good deal of merriment when my mother returned from her excursions. She sometimes used to practice her monologues on us children before launching forth, occasioning a certain amount of anxiety on our part. "Oh, Mother, it's crazy!" would be the chorus. Having an unconventional mother was sometimes hard to bear! But when she returned it was always a lark. I can still remember her standing over the hot-air register in the dining room, looking very pretty in her black lace dress, pulling off her white kid gloves, regaling us with highly colored tales of a performance before the Radcliffe Club in New York. She had wondered before taking the train whether perhaps her clothes were "too duddy; still, writers should look a bit quaint!" but had been prevailed upon by the family to wear her best party dress and "her horrible high-heeled beaded slippers" ("I'm going to have my heels cut down, style is too much for me!"). Style may have been too much for her but her account of her trip was of an unqualified success. She wrote banteringly to her mother, "I came home Thursday with an enthusiastic account of my trip; how I rocked New York to its foundations, how everyone roared with laughter at my wit, and clapped me to the echo, how there were at least fifty people there, etc. Walter came back the same evening. You ought to have been there to notice the difference in his report. No one especially there, no one

particularly interested in what he had to say, no applause worth
mentioning, only about 500 people there — I tell you — how
lovely a quality modesty is, and how rare, especially in the James
family!"

❧

My mother's running fight with the Irish politicians over school
matters may have had its lighthearted and funny side, even
though in her heart of hearts she thought most of them to be
knaves, but when it came to the battle between the Catholic
hierarchy and the proponents of birth control, the lines were
drawn with no holds barred. She was an early activist in the birth
control movement. She attended the famous Birth Control Conference in New York in 1921, writing to her mother on November
12, "Here I am, enjoying what Wilma calls 'Mother's Sabbatical.'
Mr. Crothers thinks it quaint to go off on a toot to a Birth Control
Conference, but it is proving extraordinarily interesting. . . . I
am proud to be one of the pioneers in so important a movement."

The next evening proved to be a momentous one, at which the
conference broke up in an uproar, closed down by the New York
police, and Margaret Sanger was arrested and sent to jail.

My mother reported to her mother in a fury of outrage: "I am
sitting in the train, after a night of tremendous excitement, seeing
that beautiful Mrs. Sanger arrested for holding a Birth Control
meeting, our meeting dismissed on order of Capt. Donohue of the
New York Police Dept., on the request of the Secretary of
Archbishop Hayes. That is what our land of freedom has come to
under Irish Catholic control. I am becoming a fanatical anti-
Catholic. The whole thing is terribly serious. I am going back to
put the matter to the proof, in Massachusetts, and see if freedom
of speech there is in control of Cardinal O'Connell. The blood of
my Protestant forebears is boiling in my veins!"

Her outrage continued unabated on her homecoming and she
returned to the fray: "I am still burning with rage. I know how
Latimer and Ridley must have felt when they were burned at the
stake, glad that they could testify for the truth and against tyranny
in their suffering. I wished I too could be burned or flayed for

freedom, it was terrible to be helpless. . . . Three hundred years ago Mrs. Sanger would have been burned at the stake — we have at least saved her from that, but we have come to a pretty pass if we have to ask the Catholic Church for permission to discuss subjects in which we are interested. It may be we shall be snowed under and vanquished by ignorance and bigotry, but let us at least die fighting. I am speaking at every meeting at which I have a chance, telling my experience of the conference. We must band ourselves together to fight for all that is dearest to us."

Later, in a more philosophical and perhaps more realistic mood, she commented, "I am getting back to 'normalcy' since my liberty frenzy and see that the battle will have to be fought to all eternity and probably never won."

She fought the fight for birth control for the rest of her life. She was one of the founders of the birth control movement in Massachusetts, and for many years an active member of the Board of Directors of the Planned Parenthood League of Massachusetts, serving as its president for a period during the thirties. Her profound commitment to the movement, I believe, had its roots in her devotion to her mother and her awareness of her mother's anguish over childbearing. Her mother was a bluestocking and an intellectual who often said she "was not meant for motherhood," even though she carried the burden of her large family with courage. My mother remembered her horror at the age of fifteen, witnessing the "agony" of her mother in the birth of her last child. She, who did not know the meaning of "submission," hated the thralldom in which she saw women held by the bearing of unwanted children, and felt no law of man had any authority to dictate against the right of women to determine whether or not to bear children. With the introduction of modern contraceptives, this had become a genuine choice. That this knowledge should be withheld from and denied to women by fiat of men, especially Catholic clergy professing celibacy, was intolerable. It was interesting to see the contrast between my mother's fury at the Catholic church and my Aunt Ida's appreciation of many of the priests she saw in her work, succoring the poor and unfortunates of their parishes in

their need and desperation. My mother saw the clergy only as a
body of hypocritical, bigoted, relentless tyrants taking away her
civil liberties and the rights of all women. In fact, I think she was
pretty mad at men in general as the source of so many taboos and
restrictions laid on women since time immemorial and saw her
chance to help free them from this "ultimate enslavement." She
herself was delighted with her large family and would have been
glad to have had a few more. But she had seen enough of life and
the tragedy of poverty-stricken mothers worn out by childbearing
and overwhelmed by too many children not to be outraged on their
behalf.

The first impulse of the movement had been the humanitarian
one, another landmark in the liberation of women; in essence that
had been the original touchstone of my mother's passionate involvement. As time went on, she, who like anyone else could add
two and two to make four, became more and more concerned with
birth control as a factor in curbing the population explosion. The
sheer mathematics of the increase in worldwide births as the
twentieth century progressed was so obvious. Back in the twenties, before the movement began to emphasize this aspect, she
saw with her usual clarity that there were soon going to be too
many people to feed, clothe, and care for, a phenomenon of such
proportions as had never been seen on this earth.

In her old age, she became something of an old-fashioned
fanatic, traveling to the Philippines, India, and Israel, visiting
clinics, and exchanging "lore." As a spry old lady of eighty-four,
shod in blue sneakers and leaning on a cane, she went with my
sister Linda, at that time head of an adoption agency in
Washington, D.C., to an International Conference of Social Work
in Rome. They stopped in London, then flew on to Istanbul, Tel
Aviv, and Athens, but not until they reached Belgrade did my
sister, much to her horror, discover as my mother's battered old
suitcase fell open that it was stuffed with contraceptives of all
sorts and sizes. As my sister rather bemusedly remarked to my
mother, "Why, Mother, you never taught me to travel that way!"
My mother considered herself the personal representative of the

Planned Parenthood League of Massachusetts behind the Iron Curtain, disseminating information and equipment throughout the Balkans.

She could be observed sitting tête-à-tête with the bus driver or making friends with fellow passengers, writing down their addresses in her crabbed handwriting, though how she communicated in Serbo-Croatian was a mystery. She was never daunted by a little thing like a foreign language in the pursuit of a Holy Crusade. My sister was forever having to run to the mailbox, dropping into it mysterious packages that my mother sent broadside to her new acquaintances. Hopefully, they did not get their recipients into trouble with Marshal Tito.

Abortion clinics seemed to be the chief answer to the birth control problem in Yugoslavia. My mother insisted on visiting various examples of the clinics, leading my long-suffering sister through malodorous back alleys and up fetid back stairs into these sordid establishments where she spread the word and apparently the contraceptives, for my sister remarked that when they reached Rome, my mother's suitcase was empty.

chapter six

As I recall, no one ever bothered to ask us whether we *liked* school. We went to school as one's father might go to work in the morning. It was our business, and we were expected to put in our daily stint, whether we wanted to or not. As if to emphasize this, when we graduated into the Cambridge High and Latin School from our elementary school our teachers addressed us as Mr. and Miss, and being called upon as "Miss Cannon" somehow gave a professional status to the role of high school student and endowed one with a false sense of maturity.

It was exciting to be part of the throng. We had lived such a family-oriented life that being thrown into the larger world of a public high school with all its excitement and cross-currents, its variety and fun, was challenging and exhilarating. I remember liking the anonymity of the large school where it was easy to melt into the crowd. The idea of being singled out for special attention would have been terrifying and as I look back I think this sense of privacy was for me a great boon. From my hidden perch on the sidelines I could look out and watch the passing show. It was a true melting pot of a school in those days; from East Cambridge came first-generation Italian and Portuguese and Greek "kids"; there were bright Jewish boys and girls with heavy Yiddish accents, "lace curtain" Irish from North Cambridge and Cambridgeport, a few blacks, and the sons and daughters of Protestant Yankees.

We were part of a small contingent of academic offspring, most

Memorial Hall, Cambridge

of our contemporaries having been hustled off to the "safety" of private day or boarding schools. A large number of Catholic children passed their whole educational life in parochial schools, so that the sharp divisions within the city were further accentuated by the absolute alienation existing between the various educational institutions. Harvard itself was "over there," aloof, remote, tacit in its sense of superiority, almost a rebuke to the rest of Cambridge, the "town" of "town and gown." The high school "kids" were contemptuous of the parochial school "kids"; the parochial school "kids" despised the high school "kids"; and they both combined to abominate the private school "sissies."

It was a jolly mix, but seemed not to have affected the general tone of our high school life. We were all outsiders thrown together higgledy-piggledy and the rich mélange of personality and cultures was an education in itself. We did not think much in ethnic terms in those days. Differences in background and even in religion were remarked upon but taken for granted, by them and by us. I can, however, remember us as grammar school children being little Unitarian skeptics, once baiting our Catholic playmates with questions as to the validity of the Virgin Birth, referring to what we thought were appropriate passages in the Bible to prove our point. There must have been talk around the house on the subject as the result of the Scopes Trial in Tennessee, for my mother wrote, "The children actively discuss the Virgin Birth, thanks to the Fundamentalist's gift of the subject to polite conversation. They thought it very illogical that God should be both God and Christ." But it was all rather like the blind leading the blind. I doubt that any of us knew what "Virgin Birth" meant, and we won the argument not through superior theological authority or mastery of esoteric doctrine but because they were playing in *our* back yard and there were more of us!

The question of religion was always peripherally present in high school. When we would gather from our various neighborhoods each morning at 8:30 and repeat the Lord's Prayer together with bowed heads at our desk, you could tell the Catholic "kids" from the Protestants because they always dropped off the last phrase, "For thine is the Kingdom, and the Power, and the Glory, forever and ever, Amen." The Jewish students had their holidays that seemed somehow exotic and outlandish and it was strange that no sooner had school started in September than they "got three or four days off for Yom Kippur." For Lent, girls and boys were always "swearing off" or "giving up" something toothsome for the duration, like Tootsie Rolls or Eskimo Pies, but ending up with "new outfits" for Easter. We careless little heretics never gave *anything* up, and I think we felt a bit left out of it, not partaking of this annual rite. There were no new bonnets either, as concern with new clothes for Easter was considered a leftover fetish from some idolatrous past. But I can remember once marking my forehead with ashes on Ash Wednesday and, when entering a Catholic church, crossing myself as a kind of daring gesture and feeling as though I had committed some sort of immoral sacrilege.

After our morning prayers, we pledged allegiance to the flag, standing four-square beside our desks, hand to forehead and, if you were a Girl Scout or a Boy Scout, smugly folding your little finger into your palm under your thumb. Some of the homeroom teachers were martinets; straight backs and square shoulders were mandatory, and bad posture or sloppiness here remarked upon sarcastically as Miss C. and Mr. R. were reprimanded. With the first bell, we flowed out into the noisome halls to our various classes. At 2:30, just as inexorably, we scattered to our neighborhoods, by foot or streetcar, our paths hardly ever crossing, like people working in the same office who do not necessarily see each other after office hours. We often did not know one another's first names, being invariably referred to in class, as, for instance, Miss Pofcha or Mr. DeVito, and so conventional and conservative were we as young people that if someone *did* call one by one's first name it seemed almost a breach of etiquette, a gross intimacy. How different from today!

I can still recall the splintery wooden floors of the corridors, the piercing sound of the bell releasing us for our next classes, the yellow varnished wainscoting and banisters of the stairs, heavily scarred by random carvings of names and symbols; the tired old desks with inkwells set in the right-hand corners and a lid that

could be raised, behind which one could powder one's nose unob-
served. The homeroom teacher used to sit enthroned behind her
desk on her raised wooden platform from where she could survey
our note-passing and whispering, considered sinful in those days
when discipline and order were deemed beneficial. We were
drilled unmercifully in grammar in tigerish Miss Haggerty's English class and I can still remember the lash of her tongue if some
delinquent got subject and predicate nominative in wrong agree-
ment after the verb "to be" or used the nominative case after the
preposition. We did the usual slogging through *The Mill on the
Floss* and *Idylls of the King,* French verbs, algebraic equations,
and geometry, and I remember being rather envious of the boys in
the class who went on to do "trig" and logarithms — advanced
math seemingly to be the private terrain of the male sex. Our
Latin textbooks handed on from year to year were tattered and
thumbed and so marked up with written-in translations that a trot
was hardly necessary. Not that I knew what a trot was, in my
innocence, until too late when well launched into Virgil in my
senior year. However, our Latin master, Mr. Derry, was such a
gifted teacher that we worked hard to please him, trudging
through Caesar and Cicero in a tremendous effort to keep up. His
classroom was lined with dusty, glass-doored bookcases topped
by plaster casts of Homer, Caesar, and Virgil, and he would sit in
the middle of this unpromising milieu, the very essence of an
old-fashioned schoolteacher, with his short round figure, bald
head, and benevolent eyes behind rimless glasses, and hold a
class of at least fifty students spellbound by his evocation of
classical Rome and his love for the Latin language.

The school was divided into the College Course and the Commercial Course and the communication between the two groups
was almost nonexistent. From time to time there would be an "all
school assembly" where the current ineffable mayor or one of the
orators from the School Committee would address us on days of
Patriotic Observance. The whole student body would pour into the
dusky Assembly Hall, where the squeaking of the chairs and the
general uproar somewhat interrupted the flow of their grandilo-
quences, and in spite of the turgid nature of these gatherings we

welcomed them with enthusiasm since any change in the routine was a plus. It was the one time we ever mixed with the students of the Commercial Course. The Commercial "kids" occupied a separate world breached only if one were chosen (an honor) to take a notice from the headmaster into what we considered their impossibly remote classrooms, where grizzled veterans taught such subjects as Commercial Arithmetic and Shorthand. Sometimes, when one had a free study period, it was considered daring to wander far afield and ask to study in the back of one of their rooms, where I was once regaled by one of these old girls referring to her subject as "Boo-keeping."

A lot of the Commercial "kids" even dressed differently, did their hair in "cootie garages" or wild marcels, wore lipstick and rouge, were slangy and used bad grammar; some were taking "toe" or "tap," most worked after school, and altogether, sitting in the back of their classrooms was as good as going to a play.

High school gave us ideas. We began to use lipstick, too, and powder our noses, and "shingle" our hair in boyish bobs. We cut out coupons from movie magazines and sent away for free samples of Tangee Lipstick and Pond's Cold Cream. I can still remember the feel of the delicious bump, through the brown paper envelopes, of those precious objects promising a future of unearthly beauty. We began to wear high-heeled shoes and demand something less drab than the tired brown jerseys and skirts that had been our uniforms throughout our total school existence. My father was horrified by our lipstick, thinking we were no better than fallen women, and went into a depression for days when we refused to give up the horrid habit. As for high-heeled shoes, he brought up his big guns, invoking the name and judgment of one of his orthopedic colleagues to impress us with their evil effects on the tarsal bones. But he was fighting a losing battle. Lipstick was not to be erased, and we dismissed his distinguished colleague as just one of those "fuddyduddy, stuffy Boston doctors." What an innocent and innocuous flouting of parental authority it all seems today, and yet the emotions boiling up were equal in intensity and heat to any suffered by modern fathers over the delinquency of their young, whether dropout, addict, or plain prodigal.

The competition in school was fierce. The College Course was full of bright, aspiring first-generation students determined to make their way in the world and it was quite a shock, after having been told "how wonderful we were" by our mother, who believed almost to a fault in "reinforcement," as it is called by psychologists today, that we were, after all, not *that* remarkable and had to fight hard and tenaciously to keep in the contest. It was a real rest to get to college where the pace seemed relaxed after the demands laid on us by some of our hard-driving high school teachers and fellow schoolmates.

The terror of our lives was the College Boards, looming at the end of our senior year. I can still see the shape of those fateful little white sheets of paper and feel the panic spreading as I scanned the algebra problems or the French translation, all comprehension and memory seeming to fly out the window into the balmy June air. Of course, it was taken for granted that one went on to college and would get into any college one chose, once the dread examinations were hurdled, but there was never any other college but Radcliffe for the girls of the family. For one thing, the family could not afford any institution "away," no matter how much we might have mooned after Bryn Mawr or Vassar, but, more important, it would have been a kind of *lèse majesté* as far as my mother was concerned to have deserted Radcliffe.

❧

After a dim week of school and homework, Saturday was the big day in our lives and we started early to brainwash our mother into letting us go to the movies in Boston, where we favored Loew's State and Orpheum theaters. She would seem intractable, but by Saturday noon she would have capitulated, worn out by our pleading. Off we would go, triumphant, carfare and ticket money jingling in the tips of our mittens, to drool over Clara Bow in *It;* weep crocodile tears over *Wings*, considered educational, and therefore worthy, because it was about airplanes; or swoon over

Greta Garbo in *Anna Karenina*. A welter of salty tears, flowing
unchecked and unlicked, down our adolescent cheeks, showed
we really cared for the tragedy and beauty of it all. As I wrote to
my mother in a moment of ecstasy: "She [Greta Garbo] is the most
beautiful creature I have ever seen. You ought to go and see her";
then I added prudently, "there's quite a lot of kissing in it but you
can close your eyes if you don't like it." In the same spirit we
would brag about the "stitches" we got in our sides from laughing
at Charlie Chaplin or Laurel and Hardy, or the Our Gang comedies. We prided ourselves that no one laughed harder or wept
more copiously than we.

We even got in on the tag end of old-fashioned vaudeville at
Loew's Orpheum, sitting precariously in the steep balcony seats
and laughing prodigiously, though a good deal of the patter and
double entendre went flying over our innocent heads. Farther
down toward the seamier end of Washington Street, at the Keith
Albee, we saw our first "talkie" and incidentally our first street
brawl, policemen with nightsticks laying about them on the heads
of drunken sailors as we emerged from having seen Al Jolson in
The Jazz Singer. Quite a lot of excitement for one Saturday afternoon, and we were sharp enough not to fill our mother in on *all* of
the details of our weekly expeditions. Vaudeville she considered
"cheap," drunkenness "horrid," and police brutality "reprehensible."

In those days, Boston was a marvelous theater city. The Colonial, the Shubert, the Hollis, and the rest of the downtown theaters were seldom dark but our favorite was the Copley Theatre,
long since torn down, where a remarkable repertory company
performed. On Saturday afternoons, with the marked approval of
our mother, we used to buy twenty-five-cent tickets for the second
balcony, where we sat entranced by *Charley's Aunt* or *Androcles
and the Lion* or more dour fare like *Outward Bound*. *The Ghost
Train*, that beguiling old chestnut, was produced whenever the
revenue was running low and kept the company going for years.
E. E. Clive, who later made something of a name for himself in
Hollywood, was the guiding spirit of this enterprise, and many of
his troupe went on to fame in the movies and on Broadway.

However, as we were always relegated to the second balcony, my chief impression of the legitimate theater was for years the distant square of a brightly lit toy stage with tiny figures moving about as seen through the wrong end of an opera glass. Orchestra seats were beyond the realm of possibility, to be dreamed of in some golden, unthinkable future.

When you were sixteen and the world lay before you, it was hard to decide whether to go on the stage, become a movie star, or simply be a prima ballerina. My mother had taken me at an early age to see Pavlova dance in *Swan Lake* on the theory that I was going to be the dancer of the family. I was the scrawny, wiry one of the girls, which seemed to recommend me for the ballet in her eyes. My sister Linda was to be the musician. She would practice dutifully to propitiate my mother, remarking in her humorous way, "someone has to be musical!" My sister Wilma was slated to be the artist. There was no question of her talent and, of course, in keeping with my mother's family tradition, there *had* to be an artist in each generation. My poor sister Helen was "just the baby" — apparently a career in itself until it was discovered that she had all the brains, and she was delegated to be the scholar of the family. My brother Bradford was, needless to say, to be the doctor. Fortunately, as it turned out, it was a profession that suited him admirably.

For a wild moment a career as a ballet dancer seemed imaginable, especially after seeing the Ballet Russe de Monte Carlo on its first American tour at the gorgeous Boston Opera House (long ago so tragically demolished), with its opulent crimson plush seats and tiers of boxes, its gilded putti and elaborate scrollery. The setting itself was enough to add wings to ambition, but we were timid young people at the core, and though we cast longing eyes at the footlights and the velvet curtains and cocked our ears for the plaudits of the multitudes, we renounced theatrical ambitions and went meekly off to college.

❧

My oldest sister, Wilma, seemed to us callow younger sisters to have been fashioned of finer clay than the rest of us and we held her in some awe. She had headaches and was considered in delicate health. On my mother's side, there was a good deal of tracing symptoms to relatives who had suffered similar afflictions, even as far back as two or three generations. I think there was a certain genealogical pride involved. After all, Great-grandfather Haynes had died of consumption, and this "tendency toward tuberculosis," the family taint, had tragic and romantic overtones. He had succumbed in the flower of his youth and at the threshold of a great career as a portrait painter, and my sister, who wrote poetry and drew beautifully, was considered his rightful heir. No such fate must befall her. So she was allowed to lie around and read *Lorna Doone* and *The Little Minister* while the rest of us were still playing in the back yard with the neighborhood regulars and rather resenting her absence and special treatment. Our yard was thronged with children after school playing Prisoner's Base in the fall and softball in the spring and climbing trees in all seasons. It was my youngest sister, Helen, of a naturally sociable nature, who really peopled the teams with her Agassiz School classmates. One tall, lanky boy, large for his age as a seventh grader, who used to be much admired for his tree climbing and his agility at shinnying up the porch pillars, turned out in later life to be a good second-story man and we felt he had been almost too well trained climbing up our trees and clambering over our roofs. My mother used to grow desperate from time to time with the general noise and roughhousing, writing, "Helen has filled the back yard with her friends, mostly negroes and roughnecks. It is a beautiful exhibition of democracy and as that is what mother *stands for* I have said nothing. But finally they got on the nerves of even tolerant Mother and Helen was asked to invite girls. Apparently all girls have 'bones in their legs' or something, for they don't have the dash that Helen demands of her playmates. Hence much weeping and wailing and gnashing of teeth." Some of the children must have carried off fond memories of these lively afternoons, for many years later, after our house had been moved across the street, one of the nice black boys who had been our playmate returned nostalgically to show his bride where he had played Prisoner's Base when he was a child. But alas, the yard was no more, and his playmates had long ago gone on to other things.

My sister Wilma seemed, along with all her other qualities, to have a deeper spiritual nature than the rest of us and that was supposed to be good. Besides, when she entered Radcliffe in 1927, she suddenly took a great leap forward and left us far behind. She had some serious-minded boyfriends who talked about ideas and such deep subjects as their "philosophy of life" and some more lighthearted ones who took her to Lampoon dances. Our boyfriends, if we had any, might pass us "mash" notes under the teacher's eye, which of course we would never acknowledge as a matter of pride, or leave valentines in our desk on Valentine's Day. Once my sister Linda and I went on an improbable date with two classmates, one of whom borrowed his aunt's Packard, to a ballroom at Revere Beach, where amber lights played and we were the only couples on the shiny, slippery floor. We thought this was pretty "keen" though we had to leave before the regulars arrived in order to conform to the family time restrictions, which were inhibiting to the "sophisticated" life. Needless to say, my mother knew nothing of this expedition or her horror would have been complete; Revere Beach was not exactly her beat. But on the whole, we two sisters were cases of arrested development, and whomever we may have sighed over among our schoolmates, we sighed over in our secret hearts, though we did feel sorry for the daughters of our parents' friends who went to all-girl schools and missed out on the fun.

The influence of my sister Wilma was strong, however, and there was a great deal of emphasis on being "intellectual" and having "intellectual conversations" with one's boyfriends. But having an "intellectual" boyfriend was not enough unless he had a "sense of humor," and a sense of humor was judged by whether he thought the "private jokes" that seemed inevitably to have developed in a closely knit family of girls were funny. As for "being intellectual," it was also subject to enigmatic interpretation. In my case, the name of the game seemed to be combat rather than content. Ideas were for fighting, intellectual exercise was a form of skirmish, and the summoning of argument for the final coup de

118 grace was the supreme ambition. The idea that we should refrain from argument because our adversaries were male never entered our heads and we looked with contempt on any pusillanimous contemporaries who played dumb in their pursuit of their "boy-friends." If our beaus couldn't stand the heat and didn't like being routed by "superior brain power," they could lump it! And a lot of them did.

❧

School nights were sacred to study and homework, but an exception was made for the Boston Symphony Orchestra, which in those days played a series of concerts for the Harvard community in Sanders Theatre in Memorial Hall across the street from our house. It was one time when living completely surrounded by academic buildings proved to be a blessing. People were always giving the family extra tickets, since we lived so close by and represented such a mass of humanity, and at the last minute two or three of us would throw on our coats and run across Kirkland Street to the concert.

Year after year, we took it as our due that we should be able to listen to that glorious music in our own front yard, so to speak; Koussevitzky conducting Tchaikovsky concertos, Beethoven symphonies, and Mozart sonatas; Sibelius and Stravinsky, heard for the first time; and always the fascination of Koussevitzky himself, elegant, imperious, adored! We learned not to clap between movements, fell in love with the double-bass player, and sighed over the flutist; sat on the obdurate wooden seats dreaming of fame and fortune as the long movements of the Brahms seemed to drag on forever; contemplated the enormous brass chandelier hanging perilously above the orchestra and wondered how they changed the light bulbs; tried to translate the Latin inscription on the huge lunette over the stage; and let our eyes roam over the audience, as quintessentially academic Cambridge as the Friday afternoon concerts were the essence of Boston.

Cambridge ladies were, however, even frumpier than their Boston counterparts and though often "dressed" for these occasions gave the impression of being garbed out of their grandmothers' trunks. These being evening concerts, one was at least spared the ill-favored hats worn by generations of Boston ladies, which in their Cambridge incarnation might have been even more disastrous. Not that anyone really cared or noticed. Their minds were on higher things.

Harvard University in the twenties was still a genuine academic community. Most of the senior and many of the junior faculty still lived in Cambridge; indeed most of them would have considered living anywhere else analogous to banishment to Outer Mongolia. It was a peculiarity of Cambridge that houses along "Professor's Row" and in other parts of Old Cambridge as well were never identified by street number or even by present owners. One might have lived for fifteen or twenty years in one of the comfortable old houses on Francis Avenue or Irving Street, and still have people remark in sociable conversation, "Oh, yes, you live in the Royce house," Professor Royce having been dead for fifty years, or, "Yes, that was old Professor Moore's house," though two or three other owners might have intervened.

Houses were handed on from one academic to another; even the real estate agents, with unusual sensitivity to intellectual atmosphere, seemed to conspire to maintain a high level of academic occupancy and few ringers were allowed in. It was a bizarre form of exclusion, not practiced along the more mundane lines of race, creed, or previous condition of servitude. As a result professors lived in close proximity to their colleagues and a goodly number were in faithful attendance at the Thursday evening concerts.

Thursday evening concerts were not only musical feasts but occasions for pleasant social intercourse; in fact, it seemed that to some the gathering of people in the intermission in the funereal foyer of Memorial Hall with its uneven marble floor and unheatable vaulted ceiling was the most important part of the concert. Seats were awarded hierarchically in those days and if one sat in the mezzanine out from under the balcony it was a sign of having arrived. Through the years one could watch the academic progress of ambitious young instructors, with that lean and hungry look, as they moved down from the balcony to mingle with their superiors; young assistant professors, their appointments made permanent, their faces changing, as security softened anxiety and striving, to visages of rotund self-satisfaction. Splendid Cambridge characters occupied the same seats for decades and one saw them grow old and decrepit and finally pass from the scene. There was the distinguished old lady with a large tin ear trumpet who always sat in the front row; the modest academic daughter, engaged at last to some worthy graduate student, sharing the score with him, following a Mozart concerto; and eager undergraduates, transfixed and mute with delight, sitting in the balcony. Even the orchestra shifted and changed through the decades. Gradually the double-bass player became a paunchy, gray-haired old man, the flutist retired. Munch eventually succeeded Koussevitzky, gifted graduate students grew up to be Nobel prizewinners, Sanders Theatre was refurbished, revarnished, and wired for sound, and those two immutable marble figures flanking the stage, Josiah Quincy and James Otis, turned gleaming white after a good washing with soap and water. And, sad to say, the Cambridge concerts at last expired themselves, no doubt the victims of inexorable economic forces, the same forces that scattered much of the Harvard "community" from its safe haven of pleasant Cambridge neighborhoods far and wide into the outlying suburbs.

chapter seven

In 1928, MY MOTHER PUBLISHED A BEST-SELLING NOVEL, *Red Rust*, the story of Swedish pioneers in her native Minnesota. It was her first novel, but not her first piece of writing. She had in fact been turning out provocative articles for *The Atlantic Monthly*, *Harper's*, and the *North American Review* since the early twenties on a variety of subjects, ranging from "The New Leisure to "Philanthropic Doubts," from "Can Our Civilization Maintain Itself?" to "The Crabbing of Youth by Age," a lively critique of education in the June 1923 *Atlantic*. She was obviously not intimidated by either the largeness or complexity of her subject matter and gave anything she wrote a spirited whirl.

In 1925 she had gone with her sister on a trip to the Southwest where she had become fascinated with the history of the coming of the Spanish Conquistadors to New Mexico and had come home fired with the idea of writing a children's book based on the story of Coronado. Hardly waiting long enough to unpack her suitcase (she never took more than one small one, even before air travel), she retired to the Peabody Museum and to Widener Library where she immersed herself in the literature of the Spanish invaders. She wrote her mother, "Have you ever read about Coronado's expedition into New Mexico? It makes the Pilgrims look like sybarites! I am reading all the old diaries of the explorers I can get hold of and the children say that New Mexico and Coronado are the only words they hear from morning to night."

That summer, with shoeboxes full of notes, and with one of

The "chalet"

those featherweight Corona typewriters that danced all over the table with the touch of a finger, my mother, accompanied by five children and various cousins to water down the concentrated family and ameliorate the squabbling, went off to New Hampshire to write her book.

Franklin, through the years, was the scene of feverish literary activity. On the top of every hill, someone seemed to be writing a book. In my Aunt Ida's house across the valley from ours, Miss Richmond, a distinguished pioneer in the field of social work, was writing a tome on social theory. Up the hill, Professor Robert Yerkes not only wrote books on behavioral psychology but for a few summers kept two baby chimpanzees in the old barn in comfortable cages under the haymow, with whom he began his celebrated series of experiments on the intelligence of anthropoid apes. We children were allowed every once in a while as a special treat to take the chimps for walks in the fields, holding onto their leathery little hands, or watch them re-creating their African habitat as they broke branches and built nests high in the top of the gray birches that grew along the stone walls of the cow pasture. The natives took this addition to the local fauna with their usual stolidity, having gotten used to the quirks of the "summer folks" and all those "profs."

My father wrote in his study, a tiny brown-shingled shack like something out of *Hansel and Gretel*. It was hidden away at the foot of the towering twin pines that gave our farm its name, built on top of the boulder that was the overhanging backdrop for the woodsy stage where every summer for years we put on plays. He was sometimes forced to evacuate his little aerie when it was used as a Scottish castle in *The Lady of the Lake* or a Greek temple in *Alcestis*. But usually the absolute quiet of his retreat was broken only by the sound of the crickets in the nearby field or the croaking of the frogs in the frog pond in the Yerkes pasture, though it was close enough to the road so that he could hear the mailman when he arrived. He liked to punctuate his writing by a trip to the mailbox after Mr. Watts, our laconic postman, had staggered up the hill: first in his buggy drawn by a long-suffering horse, later, at not much greater speed, in his Model T Ford.

124   My mother wrote in the "chalet," another homemade shanty perched on the side of the hill at some remove from the main house, looking out across the pasture at the sweeping view of the valley and Mount Kearsarge on the horizon. The "chalet" had been concocted soon after my parents bought the farm in 1910 by my mother and some friends out of the old collapsing hen house that had clung to the side of the barn. As a "surprise" for my father, who was off on a trip, it was moved and "reassembled" at its new site. As my father said, after his first astonishment, the "surprise" was how much work was left for him to do! The "chalet" was rather "modern" in its architectural conception, with unobstructed screened openings on all four sides, protected from the weather by wooden shutters, hinged at the top, to be raised and lowered by ropes that ran through small pulleys. It was all very well when the weather was sunny and warm but when the rains came and the weather turned cold, the little hut was like a satanic cave, lit only by faltering candlelight. Besides, the roof, though enthusiastically shingled by my mother and my Aunt Bernice, was apt to leak. The "chalet," which served as the guest house when not used by my mother as her "studio," was once memorialized in a bread-and-butter letter by Professor Pierce, after staying in it for a week. "Dear Madam," he wrote, "The Manuscript of your article entitled 'The Leaky Chalet' has been received and read with pleasure. It is superb. We enjoyed especially the chapter 'Who Sleeps Bathes' " — and he enclosed a check to pay for having the roof reshingled.

My mother used us children as guinea pigs, trying out each chapter as it was written to find out whether it was to our taste. "I read the first chapter of my book [ultimately entitled *The Pueblo Boy*] to the children and got their unqualified disapproval. As they are my audience, I wrote another chapter according to their prescription and succeeded better. I have never found a more congenial task. I leave the family to its own resources. I get up at six o'clock, order the meals with a note enclosed to tell the children what their duties are (berrying, weeding the garden). Then I make my bed, wake the maid [lucky mother!] and depart for the chalet and am at work at seven o'clock with all my jobs done. I have a view of all that goes on, see the berry pickers go by and return etc., yet am blessedly removed. And my orders are that nothing but sudden death is allowed to interfere with my morning work." She goes on: "Creative work requires this freedom from responsibility. . . . I do not see how Mrs. Humphrey Ward wrote her books, brought up her children, and retained her husband's affection. It is the kind of experience that makes one marvel that women can combine a career with home responsibilities, not so much the divided time as the divided mind."

Having satisfied, up to a point, the criticisms of her children, she finished the book and sent it off to a potential publisher. It became the first of a series on the Spanish and Indians in the Southwest that she continued to write over the next ten years.

❧

But she had gotten the bit between her teeth and as she said, "I am rather planning to tackle a novel now. Why not? Stupider people have done so. But shall I ever find such a stimulus as wonderful Acoma?"

She turned for her subject matter back to her native state and wrote of the experiences of the Swedish immigrants. *Red Rust* is the story of Matt Swenson, a gifted farm boy who spends his life trying to develop a strain of wheat resistant to the devastating rust disease that had decimated the wheat fields of the struggling Swedish pioneers. In the body of the book she paints a vivid picture of the life of the Swedish immigrants whom she had known as a child on their Minnesota farms and about whose experiences and hardships she had heard much from her lawyer father. As she wrote to her mother after having sent the completed manuscript to her family in St. Paul: "I want Papa to read it and pick out the terrible errors. He knows the Swedes in their homes from his hunting trips better than any of the other members of the family and he may pick up mistakes that the others will miss. The character of Jensen I drew from Jens, our morose coachman, and the cooks and nurses and laundry helpers form a composite."

In her research, she consulted Dr. Otto Folin, professor at the Medical School, of Swedish background, who had been brought up on a Minnesota farm and who "confirmed the rightness that oxen were used by the poor homesteaders," and was in violent correspondence with the Department of Agriculture about various strains of wheat and techniques of agriculture. Once when queried about the correctness of one of her sweeping generalizations, she observed philosophically, "Writing a book involves philology, climatology, astronomy, botany, zoology, etc., besides the mere story! The only safe subject is a love story located on Mars where no one can catch you up!" She spent many hours poring over the literature of the early pioneers. "By the way," she wrote, "I have been reading E. C. Seymour's 'Travels in Minnesota in 1849.' It is full of the St. Croix River, Stillwater, Marine, and all that region, giving the Indian background" — the area where as a little girl she used to go quail-shooting with her beloved father. She continued, "One book, 'The History of the St. Croix Valley,' by O'Neil, I think, had the lives of the Baileys, Crandons, Woodworths, Noltmeiers, etc. It seemed so odd to sit in the Widener Library stacks and come suddenly upon old friends."

She often wrote in the bathroom, the only warm room in the house, and when she wanted to get away from the telephone, importunate committee women, and whining children, would take refuge in the family car, where she would scribble away on a pad of paper propped up on the steering wheel.

Literary competitions were much in vogue in those days and in 1927 both *Harper's* and *The Atlantic Monthly* conducted them, offering prizes up to $10,000 and promises of publication. My mother, who was just as starry-eyed about possibilities of instant fame as any number of hopefuls before or since, decided to try her luck.

After clearing up the inevitable errors — "Thank heaven," she wrote her father, "you removed the tamarack from the 'deciduous' group of trees" — and after killing off the hero in the last chapter, much to the distress of her mother and Dr. Crothers, she sent copies of the manuscript, not to just one but to both contests. She never believed in doing things by halves. She reflected philosophically, "At least they will have to be read in the circumstances, though when you remember that there were 1500 manuscripts submitted last year for the *Harper's* you *do* feel that you will be tasted and rejected speedily."

In February, she received a letter from the *Harper's* editor implying that she was in the running for the *Harper's* prize. A few days later, she wrote to her mother, "I am in a pickle! After the letter from Harper's, Walter thought I ought to withdraw the novel from the Atlantic contest. . . . Mr. M. who is in charge of the contest 'refused' to return it and 'hinted' that I might get the Atlantic prize! They are to let me know in a few days. Of course, I have not had an offer from either but it looks as though the supply of books must have been meagre this year and mine the only grammatical one in the bunch."

The excitement of the family was tremendous. "The more we talk about the possibility of the book winning the prize, the more the problem of spending the money looms. Ida wants the mantel-piece repainted, Walter wants the paint around the doorknobs washed, and except for music lessons for the children, books and travel, I have no wants. The children are greatly excited. Linda says with a sigh of relief, 'Now I can have another pair of silk stockings and not have to darn all the time,' and Wilma has become so demoralized by the financial prospects that she said, 'You know, I am losing all sense of the value of money. I spend a quarter now without thinking of it.' I do not think anything has touched me so much in the whole affair as the children's excite-ment and interest in every step of the process. Bradford remarked after the first letter came, 'Well, Mother, you're quite a woman,' which from him was pure flattery."

"Did you ever hear of such a strenuous time for a quiet, homeloving woman?" she observed satirically. "The truth is that I am going to antagonize someone whatever I do, and the only question is, would it be better to be hated by a big important firm like Harper's or by my neighbor, Mr. Sedgwick." After weeks of cliffhanging, haggling, and indecision, during which she became "quite ill with emotion" and remarked that "many more days of this kind of excitement will send me to bed with nervous prostra-tion," she finally came down on the side of loyalty, withdrawing

128 her book from *Harper's* and leaving it with *The Atlantic*, which had published her articles for years.

My mother did not win the *Atlantic* prize but her book was runner-up to Mazo de la Roche's *Jalna*, both books long since forgotten. My mother, being human, wrote, "Now, of course, I wish I had stuck by Harper's. But at any rate, it was fun to have created such excitement with a first novel. When I think that last summer I should have felt myself fortunate even to be published, I cannot complain."

Red Rust was published in 1928 and became a best-seller, at one time being preceded on the list only by *Winter's Moon* by Hugh Walpole and Thornton Wilder's *The Bridge of San Luis Rey*.

My mother's book was received in Boston and Cambridge with typical cautious reserve. She reported that "one of our neighbors, a severe New Englander who is full of righteousness with a warm heart and a Spartan manner, came up to me at a tea and said, 'I want to thank you for your book.' I countered with 'When you pay a good $2.50 for a book I do not think you are under any obligation to thank the writer. I only hope you enjoyed it.' She responded earnestly, 'I was fortunate enough not to have to buy it. Someone lent it to me.' Then she looked at me severely and said, 'I did not like some of it. You cannot expect me to like much of a book about pioneers.' "

And another friend, a Mrs. B., who according to my mother lived in constant fear of sovietism in America and who saw the insidious hand of Moscow everywhere, was "big enough to ignore the title and said to me, 'I want to congratulate you on having written a Best Seller which has not a risque sentence in the book. It is a great achievement!' "

As for critical comment from the family, my sister Wilma observed meditatively, "It's awfully queer to read a book by your mother. I've already come across six words I never heard of before and I never realized my mother knew anything about 'love,' " and my sister Linda let my mother know that she thought it dangerous to write impassioned love scenes. "You might put ideas in our heads!"

A few years later, my mother received a letter from someone in the Department of Agriculture saying in part, "I have just finished rereading your book after a lapse of ten years since the first reading. . . . How such an authoritative book could be written by an 'Eastern' author appears to have been a big question in the minds of everyone who read it [i.e., the people in the Department of Agriculture, I presume].

"I have only recently learned that you were raised in St. Paul, Minn. and that your father was a pioneer of that region, which explains a great deal.

"This work of fiction appears to have created more popular interest in the control of the cereal rusts than anything else that has ever been written. It played a major role in the obtaining of funds for starting an extensive campaign against rust by breeding for resistance, a line of work that is just beginning to bear fruit. . . . In other words, the dreams of 'Matt Swenson' are finally being realized."

❧

In 1929, with the proceeds of *Red Rust,* the family went to Europe. It all began in the spring when my father came home from his laboratory one day and announced that he had just refused an invitation to be visiting professor at the Ecole de Médecine of the University of Paris in the following spring. He saw no reason to uproot himself from his work, interrupt his experiments, disrupt the even tenor of his life to lecture in a foreign language, eat unfamiliar food, and sleep in alien beds. My mother, not one to take such a decision lying down, especially one that involved travel, announced in turn to my father that he should return to his laboratory and immediately withdraw his refusal. "After all, Walter, what an opportunity for the girls." My brother, who seemed to be perpetually being educated, had to stay home and keep his nose to the grindstone, as he was firmly launched in medical school and could, it must be presumed, do without the European "polishing" reserved for his sisters.

My father went back to his laboratory and withdrew his refusal, though he stood his ground, deciding that half a year was enough for him. My mother, however, had other ideas for herself and us girls: three months of "Art Awheel in Italy," before we met again in Paris for Christmas.

chapter eight

It must be remembered that going to Europe in the late twenties was still a great adventure, something that was planned for months if not years, and not undertaken lightly, at least in our modest academic family. So we began our preparations. First we bought an impossibly large but "spiffy" second-hand Cadillac touring car with jump seats, which when swung off the *Roma* in Genoa missed falling into the harbor by a hair's breadth. The Italian dockers seemed never to have handled anything so cumbersome or so monstrous. My father, with his usual ingenuity, built covered boxes along the running boards fixed with strong padlocks to discourage pilferers. In them we stored our meager wardrobes — one dress, one suit, a sweater or two, a pair of shoes, and two pairs of stockings apiece for a year's travel! Present-day hippies couldn't do much better when it came to reduction to essentials. We girls were fitted with harnesslike contraptions hung around our waists under our clothes, which contained our passports and which we referred to as our chastity belts. We soon discarded them as ridiculous. My mother, however, continued to gird herself, not only with her passport but with "the letter of credit," a sacrosanct document, precursor of the American Express card, and rather less convenient, for my mother had virtually to disrobe in front of the bank teller's window in order to cash our dollars into lire.

We were met at the dock in Genoa by the sixth member of the group, my mother's sister, Aunt Margaret. She was an artist and a

Looking down over Florence

sculptress, who had studied in New York with Augustus Saint-Gaudens in her youth and had once written a letter home to her mother passing judgment on the master: "I have had St. Gaudens' criticism and I was not as impressed with him as I had expected. He is not at all an educated man!" But she went on to add, "I like Mr. St. Gaudens' dog so much. One feels it an honor when he takes notice of you." Such a remark was typical of her sweet-natured moony personality as well as of the rigorous standards of "education" that her mother had inculcated in her. She quickly established her little nest in the car in one of the jump seats, with her paint bag, her purse, and her suitcase somehow deposited under her feet and a pair of stockings perpetually hung out to dry on the blanket rope that festooned the back of the front seat. She was a gentle counterfoil to our adolescent brashness, a romantic who saw in every distant shepherd sitting on a rock a "possible Michelangelo, if only we could give him a chisel" and would remark dreamily as we drove into Florence or Assisi or Rome, "So *this* is Venice!"

My mother was determined that our time should be well spent. Art was to be our Muse; and to this end, like genteel English travelers of the nineteenth century setting out of the Grand Tour, we supplied ourselves with watercolor blocks, canvas-covered sketchbooks, paint boxes, and a couple of collapsible stools with which to paint our way through Italy. In our "touring car" we traveled in a leisurely fashion for three months from Venice down the full length of the peninsula to Sicily, scraping our way through miles of village streets too narrow for such a preposterous vehicle and enlivening the life of the natives of many a tiny hamlet as we sketched onion-domed churches in the Dolomites, villas in Tuscany, Roman ruins in Pompeii, peasant huts in Calabria, and the Greek theater in Taormina with Mount Etna in the distance in mild eruption.

Within our ranks all was not always peaceful contemplation. The anguished cries of "How do you *do* shadows?" and the unbearable realization that "Your trees are better than mine," combined with the furious screech of ripping paper, were all too common sounds disrupting our idyll. Settling on "a subject" could also be a source of conflict, though ruins were popular, perhaps because it did not matter whether the lines were straight. No matter how frustrated one might be by the inability to get the perspective to "go away" or the arches of San Marco to "match," the confrontation forever imprinted special landscapes and certain buildings on our minds. The frustration itself was a kind of spur, and the excitement of each challenge had an almost physiological effect. The adrenalin began to flow, the heartbeat increased: "Will I or won't I be able to pull it off this time?" Sometimes one did, more often one did not. But who can forget the tension of the attack: choosing the colors, rearranging the trees, delineating the composition, abolishing whole villages if necessary, or banishing an inconvenient figure or an intrusive cow as being too difficult to draw. Such are the privileges of the artist, a rather low-level exercise in playing God.

Recently I was stirring around in an old trunkful of paintings and drawings of our Italian trip, and fell to wondering how my mother was able to achieve such command without alienating us for life. I cannot imagine her getting away with it today, but we tagged along, amazingly docile, as I look back on it. Perhaps it was because she was such an irresistible, joyous force, sweeping us along in a whirlwind of high spirits and positive action. We simply did not want to be left behind and miss the fun. Whatever the reason, my sisters and I caught the fever. Through the years we have packed our paints whenever we have traveled and by now, between the combined efforts of all four, few parts of the world have escaped our brushes, from the mosques of Isfahan to the ruined abbeys of Ireland or the looming mine heads of Montana and, long ago, the Chinese Buddhist temples in the hills of Foochow on the Min River.

The bonuses have been great. To sketch a country is to look at it in a unique manner and in turn it is a rare way to get to know the natives. If you are foolhardy enough to sit down in the open air to paint, you are as vulnerable to the attention of the masses as honey is to a swarm of bees. People will happily stand ten-deep behind one's back trying to get a peek, and will stack themselves ten-deep in front as well, therefore successfully cutting off the landscape. With the population explosion, the going has become even more hazardous, especially in so-called underdeveloped countries where the populace seems to have endless time on its hands, in particular, the little "connoisseurs" between six months and six years old.

On the whole, I am against guides, as I like sight-seeing on my own terms, but in places like India they can be a godsend for the itinerant painter. Not only will they perform the usual function of running art critic, but they will tote gear, ward off inquisitive children and pariah dogs, fetch chairs from accommodating householders, refill the paint cup with water, and above all shoo away sacred cows who have a talent for standing moodily in the view.

In Mohammedan countries one can scatter the girl children and women by drawing their likenesses, for they dread the evil eye, feeling threatened in some primordial way, fearing that some dark essence is being stolen from them by such depiction. The young ones giggle and run away; the women wrap their robes or saris more closely around their infants or pull their veils over their faces. But the little boys, all bristling male ego, are insatiable models. They preen and strut like turkey cocks, and find it incomprehensible that they might be considered little pests, and the inevitable smart-alec young blades, who brazenly insert themselves between you and your subject, feel they are Allah's gift to women. But on the whole, people are neither threatening nor ugly, simply curious, feeling fully justified in scrutinizing every brush stroke, pointing out all omissions, and passing comment, usually mercifully in some incomprehensible language. Italy, in 1929, with its "large leisure class," as my mother remarked about the hoards of followers who attached themselves to us in every Calabrian village, prepared us for all the pitfalls as well as the pleasures of our future as wandering painters.

I do not wish to leave the impression that we were a carful of Pollyannas, for from time to time there was no lack of grumbling and dissent in the ranks. A revolt occurred in Venice over my mother's energy and decisiveness, which was deemed "numbing" to everyone else's initiative. It was decided by popular consent that the running of the trip was to be handed over to us girls, and our mother relegated to a comparatively mute role. As my mother wrote to my father, "Wouldn't it be wonderful if I could put it through [i.e., abdication]! It would be a bonanza for you, wouldn't it? I am to carry the purse but the girls are to pay the bills. They say my chest alone is adapted to the letter of credit. My character is to suffer a revolution. If only the fates that presided over my birth will give me the good gift of acquiescence." My sister Helen, however, remarked perspicaciously, "Some centuries from now there will be a St. Cornelia [we were well up on saints and their symbols by now], a martyr to keeping silent, who finally had to have her head cut off to accomplish it."

It was a rare time to have traveled in Italy, before tourism had overwhelmed it. All galleries were our province; churches, frescoes, and mosaics our daily fare. My sister Wilma, fresh from the rigors of a fine arts concentration at Radcliffe, was our docent, perhaps a little prolix at times as docents are apt to be, but enthusiastic and knowledgeable, and a lot of it rubbed off on the rest of us. We all chose our specialties: my mother, sarcophagi; we younger sisters, coats of arms, costumes, prehistoric remains; my sister Wilma, Romanesque architecture; and my Aunt Margaret, the whole field of sculpture. By the end of our three months we became a veritable phalanx of art authorities. So deserted were the churches that we were able to see the sublime Piero della Francesca frescoes in Arezzo only by whistling up the old verger to unlock the church doors. Once inside, we sat in the empty choir stalls behind the high altar undisturbed in our contemplation except by the verger boxing the ears of a small boy amidst a noisy colloquy. The child was apparently bent on unlocking the dusty postcard cabinet behind the same altar, presumably in pursuit of a sale, which we would have thought was considered a worthy enterprise anywhere in Italy. We wondered at the severity of the custodian and reflected that perhaps he was one of those rare ecclesiastical officials who put aesthetics before commerce.

We came upon the lovely Church of Sant'Appollinare in Classe in Ravenna in the soft early light of a September morning, finding it equally empty and deserted; and seeing its magnificent Byzantine mosaics without the intervention of guides or importunate small boys gave us almost the sense of being explorers stumbling on undiscovered treasure for the first time. And so we zigzagged from the Adriatic across the Apennines, through the charming hill towns of Gubbio, Urbino, Assisi, and Perugia. In the valley of the Clitumnus, St. Francis's "sweetest valley in the world," where he lived and preached, we spent the night in the Eremo Franciscano, a lovely little convent high on the rocky hills above the valley, built on a site where St. Francis was said to have preached and slept. We had climbed the long stony goat path through dim silvery olive groves, our way lit by a full moon, to be greeted by the convent bell, rung to welcome the wandering strangers. The eight sisters of the little secular order were living strictly by the precepts and example of St. Francis, and in their gentle goodness took us in, found beds for us in tiny whitewashed anchorite cells dedicated to St. Girolamo and St. Bernardino, and fed us with tea, bread, and jam of their own making and ripe olives from their trees. So moved was my mother by the radiance and beauty of their lives of selflessness and dedication that she wrote, "They made a picture which will never leave us, the eight women, one blind, two little dark Calabrians, one old frail Sister with white hair, a red haired novitiate, a plain hewn Sister who did the cooking. Sorella Rosa, who looked like a Melozzo da Forli angel from her lovely face to her beautiful bare feet slipped into rope sandals and at the heart of it all Sorella Maria herself with the asceticism of the saint withdrawn and the tender approachableness of the Mater Dolorosa. One could think of no sin she could not pity or forgive, no love which would not be the richer for having been shared with her. Gentleness, pity, understanding, spoke in her every word and gesture."

I can remember a certain wonder at seeing my mother so affected by things of the spirit, yet as I grew older I came to recognize more and more that beneath her slapdash, uninhibited exterior she was a woman of deep sentiment and feeling.

And so we said our farewells the next day under the arches of the sunny cloister ablaze with scarlet geraniums, and picked our way down the stony goat path, our ears still attuned to the chanting of the evening prayers, which had lulled our sleep, and to the sweet farewell song sung by the eight sisters as they stood at the convent gate and waved good-bye. We took to our wanderings once more and at last dropped down into the valley of the Arno and the city of Florence.

Florence was our shrine! We had all faithfully read *The Medici* in preparation for our pilgrimage; had been conditioned since childhood by the sepia reproductions and photographs of the Bargello, of Michelangelo's *David*, of the swaddled babies of Luca della Robbia and the *Annunciation* of Leonardo da Vinci, which my Aunt Ida hung on her walls; and were well versed in the romance of Elizabeth Barrett and Robert Browning as told and retold by my mother, brought up as she had been in the age of genteel romanticism and the Browning Societies.

In fact, my mother was overflowing with lore. We passed over the Po River where "Hannibal had crossed with his army and his elephants" and crossed the Rubicon to the accompaniment of the "marching legions of Caesar's army." She could not resist seeing Caesar "returning to Rome along the Via Cassia, with chariots, slaves, horses, and poor Caesar jerked in a springless vehicle over the stones of the great road, a triumphant victor and a very uncomfortable man, envying the ladies of 2000 years later rolling along in their rubber-tired Cadillac over roads he had built." She had a seemingly bottomless grab bag of pertinent facts (or near facts) and classical allusions (left over, one supposes, from teaching Latin for two years after she graduated from Radcliffe), which she produced at appropriate moments. Although she claimed that "I always like to unload my information as soon as I acquire it. I don't like to have it cluttering up my mind," she had in fact stowed a good deal away through the years for future reference.

Florence may still have been the city of Henry James, of the

Sitwells, and of Bernard Berenson, but it was also the refuge of English maiden ladies of small income but artistic sensibilities, impoverished young art historians, and culture-seeking German couples, a goodly number of whom were living in the pension looking over the Arno in which we stayed. No Grand Hotels for us, alas; the pensions of Europe were our fate! They all seemed to share certain characteristics in common; the lugubrious foyer, dark, scabrous wallpaper on the walls, and lumpy beds with bolsters, from the feel of them, stuffed with rocks. As was often the case, our pension in Florence had once been an establishment of some distinction that had fallen on evil days. The ceilings were fifteen feet high with elegant moldings and the parlor and the hallway were adorned with dim reproductions of Botticelli and Fra Filippo Lippi Madonnas hung against faded brocades. Heavy neo-Renaissance tables of unexampled ugliness stood against the walls and rusty green velour overstuffed chairs with lace antimacassars were arranged stiffly in the salon. All was bathed in a sepulchral light owing to the inevitable fifteen-watt bulb hanging from the ceiling. The dining room, equally mournful and ponderous, was hushed at mealtime; an air of nineteenth-century decorousness clung about the dinner table where one felt that conversation was frowned upon, and if held at all must be conducted in lowered voices. Furled napkins in napkin rings lay on the sideboard and in the land of Lucullus, watery soup and indifferent pasta and veal were our daily regimen.

However, pensions in those days had redeeming features. They always seemed to contain libraries of tattered Tauchnitz editions, no doubt left behind by indifferent patrons. Some of them must have had exotic tastes, for it was in the dark of the night, lit, if I was lucky, by another fifteen-watt bulb by the side of my bed, that I first read Hemingway, Dos Passos, and Fitzgerald. *Lady Chatterley's Lover*, too, fell into my hands, all unsuspecting, and I can report that the leap from *The Mill on the Floss* to D. H. Lawrence was achieved not without a certain amount of confusion as to what was going on. My seventeenth year was a seminal one, to say the least.

I am always grateful that it was in such a bizarre twilight world of European hotels and pensions that I was first exposed to volumes like *The Sun Also Rises* and *Tender Is the Night*. Not only was the atmosphere of Italy and France still that of the hectic postwar world of the American expatriates, but the characters were still around: the narcissistic heroines, the hedonistic heroes, the bombastic artists, brooding poets, and tense young writers. I would glimpse them in restaurants, in galleries, in street cafés still acting out their roles and in my burgeoning adolescent heart longed to be part of their scene, a life that promised unimaginable joys and excitement. As time went on I must have been a trial to my sisters and my mother, for I was apt to put on airs and complain about my superior "sensitivity" and let it be known that I felt I was traveling in the company of unsophisticated Philistines. "Marian and her highfalutin tastes" became a family battle cry, as I sighed after and longed to possess "beautiful objects" or "expensive dresses" or "fancy food." After apostrophizing other occupants of the car in a long verse poem my sister Wilma wrote about the trip for our father at Christmas, she put me down rather neatly, having already paid tribute to my sister Linda —

> *Next Linda, born her mother's joy*
> *The best chauffeur in our employ.*
> *She honks at corners, travels slow,*
> *And always goes down hills in low.*
> *One problem did this pearl present*
> *Her energies possessed no vent*
> *Till God, who every sparrow sees,*
> *Expressed her Marian to tease.*
> *Alas, the denouement was swift*
> *No cherub was this God-sent gift*
> *(His cherubs live on air alone . . .*
> *Our must be stuffed with Toblerone)*
> *We tested her with Heaven's vaults*
> *By HARPING GENTLY . . . on her faults*
> *The worldling said it wasn't funny*
> *And out she swept to spend some money.*

However, in a different mood, I went through the Uffizi Gallery with my sisters in a state of suspended animation and intoxication. My sister Wilma wrote to my Aunt Ida about her first visit to the gallery, "It was like opening a Christmas stocking, each present just what you wanted most, and then a glimpse ahead into the little room beyond, like packages deeper down in the stocking which have bulges so full of meaning but which you just will not rush ahead to until you have seen everything above."

We used to play a game of identifying painters as we went from room to room and got quite expert at recognizing saints by their symbols, making a specialty of the good St. Jerome removing the thorn from the paw of the lion, whose soulful eyes and doleful expression as depicted in Italian Primitives reminded us of our cherished Irish terrier we had left behind us at home. Such was our lighthearted approach to the subject of Italian art.

We would make fun of my mother and my Aunt Margaret for their addiction to the Baedeker lest they miss something three-starred. We had set forth with a whole library of Baedekers of all ages and in all states of repair, lent to us or given to us, dusted off from previous trips to Europe, and referred to religiously by the two adults of the trip. My sister's long poem included a short verse celebrating their virtues.

> . . . *the Baedekers en famille*
> *Who range in age from fifty three*
> *To seven months — a high brow band.*
> *They led us firmly by the hand*
> *And showed us what we* ought *to see,*
> *We learned this — when they disagree*
> *The younger ones are always right.*
> *In* Life *and guidebooks this hold tight.*

We girls scorned such aesthetic crutches and were determined to make up our own minds as to our likes and dislikes, becoming quite vociferous about our reasons, especially at mealtime. The tendency to reproduce the Cannon breakfast table was all very

142 well in the little *albergi* of Sicily or Calabria where our voices
were thoroughly drowned out by the natives, but it caused some
dismay, I fear, in the hushed atmosphere of the genteel pensions
where the "regulars" usually ate their soup in stony silence.

It is hard to believe today that cars in Italy in 1929 were
comparatively scarce and that behemoths like ours, driven solely
by women "without a man" were so rare as to be beyond the realm
of credibility. Even in Florence and Rome we were viewed with
amazement, but south of Naples it was as though an invasion of
creatures from another world were taking place. Little boys
chased us through streets and at the least sign of our slowing down
settled like locusts on the running boards of the car. In order not
to crush or extirpate half the population we had to ward them off
with the stick with which we measured the gasoline in the tank,
often so vigorously that my sister Linda ruefully remarked, "We
shall be known as the Simon Legrees of Italy."

The seating in the car in time took on a certain pattern. My
sister Helen, fourteen years old, the youngest and the best organized, sat in the front seat next to the driver, the maps firmly in
her hands. My sister Wilma's verse describes her charmingly —

> *Here find you in my travelogue*
> *That silent and efficient cog*
> *Which makes our tumbling world go round.*
> *Helen's her name. She can be found*
> *In front upon the right hand side*
> *Behind a map or Michelin Guide*
> *Or buried in the Rest Tour Book*
> *She is our private Thomas Cook.*

In the coolest and most extraordinary fashion, she guided us
without fail through the Dolomites, down into Venice, along the
Adriatic shore, over the Apennines, and through the Umbrian
countryside. The maze of the narrow streets of Florence was no
puzzle to her nor did she lose her nerve or her sense of direction
in the intricacies of Roman traffic. I remember that she was
neither fussed nor confused when my sister Wilma insisted that

we turn off the main road north of Rome to see the beautiful Renaissance gardens of the Villa Lante, though no one knew exactly where it was. She found it and guided us to it, back in those remote days when no one but art historians or avid art students like my sister ever visited it. It was just part of her daily stint. The driving fell mostly to my sisters Wilma and Linda, though my sister Wilma's driving was considered hazardous as she was apt to moon over the view. I was too young for an International Driver's License, though on lonely stretches free of *carabinieri* I took over the wheel. My mother was immobilized in the middle of the back seat where she could be "kept down," for in spite of her lighthearted ways, she was nervous about narrow, cliff-hanging roads, on-coming charabancs, and flocks of sheep blocking the way.

The culture of the road had a drama and tension all its own. High passes in the Apennines and lonely stretches of road in remote parts of Sicily have been forever etched in our memories by the dread disaster of a flat tire; out of nowhere, groups of useless, black-clad males would gather, while my sister Linda and I changed the tire. At one such time, my mother, who was apt to get overwrought when things went wrong with the car, insisted that "someone had to put on the beautiful overalls" that had been brought along for such emergencies. My sister Wilma, sensing the situation, immediately got into them, thus soothing my mother considerably, even though "it did not make a mechanic out of Wilma." Something was always getting out of whack in our over-sized equipage so that our contact with the garagemen of Italy soon became our profoundest social relationship. Broken springs, squeaking wheels, a leaking gas tank, determined the quality of our lives and a good mechanic took on the ambience and desirability of a Giotto fresco. As my mother commented, "It amazes me to see how easily I get on in Italian. When I am able to make a mechanic understand in Italian what I do not understand in English, I call it a triumph."

The problem of finding a garage every night for our Juggernaut was another never-ending comedy. We bedded it down in empty churches, front parlors, and, in Syracuse, in someone's bedroom, with an inch to spare on each side of the entranceway. When it was discovered that the door could not be closed, my mother asked whether it was "*sicuro*." The patron and his wife answered that it was supremely safe, in the bosom of the family, as it were, since they *slept* there! Where, my mother could not figure out, as there was no extra space for their beds, unless they abandoned their mattresses and curled up in the seat of the car.

In Rome, my sister Helen remembers that the fact that she was diagnosed as having a case of scabies brought about our introduction into Roman society. She had for some time been scratching herself unduly and we naturally thought she was suffering from fleas, an apparently inescapable fate in Italy in those days. To be sure, the rest of us seemed immune and we surmised that it must be her pale blond flesh that attracted the Italian fleas as her pale blond hair and her blue eyes attracted the Italian male. But by the time we reached Rome it had become something more than fleas. A fashionable Roman doctor diagnosed scabies, a skin eruption probably picked up on the *Roma* en route to Genoa, though, as my mother wrote, "One did not want to hurt the national feelings of the Italians by mentioning it." However, the doctor whose clientele was composed of the most exalted marchesas and contessas seemed to think nothing of it and attempted to comfort Helen by saying, "You must know that princesses have scabies," thereby confirming his credentials and cheering her up to be in such imposing company! The rest of us felt compassion but a certain smugness at having avoided such a fate until we learned that we all had to be covered with a medicinal grease from head to toe for twenty-four hours. I remember that we lay around our pleasant pension room looking like Channel swimmers while my mother read aloud *The Life of Isadora Duncan*. The doctor had two handsome nephews and two sleek young sons and as a result of Helen's scabies we entered Roman society, as, in our fumigated clothes, we stepped out to the opera with these beautiful scions. When we were invited for picnics and horseback rides in the park and things seemed to be getting out of hand, my mother, smelling danger, hustled us out of Rome, and with fond backward glances we were soon on our way.

We may have moved in social and intellectual circles in Rome and Florence, but our real connections were in Calabria. My mother's Minnesota relatives had various "little Italian cobblers" and "little corner fruit-sellers from Calabria" in St. Paul and they in turn still had ancient relatives living in tiny hamlets in that remote region of the country. Armed with names, photographs, and letters of introduction to these unsuspecting uncles, aunts, and mothers, we plunged south in search of them. In Rome and Naples we had been endlessly warned against the perils of travel in Calabria; the roads were terrible, the brigands rampant, the hotels nonexistent, and the risks overwhelming; just the sort of strictures that whetted my mother's appetite.

The roads, which turned out to be eminently passable, went high up over the mountain passes, through great forests of yellowing chestnut trees under which old women in heavy kerchiefs and full woolen skirts were pasturing their pigs, poking in the leaves for chestnuts, while the haughty pigs waited to eat them after they were found. On the high slopes, wisps of smoke drifted up from the fires of the charcoal burners and on the narrow roads loaded donkeys and black-garbed women with bundles of sticks on their backs made way for us, startled with disbelief at our huge car and its totally female occupants.

The villages were like scenes from a De Sica film; when I saw one decades later, it brought forth a rush of nostalgia, memories of the hordes of black-suited men that thronged the village squares, their mouths dropping open with amazement as we stopped to ask directions. Inevitably, the local American returnee was usually produced to translate for us. Although we had our dictionary handy and were rather pleased with our Italian, it seemed to be a point of pride with the men to cosset the "helpless" ladies; Italian machismo was at stake, or perhaps they thought we might be a bad example for their womenfolk. There was always some former citizen of Cicero or Little Italy whose command of the language consisted of "Goddamn" or "I want to get the hell out of here," who would thrust himself forward, puffed up with pride, elbowing humbler and less worldly villagers aside as he assumed the role of guide, protector, and general nuisance.

We came to Petrona, the native village of "the little cobbler's" old mother, on a dark, rainy night. Hardly a light was burning, and the narrow cobblestone streets were slick with sewage and refuse. When we asked some bewildered inhabitants to take us to Signora Santa Colosima, their wonder was even greater, for she was the poorest of the poor. They led us to her darkened doorstep where amid excited shoutings and explanations we were described as intimate friends of her son in far-off America, which we echoed with rather excessive animation in view of the fact that none of us had ever seen him.

Signora Santa Colosima had not heard from her son in Minnesota for years, a letter hardly ever penetrating this fastness from other parts of Italy, much less America. But she rallied to the challenge with simplicity and charm, throwing her arms around my mother's neck in an affectionate gesture of welcome, and inviting us into her sparse peasant house, its cavernous interior lit by one dim lamp burning olive oil as in Roman times.

In a brief time, the word of our bizarre visitation spread through the tiny hamlet, and all the relatives and cousins to the nth degree began to push into the large square room. Disgruntled chickens roosted on the ladder leading to the loft, and cornhusks, dried ferns, heaps of straw, and baskets of chestnuts were stacked against the stone walls. A subtle smell of pig suffused the atmosphere. More people arrived until the whole population of the village seemed to have crowded into the room and a party got under way. Native cured hams, bread, apples, chestnuts, and bitter wine were produced in a gracious gesture of hospitality from these grindingly poor people. The inevitable returned American pushed in officiously, bragging of having worked for "Henriferd" in Detroit, and apologizing for the town and all its inhabitants, his vocabulary generously sprinkled with "By golly" and "Hell," showing an easy familiarity with the language. But no one paid any attention. Even the intrusion of two members of the *carabinieri*, resplendent in their gold-buttoned uniforms, long capes, and shiny tricorn hats, did not dampen the gaiety and high spirits of the company. They even joined in the singing, and clapped as the men and girls danced the tarantella to the accompaniment of four guitarists. It was an unforgettable scene: the hatted men, the women with scarves on their heads and bright pleated skirts, the tatterdemalion orchestra, lolling on chairs, plucking their instruments, and the tall gold-laced officers, clean and tailored, all lit by the dim, flickering lamps and the light of the dying fire, like a painting by de la Tour.

Since there was no inn in the town or for many miles around, we were invited to sleep in the two huge family beds on two floors of the old farmhouse. Where the usual occupants slept, we never discovered, but before we lay down exhausted, three small children were extracted from one of the beds, like eggs plucked out of a hen's nest. A rooster was the other occupant of our room. Throughout the night one could hear the crow of a cock in some far-off roost, and knew that the cry would be taken up by the intervening fellow roosters until the piercing answering screech of our particular chanticleer would shatter our repose. And so we slept (more or less) under clean, handwoven sheets and woolen spreads hand-loomed by the women of the family from the wool of the sheep on the mountains and brought out of the wedding chest to make up our beds. In her usual fashion, my mother was up with the sun, her rising having been encouraged by the various animal noises around the room and under the window, especially the snuffling of the pigs rooting in the refuse and the honking of the geese and the braying of the tiny donkeys in the neighboring farmyards. At her request, she was carried off to see the village school, which needless to say was quite deserted of children, since they were all following her around the town. It was a dark little hovel of a building, one room with one window for light except when the door was left open to further dissipate the gloom. "It was so dark, that we could hardly see the children's faces, and the pleasant intelligent looking teacher deplored the fact but seemed to accept it [the lack of light] as one of the inevitable laws of nature. I wanted to knock out some stones all along the side *right then and there,* and let the light in, but the children repressed me."

It was so characteristic of her, on seeing a problem that could be solved by simple and straightforward human exertion, to want to *act*.

She was something of a one-woman Peace Corps in her many travels during her lifetime long before the whole idea was dignified by government sponsorship, and she got off to a good running start in Petrona. We were taken to meet the "rich lady" who in medieval fashion owned the hamlet and all the surrounding lands, and who lived in a remarkably ugly villa on the hill above the town, resplendent with gilt furniture, yellow brocade curtains, gilded mirrors, and Venetian glass chandeliers. My mother, without missing a step, immediately challenged the dumbfounded marchesa by suggesting that she should *do* something about the school: "for instance, get all those idle men sitting around the village square to whitewash the school room and cut out some windows for light." For years after our visit to Petrona must have entered the local folklore, my mother used to send copies of the *National Geographic* to the village school and letters to the marchesa, urging her to action and the betterment of her domain. Her concern was in large part for the poverty-stricken inhabitants but also because she felt the marchesa should be up and doing and "the better for it."

She did not save her reforming attentions just for the blameless poor or heedless upper classes of foreign lands but even-handedly ladled out equal doses of uplift to her fellow countrymen. I remember many years later, when we were driving together through one of the "hollers" in the mountains of eastern Tennessee, stopping to see a little one-room schoolhouse that was just as gloomy as its Sicilian counterpart with few windows and dark unpainted walls. When she got back to Cambridge, she sent the sweet young teacher a check for paint and suggested that she get the men of the tiny community to spend a Sunday afternoon whitewashing the interior of the schoolroom. It was characteristic of her that besides everything else, she wanted to "brighten things up" and a coat of paint seemed to be one of the ways of accomplishing it.

She was always interested in helping people to help themselves, even though they often resisted, not only because she was

a believer in the dignity of the individual but because she felt that
it was a sensible way to accomplish things. It was for this reason
that she was thrilled by her visit to Israel at the end of her life
where her natural impulse to "get things done" seemed to be so
wonderfully echoed by the zeal and efficiency of the young Is-
raelis, while "those lazy Arab men sat around doing nothing" with
their veiled women and their numerous progeny "overpopulating
the world." She had no patience with the finer points of politics
when they interfered with what she felt to be human progress. The
poor Arabs got short shrift!

And so we left Calabria, "that beautiful, maligned region," as
my mother wrote, poverty-stricken, fascinating, steeped in a
mysterious past and a strangely malignant present, its quality
caught forever in Carlo Levi's book *Christ Stopped at Eboli* and in
the sketches and text of Edward Lear's *Travels in Southern Italy*.

In our riotous progress from the Dolomites through the Straits of
Messina, in which the clanging of church bells, the braying of
donkeys, the honking of horns, and the piercing voices of the
populace seemed never to slacken, we found, at last, in Sicily, a
place of perfect solitude and perfect silence. We came one
morning upon the ancient Greek temple of Segesta as it lay on its
sweeping hillside, cream-colored against the gray mountains,
facing out from its majestic site, across the amplitude and empti-
ness of the land, toward the "wine-red" sea of Ulysses and the
Argonauts. No sound broke the utter silence. Nothing was in sight
except feeding sheep and two shawl-wrapped shepherds, and for
once our caravan of vociferous females was struck dumb. My
mother and I climbed the long path to the Greek theater far above
on the mountainside behind. "We came to the theatre," my
mother wrote, "from the hill and the lovely view burst upon us,
the sea, the red land, the distant gray mountains, all framed in
the stone wings of the theatre, the land dropping off abruptly
behind the stage so that it seemed to sit on the edge of the world.
Not a sound anywhere; an occasional bird flew across the valley in
front of us, white sails dotted the sea, far below a man was
plowing, slowly turning the red furrows as he went. One shepherd
boy came and tried to sell us some Greek coins, but when he

found we were not interested, he stood without stirring, his shawl slung over his shoulder, content to look with us at the pale distance, without thought or motion." She pictured *Alcestis* and *Iphigenia in Tauris* given on this stage (in some contrast to our pine-needle–scattered stage in New Hampshire) and the Segestan Greeks gathered from the hills and valleys, "perhaps ancestors of this very boy who idled beside us," and quoted Professor Whitehead's words, "Religion is the use man makes of his solitude. If he is never alone, he is never religious."

Then, descending the steep path, we rejoined our fellow travelers and once again plunged into the vivid, tumultuous life of our wanderings through Italy.

Temple of Segesta, Sicily

chapter nine

WE ARRIVED IN PARIS IN TIME TO MEET MY FATHER A FEW DAYS
before Christmas. Some guardian angel directed us to the Hôtel
de l'Université, a hostelry beloved in the late twenties and early
thirties by genteel, well-heeled Americans, many of whom had
been scattered back to the States by the stock-market crash that
fall of 1929. So there was room for our overflowing family, at a
price, which my mother, in a fit of uncharacteristic extravagance,
decided to pay! "After all," she reflected, characteristically
finding some plausible means of salving her conscience, "Father
needs a peaceful place to practice his French and get his lectures
organized. The Ecole de Médecine is close by, too. Besides, who
knows, we may only be in Paris together this once!" So heigh-ho,
over the moon went her cap and, to be sure, we were never again
all together in Paris in the course of our lives!

Our attic rooms were certainly not the haunt of a Mimi; the
walls were bright with toile, the plumbing worked, and even
though we girls occupied garret rooms looking out across the roofs
and chimney pots of the Left Bank, a jolly chambermaid delivered
chocolate and croissants every morning for breakfast and there
was steam heat in the radiators. So we pretended to the role of
"artistes" with none of the discomforts of Bohemia, read
Baudelaire's *Fleurs du mal*, and dined in the tiny hotel salon on
some of the best food in Paris.

The hotel was a family affair. Mme. Triaureau, the handsome,
well-corseted proprietress, her hair dyed a rich chestnut, with

View from our Paris window

154 the graces of a grande dame and the sharp eye of a croupier, presided over the desk, ordering the maids and the garçon around, while her husband, once the premier chef at the Paris Ritz, dazzled us with the haute cuisine of France at every meal. Our introduction to cordon bleu cooking after the simple fare of Cambridge, Massachusetts, was not unlike the experience of the natives of underdeveloped countries moving from the ox cart to the jet airplane in one giant leap. However, unlike the New Guinea cannibals, we suffered no period of adjustment to the cultural shock. At our first dinner, M. Triaureau bore to our table with his own hands a perfect fruit soufflé *à pointe*, which elicited from my mother: "Our first dinner was as definitely a work of art as Botticelli's 'Spring'!" That she should be moved to such ecstasy over food, she, who usually thought of eating as merely a perfunctory exercise, basic to the support of life, gives some idea of its ambrosialike quality.

It was in Paris that my mother's mastery over us began to disintegrate. Her fledglings decided to try their wings. To be sure, after a week of reconnoitering we were deployed into various academies, art classes, lycées, and studios: my sister Wilma to study fresco with M. Baudoin, and my sister Helen, reluctantly, to the Lycée Victor Drury. I was apprenticed to a studio of etching and lithography that turned out to be a sort of finishing school for *les jeunes filles bien élevées* where no one spoke to me for three months, and my sister Linda became a student of *l'affiche* with "an artist named Ferdnand Leger."

We were timid at first, having been raised on the general premise that around every Paris street corner lurked an "apache" ready to pounce and spirit us away into the white slave trade, to some steamy bordello in far-off Brazil. But, mastering our fears (they were more mine, I confess, than any of my sisters'), we were soon swinging into buses, solving the intricacies of the Métro, and exploring the maze of neighboring streets bordering the Seine, with their antique shops, secondhand book shops, patisseries, and boutiques.

What a lovely moment it was to be in Paris for the first time! The automobile age had not yet arrived in full force and still, as in ages past, it was a city made for strolling. We found ourselves set down in the midst of great French institutions; the Ecole des Beaux Arts around the corner, the Institut de France a short walk along the quai, farther on, Notre Dame and Sainte-Chapelle, and across the Pont Royal, the Louvre. Two blocks away was the ancient church of Saint-Germain-des-Prés and across the *place* the Café Deux Magots, already beginning to be a gathering place for visiting Americans, where our tastes ran to hot chocolate and patisseries rather than absinthe or a *fin*. We used to loiter along the Rue de Seine and the Rue Bonaparte, pausing to gaze into the little galleries that clustered there, seeing for the first time in all probability paintings by Braque, Utrillo, Vlaminck, or drawings by Matisse and Picasso. No matter how much we prided ourselves on our recently acquired expertise in the Italian Renaissance, we were tyros when it came to modern art, though my sister Wilma and I had spotted Modigliani in a Milan gallery and were immediately won. We often sighed in after years that if only we had had some cash and the nerve to follow our instincts we would both be millionaires by now; but I fear there was nothing of the plunger in us and, besides, neither of us had ever handled anything much larger than a five-dollar bill.

Each excursion was an adventure, for in those days, Paris was still the undisputed art center of the world. No matter how unknown the works and the names of many of these artists may have been to me, I think they must have registered in my mind's eye in a subliminal way, for when I came later to know their paintings, I seemed somehow to have been familiar with them in some previous incarnation.

❧

Most diverting of all were the art stores, the haunts of the architectural students and painters and sculptors who flooded the quarter. Like many shops that cater to a special clientele, whether it be for plumbing supplies, musical instruments, or hardware, they held a special fascination. Shelves reaching to the ceiling were lined with bottles of dry pigment; crocks bristled with brushes and pens; there were boxes of Conté crayons and sets of pastels, drawers of oil-paint tubes and cakes of dried watercolors, rolls of Belgian linen canvas, enormous wooden palettes of swooping design hanging from pegs in the wall, canisters of modeling tools, calipers, wooden manikins, with articulated knees and elbows and feet and hands, and above all, drawerfuls of handmade papers: watercolor papers, tinted charcoal papers, the kinds of paper on which Ingres drew his meticulous pencil portraits, or Degas his dancing girls. The voluptuous feeling that must overcome a glutton on entering a pastry shop had nothing on the sense of riches and plenty one had on coming into one of these Left Bank stores. One felt part of a great tradition even though one's purchase might be a single sheet of watercolor paper, a bottle of sepia ink, and a steel drawing pen. But with what nicety the nib was selected, the feel of the paper assessed, and the ink held to the light to calculate the color; no great French master could have used more care or scrutinized the alternatives with closer attention.

People who employ tools, no matter what tools, and who exact the best, the most precise, the most sensitive performance from those tools know something of the emotions of which I speak; whether one be a master house painter with the perfect horsehair brush, or the cabinetmaker, with wood chisels razor-sharp, or the barber, with scissors honed to the finest edge, or even the tennis player, racquet faultlessly balanced and strung. To have the perfect tool with which to do one's job or practice one's art is one of the great satisfactions of life. And I think I received my first lesson in the materials of the artist's "trade" in these richly stocked Parisian art shops.

In later years, in my travels as a peripatetic sketcher, I made it a habit to haunt shops selling art materials wherever I went. In the bazaar in Old Delhi I found a perfect pen, a thin black thorn sharpened at one end, the kind with which the schoolchildren write out their lessons. It probably cost me less than a mil. In Japan, I knelt on the tatami-covered floor of a little shop completely devoted to the sale of brushes while, in what I assumed was a time-honored custom, drawers and drawers of them, fastidiously arranged as to size and shape, were presented for my inspection. No language barrier ever seemed to exist on these occasions. With gestures of utmost refinement, the salesman removed the elegant bamboo casing, with its red or black loop at the end, and handed me the brushes one after another. I then held them in my fingers, examined the bristles, felt the point, observed the thickness of the shaft, laid down one brush, and took up another. All the time both of us observed a decorous silence, an unhurried and undivided attention to this almost ceremonial transaction. After I made my choices, the salesman, creeping noiselessly over the tatami floor, replaced the shallow drawers, and after putting my brushes in an exquisite wooden box, wrapped them as though they were crown jewels with such art that one hardly wished ever to undo them. Then amid much bowing, scraping, and smiling, I departed, having, as it seemed to me, taken part in some ancient ritual.

My mother wrote to my brother, in the somewhat overblown style that she adopted when she was in an ebullient mood, "We are like the man wrestling with the angel in the desert — we will not let Paris go until it has blessed us!"

In her first assault on Paris, in order further to widen our contact with the great world she took us to call on Gertrude Stein and Alice B. Toklas in their apartment in the Rue de Fleurus. Gertrude Stein had been among her contemporaries at Radcliffe with whom she had attended one of William James's seminars. She remembered her in later years as "very brilliant and erratic, not admirable" (this latter comment was a typical flourish of my mother's, who had rather a strict moralistic view of the world in some things). I remember the atmosphere of the dimly lit, high-ceilinged room into which we were ushered as being somehow fantastic and unknown, intimating another world I had never experienced before.

I was at that unpleasant age when much that my mother said in public embarrassed me as being too simple-minded and unsophisticated and I can recall feeling that this was not her type of social situation. She was unperturbed, talking animatedly, her plump figure almost lost in the greenish overstuffed chair as she sat opposite her ponderous hostess. My sister Wilma remembers Miss Stein sitting in a low chair with her long woolen underwear showing, laying down the law in a very determined voice to my mother, as they discussed the problem of American writers living abroad. My mother, uncowed, countered in her usual brisk way, maintaining hotly (her Middle-Western blood beginning to boil) that "no expatriated American can understand America truly," to which Gertrude Stein crushingly replied, as though squashing a bothersome insect, "I have it all within me!" as she tapped her ample bosom with both hands.

My mother's staunch nativism, which was such a strong trait in her character, was forever bursting out. She once wrote after reading a collection of Henry James's letters in the 1920s, "The thing I do not understand is why he is so contemptuous of the America of his youth as being hopelessly provincial and unintellectual" — a comment examined from another viewpoint in a witty entry in her diary by Mrs. Henry Adams: "High time Harry James was ordered home by his family. If he wants to make a lasting literary reputation, he must settle in Cheyenne and run a hog ranch."

Since apparently *everyone* has a memory of Alice B. Toklas and Gertrude Stein, whose afterlives seem to have the length and intensity of atomic waste, I will add my single, earthshaking remembrance of the occasion. It was not of the imagist poet, one of the fellow guests, who immediately sensed a kindred soul in my sister Wilma; it was not of the Matisses and Picassos that lined the walls four- and five-deep, which I must have looked at with unseeing eyes. It was not the thought of Hemingway and Fitzgerald frequenting this salon; no matter that I had read them by the light of my fifteen-watt bulb, I was too naive and untutored to make the connection between their world and this. No, it was the memory of Miss Toklas passing me the salted almonds, whose taste I shall never forget. Who knows what remembrance of things past the flavor of those nuts may have put in train! So much for the seventeen-year-old would-be worldling whose preoccupation with food seemed to be paramount.

My father's colleagues at the Ecole de Médecine and at the Sorbonne with charming hospitality asked us all to teas, family dinners, and evening receptions. After one of the latter, an evening of talk in French with professors and students of physiology, my sister Linda complained that continuous effort in a foreign language "made her lame in the back," but my sister Wilma, who was rather a dashing linguist, came through without physical trauma.

Across the street from our hotel, in the same mansion that housed the *Revue des Deux Mondes*, lived the distinguished physiologist and Nobel prizewinner Charles Richet and his family in an elegant apartment where one day we took tea in the beautiful library, two stories high with handsome mahogany library steps. The lofty windows, along the whole length of the room and reaching almost to the ceiling, looked out on one of those leafy, intensely green gardens, full of box and shrubs and huge chestnut trees, that are hidden behind many of the ancient *hôtels* of the quarter. I recall Richet showing us his Nobel prize medal and the sword and regalia of the French Academy, and other ribbons and medals all carefully displayed in a velvet-lined case in the foyer of the apartment. It seemed to have the aspect of a shrine, for I recall that we admired and commented on the contents in whispered and almost reverential voices as though viewing sacred relics. But then, European professors in those days, and perhaps still, occupied a special status, venerated by their students as superior beings and approached by them with deference and often with fear. My father's foreign students could never get over their amazement at the informality and openness of his laboratory, and his own kindliness and lack of arrogance or hauteur.

I must have been susceptible to atmosphere in those days, for the ambience of those rooms and their distinguished occupants is a vivid memory still. It is a memory that through the years has enriched my reading of such authors as Henry James and Proust; those rooms, the cool, deep garden, and the magnificent library serving as paradigms for the great houses of the Faubourg Saint-Germain described in *The American* and *Swann's Way*.

We all attended my father's first lecture at the Ecole de Médecine, on the emotions, wishing him well in his battle with the French language. On his arrival in Paris my father had employed a charming young Frenchwoman to come and soften his American accent and teach him conversational French to relieve his agonizing over the language, much as a masseuse might be hired to relieve a painful muscle spasm. But even so, as he wrote to my brother, "I'm rather an old bird to learn to sing and my tongue no longer rolls its R's as it used to when I was an inhabitant of the Mississippi valley . . . you can imagine my plight at the first lecture when I was met outside the lecture room by the Dean of the Medical School, the Rector of the University of Paris, and the Professors of all the main departments of the Faculty of Medicine and the Faculty of Sciences of the Sorbonne. And then we marched in together to face a big audience entirely French except for Mother and your sisters. I was surrounded by the academic elite and facing a critical audience, expected by both to address them in their native language." All apparently went well, for a colleague from the Rockefeller Foundation who knew France well commented rather ambiguously that "the audience was exceptionally attentive, for a French audience."

My father had last been in France during the First World War as a member of the Harvard Hospital Unit headed by Dr. Harvey Cushing, one of the early American medical teams to be sent to the front. There he had worked with British and American colleagues on the problem of wound shock in the terribly wounded soldiers brought into the base hospitals at Béthune, at Dijon, and at the end of the war at Ecury during the last great German attack in the Châlons-sur-Marne area in 1918. When he first arrived in France he was assigned to the British army to work at Béthune where a British team of investigators were already functioning. He tells a funny story in his autobiography about his superior officer getting permission from General Pike, the chief medical officer of the British army that governed Béthune, for my father to enter the area. In order to certify him as an investigator, his colonel

explained to the general that he had invented the bismuth meal. 161
My father reported that General Pike, an obviously bluff army
type, replied, "Send him along! Send him along! I had to take a
bismuth meal once and I'd like to knock him down."

At that time, traumatic shock was a little-understood
phenomenon and many of the observations that he and his colleagues made and that he described in his book *Traumatic Shock*,
published in 1923, still hold today even though interpretation of
some of the data on shock has changed as time has gone on.

He had reached Paris from the front on the day after Armistice
Day, November 11, 1918, having traveled with fellow officers
Lieutenant Colonel Alexander Lambert, chief surgeon of the
American Red Cross in France, and Lieutenant Colonel Simon
Flexner, director of the Rockefeller Institute in New York City,
from Dijon through Sommerance, where they first heard that the
war was over. He reports a nice story about the "practical value of
internationalism in science" when the big French touring car in
which they were being driven to Paris broke down in the desolate
muddy countryside near the little town of Epernay. The
townspeople were celebrating the Armistice and all the hotels
were closed. But a French medical officer whom they met invited
them to stay in the local hospital. The doctors and nurses were at
dinner celebrating the victory. "We introduced ourselves. The
doctors knew of the discovery of the bacillus of dysentery by
Flexner; they were aware of Lambert's services through the
American Red Cross; and one of them happened to ask if I was
the Cannon who had made 'classic' studies on the stomach. Thus
we were properly identified and were warmly welcomed. . . .
Speeches were exchanged, toasts were drunk, and in spite of our
failure to reach Paris we thought the day well ended."

His return to Paris, then, in 1930 was full of memories of an
extraordinary time in his life, "the parenthesis of war," as he
called it. It also meant a renewal of friendships with French
colleagues whom he had known during the war or who had worked
in or visited the physiology laboratories at Harvard.

162   Having seen our father safely through his first lecture and well launched on his scientific activities, we returned to our light-hearted pursuit of culture and entertainment in the highways and byways of Paris. We haunted the Opéra, went to concerts at the Salle Pleyel, and tested out inadequate French at the Comédie-Française. My mother wrote to my brother, expanding on the joys of the creative life, "Linda and I finished our course at the Alliance Francaise . . . and so to freedom, like colts turned out to pasture. We celebrated by going to an exhibition of New Painting. We devour Ultra-Cubism! I have gone over utterly to the New Art, am painting cubistic pictures daily and am tremendously pleased with the results. I have hung them on the wall to the horror of your sisters. They really are interesting to do and since they require no possible technique [Picasso please note] are my *meat*."

We even went to a grand French *bal* in the city hall of one of the Paris arrondissements. There must have been over three hundred people in the lovely white marble building, with red carpets covering the sweeping staircase and brass-helmeted members of *la garde républicaine* standing at rigid attention on every step. My mother, always ready to draw analogies involving the municipal deficiencies of her native city, "wondered how elegant a ball would be given by the city fathers in our Cambridge City Hall! I only hope Mayor Russell has been able to have the floors scrubbed, the cuspidors emptied and the cigarettes removed."

Paris was full of tiny experimental film houses where we first saw *The Cabinet of Dr. Caligari* and *The Blue Angel* and early Man Ray and Cocteau films, rather a change in diet from Clara Bow and Eddie Cantor and the Our Gang comedies. They made a profound impression. The morbidity and malignancy of the foreign films seemed the highest artistry and enhanced our sense that we were experiencing life and were part of the Parisian avant-garde. My mother's memory was of a different sort. She recalled attending one of these exotic screenings where "in front of us sat a large man and his wife and two dogs, one a huge Russian wolfhound. They barked a great deal when anyone came in but no one paid any attention. The little one, a fox terrier, got restless and his master tried to hold him, but by virtue of his high living being unendowed with a *lap,* had to wear his canine pet like a watch chain on his front!" It all seemed in keeping with the grotesques of the screen and greatly added to the surrealism of the scene, a possible script for a Renoir comedy.

My sister Wilma fell in with some radical students and she and I went one evening to a large party in one of their attic rooms. The air was thick with the fumes of Gaulois cigarettes, and we sat on the floor, drinking cheap red wine and arguing politics. I remember that the atmosphere was crackling with political passion, for many of the students were Central Europeans and many, no doubt, were Communists, rigorous Marxists, seething with violent emotions, about the evils of the Versailles Treaty in particular, and the capitalist system in general. Since many of them spoke French with heavy Polish or Czech accents, making their French almost as bad as mine, I could follow the argument and even put in my oar from time to time, though I was way beyond my depth, being completely ignorant of most of the issues. But the atmosphere somehow demanded participation. It was my first experience of political argument outside the running battle of my mother with the Cambridge "pols," and it was an unforgettable glimpse of the revolutionary frenzy and passion that motivated so many of these young intellectuals as they prepared to return to their native countries to participate in the violent upheavals of the thirties.

Spring arrived and the weather softened; the Luxembourg Gardens came alive with children, smartly dressed in their neat little coats and round sailor hats, with their hoops and sailboats. The air was full of the sound of their sibilant French, so enchanting on childish lips, and so comprehensible to an apprentice in the language like me; elderly custodians demanded a sou for the iron chairs set out along the pebbled paths, and the chestnut trees bloomed and perfumed the air, and all along the banks of the Seine the booksellers had opened their little booths. We found a copy of my mother's book *Red Rust* in one of them, recycled, we felt, a bit too soon! I had tea with a distant and exotic cousin who lived on the Ile de la Cité in an apartment looking over the Seine and painted pure white! That was stunning enough after a homely diet of dun-colored flowered wallpaper and dusty grass cloth in our Cambridge house.

There was a bunch of spicy aromatic freesias on the tea table, a gentle breeze blew in off the river, and my cousin, a veritable Hemingway heroine, brittle and chic and "living in sin" with a married man, exuded an atmosphere of almost overwhelming panache; besides, she good-humoredly filled me in on a number of facts about sex that somehow had been overlooked in the course of parental guidance.

We said good-bye to our various art academies and lycées, dawdled once more along the Seine, and sat for the last time under the eaves on the window seat of our tiny room, imprinting the roofs and chimney pots of Paris forever on our memories. Everyone has a first experience of Paris. And though we might some day return with lovers, husbands, children, or friends, nothing could erase that poignant, almost painful delight of the first discovery.

My father's schedule of lectures in the provincial medical schools of France took us crisscross through central and southern France. The big Cadillac, already bursting at the seams with baggage, art materials, and bodies, still had room for my father and his scientific paraphernalia. The fact that each of his daughters went through Europe with the aforementioned skimpiest of wardrobes probably explains why *anything* more could have been added. As my mother wrote: "We are weighted down with baggage, Father has to take his lectures, film, etc. [of one of his complex experiments in denervating the nervous system of a cat — a delicate operation — with significant implications], clothing, formal and otherwise. He is like a traveling clown with multiple costumes and favorite tools of the trade." He was, however, a nervous traveler, who would, I feel sure, have preferred a more decorous form of tourism, though I am certain that as he looked back on the vagabond wanderings into which the females of his family led him, he thought he enjoyed himself. My mother remarked, somewhat nostalgically, after my father took the car in hand as we left Paris, "Those glad, carefree days of limping

A Romanesque chapel in Spain

through Italy with a car held together with strings and surgeon's plaster, singing as it went, are gone forever."

My sister Wilma used to read aloud to us of an evening in our musty hotel bedrooms the lurid French murders from the daily newspapers — *Encore un cadavre coupé en morceaux* — stimulating a rush to the battered Larousse dictionary, but my tender-hearted Aunt Margaret, who not only bled for every beggar but for every stray cat, objected with hurt sighs. So the subject was shifted to Romanesque architecture, which was the "course" we were taking under my sister's remorseless lead. No village church within ten kilometers of our itinerary escaped, and when we got to Spain the pace quickened, since almost every hamlet in Catalonia had its enchanting Romanesque chapel.

Our last stop in France before passing over into Spain was at the ancient university city of Montpellier; its medical school is said to be the oldest in the world, where medical teaching began in the ninth century. Its marvelous collection of old manuscripts and portraits includes one of Rabelais, who was one of its teachers. The most interesting thing about Montpellier, however, was our visit to the commune for foreign students in the university, established on the outskirts of the city by the Scottish biologist and sociologist Patrick Geddes. As my father wrote, "Geddes, an associate of Huxley's, had taught physiology [J. S. Haldane had been one of his students], had gone from physiology to sociology, had travelled all over India, knew Gandhi and Tagore, also many friends of ours, such as William James and was overflowing with interesting ideas. I had many years ago read a very interesting book by Geddes and Thompson — Patrick Geddes — and I asked him whether he was by any chance related to Patrick Geddes. 'I know only one Patrick Geddes,' he replied, 'and I am he.' Later one of the members of the colony asked me in his presence about the name of my book on the emotions and I gave him the full title, 'Bodily Changes in Pain, Hunger, Fear and Rage.' He then exclaimed, 'Oh, you're the Cannon who wrote that book!' And we were at last introduced to each other."

He and his wife, both in their seventies, lived with the students on a rocky hillside covered with a flowering garden in a quaint old

house where they created an atmosphere "like Brook Farm enthusiasts of Emerson's time," as my mother wrote, "who established a communist colony of idealists and freaks, living on pulse
and honey, and talking philosophy all the time. Poor Mr. Geddes,
dreamer of a better world where all nations shall lie down together
like lambs, has collected the weirdest students, several soft-
handed Hindus, some angular English, a weak young man from
Philadelphia . . ." and so on, mostly long-haired, barefoot, or
sandal-shod. We all lunched together at a long trestle table set
out on the sunny terrace on what seemed to me the most rare and
delectable food: a huge bowl of green salad and raw vegetables,
loaves of fresh bread, and a tray of cheese. The utter simplicity
must have struck me after our rich diet at the Hôtel de l'Université, for along with Gertrude Stein's salted nuts, this reductionist
meal has stuck in my food-obsessed memory. It is, of course, the
way many of us eat today, but back in the bread, butter, and
potatoes days of my childhood, it seemed a culinary revolution.
So did this atmosphere of plain living and high thinking
foreshadow the style and quality of life made prevalent by the
social upheavals and changes in mores of the sixties.

Italy had been sunny, welcoming, somehow recognizable. One
saw at every turn the counterparts of the old Italian women in
their black shawls who used to come every spring from the far
reaches of East Cambridge, settling like a flock of blackbirds on
the grass of our back yard to dig up the dandelion greens for their
soups and salads. One was always recognizing some well-
documented monument like the Leaning Tower of Pisa or the
Bridge of Sighs or the Roman Forum from a much-thumbed Latin
grammar. As for France, we had been brought up on French folk
songs, had read *The Helmet of Navarre* and *The Count of Monte
Cristo*, and wept along with my mother as she read aloud *A Tale
of Two Cities*. France was the continuation of an experience already half-begun. But Spain was alien, mysteriously beautiful,
with the sweep of its dry empty plains, and spectacular mountains, its courteous black-clad peasant men and women, its bold
"raggle-taggle" gypsies living in the caves of Andalusia, and a
latent violence that one sensed just beneath the surface.

As we came over the Pyrenees, still white with snow in the early spring, stern border guards examined our papers with suspicion and concern. There seemed suddenly to be an atmosphere of menace in the air and when we stopped at a flea-bitten inn high up in the mountains on our first night, a satanic-looking ruffian, wrapped in a heavy black wool cloak, insisted on sleeping across the threshold of our bedroom, for good or evil, we could not tell.

In Seville, during Holy Week, one of our party had his trousers slashed by an enterprising pickpocket and in the great cathedral, while the catafalques of the Virgin were borne on the backs of an army of evil-looking toughs to the chancel, lighted by thousands of candles, we girls were goosed and pinched black and blue by the caballeros of Seville.

It was in Seville, also during Holy Week, that we saw the king and queen of Spain walking through the streets observed by silent and indifferent crowds. General Miguel Primo de Rivera, the dictator of Spain, had been driven from office two or three months before and I can remember the French papers' screaming headlines announcing his defeat and decampment with his mistress and his retinue to Paris and the Rue du Bac, just around the corner from our hotel. We had already sensed the tension of Spanish politics in Paris where Rivera and his partisans had set up their headquarters in the Hôtel Lutétia, also not far from where we were staying.

In Barcelona, where my father lectured at the medical school, many of his Spanish fellow scientists, some of whom had been Fellows in his laboratory at Harvard, spoke enthusiastically and freely about the inevitable coming of the Republic. My sisters and I went for a long hike with my father and a group of his Spanish colleagues along the ridge of Montserrat, the mysterious sacred mountain outside Barcelona, where the scenes of the opera *Parsifal* are laid. There was much discussion of the political iniquities of the monarchy and of the late dictatorship of Primo de Rivera and of the Catholic Church and the hopes for a Republic, either by ballot or by revolution. It was heady talk for a political *naïf* of seventeen, like myself, for even I recognized that this was not just theoretical talk by a lot of intellectuals but deadly serious — as, in fact, it turned out to be.

My father and mother were not particularly political in the sense of belonging to or being faithful partisans of any political party. There was no tradition of party politics in the family; no child among the relatives through the years was ever named after Ulysses Grant or Grover Cleveland by admiring parents. The family was reactive, outraged by cheating and dishonesty; idealists rather than ideologues, suspicious of isms, passionate believers in inevitable progress, and imbued with the idea that good would win out in the end if all would pitch in and work together. They were, in short, devoted democrats and independents, so that the fervor and idealism of the intellectuals whom my father saw in Spain made a profound impression on him. The names of many men later prominent in the Republic were inscribed on the menu of a dinner given that spring at the Madrid Ritz for my mother and father (with us girls in attendance in our rumpled silk dresses), among them the distinguished man of letters and medical doctor Gregario Maranon, and Dr. Juan Negrín, a fellow physiologist, later premier of Spain during the final desperate days of the Spanish Civil War.

My father's admiration for and friendship with many of these men with whom he shared, as in the case of Juan Negrín, "a veritable passion" for personal freedom (described by Hugh Thomas in his *The Spanish Civil War*), as well as a deep-rooted humanitarianism, were instrumental in his later efforts on behalf of the Spanish Republicans. As Jean Mayer, the present president of Tufts University, wrote about my father after his death, "The fact that Dr. Negrin was a physiologist probably gave Prof. Cannon a feeling of kinship with those men that were fighting what should have been clearly recognized as the first round of the defense of Western democracies against the greatest threat they had ever faced. Walter Cannon braved the criticism of the isolationists and the Fascist sympathizers in this country to organize medical help for the Spanish Republic."

He became chairman of the Medical Bureau to Aid Spanish

Democracy in 1936 and during the next two years oversaw the raising of money for ambulances, for the shipment of drugs for the wounded, and for the sending of personnel and hospital equipment. The Communists and Communist sympathizers attempted to use him, like many others whose commitment to the Spanish Republicans was idealistic and compassionate, and his influence for their own ends as the grip of the Comintern tightened in Spain and the fortunes of the legitimate Republican government waned. He kept up a running fight with them on the one hand and on the other accepted the obloquy heaped on him by the conservatives with philosophical calm. He never lost his wry sense of humor. When he received a cable celebrating the New Year from some Russian scientists in 1938, he commented, "How sadly my reputation for respectability would suffer if *that* became public." At one point when he was being crucified for "being a Red," he admitted to Professor Frankfurter that he had voted for Landon and was much amused when Frankfurter remarked, "No impeccable past can save one from the accusation of being a Red."

His overriding concerns were always the alleviation of human suffering and the cause of human dignity. The background of the Spanish conflict, rooted in the misery and degradation of generations of poverty-stricken peasants and workers, the Byzantine complexity of the politics that led to the catastrophe, and the cynical exploitation of the bloodshed by the European powers for their own ends were only partially known to many who stood squarely behind the Loyalist cause. Imperfect though their knowledge may have been, they were responding to the rights of oppressed people to be free of ancient bondages. Forty years later, many of those rights fought for with such bitterness in the bloody and violent civil war have apparently at last been established.

chapter ten

ON A MORE BUCOLIC NOTE, OUR EUROPEAN EXPEDITION CAME TO an end in Cambridge, England, where we went mothing in the fens and punting on the Cam, and prepared ourselves to sink back into the womblike security of academia and familiar Cambridge, Massachusetts, as the momentous decade of the thirties began.

We returned to our house to find that it had been moved across the street and set down behind the present Busch-Reisinger Museum. Beloved beds of violets and lilies of the valley no longer grew in secret nooks along the board fence; the sun shone into the well-remembered rooms at strange angles, and the dining room windows, which used to look out on a tangled mass of sweet-smelling old-fashioned roses and across the lawn to the rustic "summer house," now gazed onto the back yard of the neurotic Peirce sisters and their numerous cats.

I do not remember being particularly affected by the Great Depression, which was in full swing by the fall of 1931, and I am amazed as I look back at how sheltered our existence was. No one we knew ever jumped out a skyscraper window because of financial reverses. We hardly knew what a stock or a bond was, had never met a banker, and the only businessman of our acquaintance was a wholesale grocer cousin in St. Paul who was said to be "having trouble." Actually, in an unusual shift, academic families prospered, comparatively, during the Depression if the breadwinner did not lose his job. Prices fell; my father's modest salary remained modest but steady. My mother, who had always

Music in the Harvard Yard

been thrifty, followed her usual pattern to such an extent that her sister in St. Paul finally sent her a check to pay for fresh carbon paper and new ribbons for her typewriter on which she wrote her far-flung letters to family and relatives, letters that had become unreadable.

My parents were able to put four daughters through college and my brother through medical school without perceptible trauma. When it was announced by the University that there was to be a cut in salary across the board for faculty members, my mother's reaction was characteristic: "I shall not deplore it. We are due a little suffering, too, if so trifling a thing as a cut in pay can be called by such a name."

To be sure, I recall a certain gloom and tension around the house on the part of my father when the news broke of the collapse of the Swedish match king Kreuger's financial empire and the resultant demise of his backers, the highly respected Boston investment firm of Lee, Higginson and Sons. My father, in an uncharacteristic essay into the money world, had encouraged my mother to invest a large part of her earnings from *Red Rust* in the "solid gold" stocks of Kreuger and Toll. I always thought that he had been stimulated to this act by his loyalty as George Higginson Professor of Physiology, and the belief that any firm with the name Higginson attached to it could do no wrong. Nothing was ever said in the hearing of us children, but my father was obviously overcome by guilt. My mother, who considered talk of money, much less preoccupation with it, in the worst possible taste, never for a moment let such a minor disaster bother her. She thought the publication of her book a great piece of luck in the first place and since its earnings had seen us through our European odyssey, she felt they had fulfilled their purpose.

I do remember the profound impression that the desolate groups of unemployed mill workers in Lowell and Lawrence made, as we drove through the cavernous streets of those mill towns on our way to Franklin. The great textile mills had long been familiar to us as children, since the route of our yearly trek north skirted their smoke-blackened brick walls, the hum and clatter of their machinery audible through the open windows on a hot summer's afternoon. The factories were busy then, and I can recall the drab lines of workers, the men with black tin lunch boxes, the women in shabby coats with scarves over their heads, pouring out of the Amoskeag Mills in Manchester, New Hampshire, across the bridges over the canals, as the late afternoon shift came away from the looms. My mother once told me of an old maiden cousin of her grandmother who had worked in the Lowell mills in the early decades of the nineteenth century, one of the "mill girls" who had lived sequestered lives in the mill dormitories, closely supervised as to their morals and behavior. She had spent her whole life working at the spinning jennies and I recall the sense of tragedy with which my mother had invested her pathetic existence. (It was not for nothing that my mother was a great "reader-aloud" of Dickens to us when we were children and our tears mingled with hers over such damp volumes as *Oliver Twist* and *Dombey and Son* in an orgy of woe, for she invested every grief-ridden scene with her undoubted flair for drama.) At any rate, I must have extrapolated the emotions aroused in me by her story to include all the workers in those mills, so that I never forgot the sight of their misery in the depth of the Depression. But I fear that these emotions were fugitive at best; the fate of these mill workers had no connection with my heedless life. We went gaily off to college, thinking it our due, and forgot the world around us.

Other changes besides the removal of our house to new surroundings were taking place in Cambridge. President Lowell had inaugurated the House system, and splendid Georgian buildings were being erected along the Charles River to house the undergraduates in unparalleled comfort and luxury. In the process, there was a certain amount of cannibalization of real estate and "homes"; ladies who ran boardinghouses for students were being done out of their livelihoods, and hash houses where the undergraduates used to feed in the pre-House days were shutting down. All this did not sit very well with the city fathers. The relationship between town and gown, always edgy, took a distinct turn for the worse. Some of the awe and respect with which the University had been viewed in earlier days by the "rest" of Cambridge had been eroded in the last few decades and Councillor Toomey, "carrying the ball" at a meeting of the City Council late in the thirties, listed the ways Harvard "had done Cambridge wrong" and called loudly for the sundering of relations between the City of Cambridge and Harvard University. In other words, a request that the University should *get lost!* The *Cambridge Chronicle* in a rueful editorial opined: "If they [the councillors] succeed in severing Harvard from the body politic, they will have to pay for their football tickets. We are sure they must have forgotten that item, for a councillor buying a football ticket is even rarer than a heath hen's egg."

Harvard had a nice opportunity at the time of its Tercentenary Celebration in 1936 to improve its relations with the city, when another councillor, Mr. McNamara, of a more propitiatory cast of mind, suggested that Harvard make a present of $300,000 to the city, $1000 for each year of the University's existence. It was to be given not only for sentimental reasons but "because Harvard has received many benefits from Cambridge and now when the city is in need, Harvard should come to its aid." "After all," he added, "thirty million dollars worth of real estate has been withdrawn from the tax rolls because of its status as a tax-free educational institution."

The suggestion, needless to say, was turned down rather huffily, the University's spokesman being quoted in *The New York Times* as stating: "Harvard could not properly comply with the Council's request for a gift of $300,000 on the occasion of the 300th anniversary. . . . Huge gifts *have* been received 'in trust' for educational purposes and cannot be diverted to other purposes."

And so Harvard continued in its lordly ways, condescendingly amused by the Toomeys, the McNamaras, and the Sullivans, even in the face of such broadsides as "Harvard is tolerant when things please them, but when they do not please them it is different, so that is what they mean by seeking the truth!" and "Wake up, Harvard, and cut out the clowning and talk about more serious things such as unemployment and taxation!" Such problems and confrontations were brushed aside as though they were bothersome gnats on a hot summer's day. In fact, the "town" of "town and gown" was often treated like a backward native country in the heyday of the British Empire, patronized, exploited, and ignored by the other end of Cambridge.

There were various efforts on the part of righteous and conscientious citizens, feeling that The Boys at City Hall had had a free ride long enough, to clean up city government. But they were invariably slapped down by the entrenched "pols" who continued to put their relatives and political cronies in school jobs, the library, the sewer department, and the trash division without benefit of talent, training, or so-called examinations. The Public Library, today one of the city's favorite institutions, was then described as "a political pond in which any politician can drop his line and come up with a job for some relative or crony." My mother at one point during this doleful period described going to the library to find Pearl Buck's translation of the Chinese classic *All Men Are Brothers*. When she went to the desk to ask a rather aged female why they did not have it, she replied, "Oh, a party I know read it and said it was just trash, so we did not get it."

When an exasperated taxpayer complained about the lack of snow removal, one mayor reiterated the sentiment originally voiced by Mayor Curley of Boston, "The snow was an Act of God. There'll have to be an Act of God to take it away."

In spite of the bombast of city councillors like the ineffable Toomey that the "Marxists from 'Hahvad' were taking over and that new Littauer Center [offices of the Graduate School of Public Administration] might become the new City Hall," by the end of the decade a reformed Plan E system of proportional representation and city manager form of government was put through, much to the anguish of the old City Hall gang. Even so, the fun and games at "Hahvad's" expense did not stop. On the occasion of the one hundredth anniversary of the founding of the City of Cambridge, which coincided with that of Milwaukee, Councillor Michael Sullivan, a well-known joker, suggested that Milwaukee exchange three railway tank cars of beer for three surplus Harvard professors, with Cambridge obviously coming out on top in the swap.

Even the academic community was showing subtle signs of

change. The student body had grown over the decades and become more cosmopolitan and in the early days of the House system a kind of true identification with the individual Houses took place. Faculty members became integral members of the Houses, dined there, and mixed with the students in a way that after the Second World War, with the enormous expansion of the student body, was never to be repeated in the same intimate manner. For a few years, the system fulfilled to a degree the ideal of an intellectual fellowship, which had been Lowell's hope in the first place.

The Business School was a community in itself, sealed away from the rest of the University in its neo-Georgian compound and rather despised by the intellectual snobs across the Charles as being a "trade school." As for the Massachusetts Institute of Technology, it was still impossibly remote for most Cantabrigians, a cold, classical pile in the middle of a matrix of down-at-the-heels factories in the nether regions of Cambridge where students learned to build bridges and experiment with wind tunnels, a far cry from the genteel world of the classics and the more esoteric humanistic disciplines. In fact, for the Cantabrigians from the other end of Cambridge, it hardly counted in their view of the world. Academia meant Harvard, and that was that!

Yet even Harvard professors, whose lives in the past had seemed cloistered and parochial, were beginning to break out of their mold. Numerous bright instructors in economics and government and some senior professors, together with the yearly complement of clever young law-school graduates going to serve as law clerks for such Supreme Court Justices as Brandeis and Cardozo, had begun the trickle down to Washington to work for the Roosevelt New Deal, the trickle that became a veritable flood during the Second World War and one that has continued unabated ever since.

But Harvard professors still trudged across the Cambridge Common to repeat their lectures, delivered in the previous hour to their male students in the unpolluted classrooms of Sever Hall, for the Radcliffe girls, so that there would be no unseemly cross-infection. Many a faculty baby's birth was financed by the extra dollars earned by its father in these biweekly treks to the hinterland. Though Radcliffe girls were allowed to use Widener Library, it was considered a bit wild and dashing, not to say "provocative," to make the trip, and they were segregated in the upper reaches of the library in a small cell into which they were permitted to retire discreetly with their books. In the handbook for my class of 1934, we were requested to wear hats at all times when going to the Square, having made no progress on that front from the days of Mrs. Agassiz and the "Harvard Annex." As for the parietal rules listed in the same handbook, in the atmosphere of today they read like the strictures laid upon novices in a nunnery. In fact, the implicit sexuality and fears for the virtue of all Radcliffe undergraduates insinuated in these blameless little red pamphlets have a piquancy as read today that I feel sure the original authors never dreamed of. Or perhaps they did!

The rigmarole attached to going to a party in someone's room in one of the Houses was of unbelievable complication — Head Tutors had to be alerted, chaperones provided, and witching hours observed. The final conclusion after all this exhausting experience on the part of the "fast" girls in my class was — a student with an apartment of his own was no longer a *student* but a *man*. Why bother with the others!

There were, to be sure, certain professors that looked with horror at the incursions of women even at the safe distance of the Radcliffe Yard into the sacred precincts of Harvard College and would have nothing to do with the academic arrangements by which their colleagues taught the Radcliffe girls. Professor Roger Merriman, for example, the first Master of Eliot House and a professor of history, would not have been caught dead teaching a Radcliffe class. It was still the time of the gentleman's C among certain of the prep-school graduates and the "clubbies," who treated "greasy grinds" who got A's with contempt and looked upon Radcliffe girls as "bluestockings" to be avoided at all costs. There was still a sense in which the families of these scions, in some ways the most parochial society in the country, considered professors hirelings who taught their young princelings but were considered otherwise rather like exotic zoo animals. As for professors' children, they were unplaceable!

Recently, I was discussing with a contemporary of mine, the son of a distinguished professor of mathematics who was a member of an old Boston family, the peculiar isolation that we felt as children of academics as we grew up. I recall saying to him, "You, Tom, mustn't have felt that sense of not belonging that we did as children. After all, your family has been around for generations." "Not at all," he answered. "My father felt isolated from the Harvard community because he was a Bostonian and was in turn treated by his Boston friends as a 'queer duck' because he was a Harvard professor."

Radcliffe in the thirties, during my undergraduate days, was considered something of a poor relation by the other women's colleges. The chic girls went to Vassar, the intellectuals to Bryn Mawr, and the comfortably placed bourgeois types to Wellesley and Smith. At least that was the way it seemed to us. We may have been Cinderellas but we knew something our haughty stepsisters did not; we were getting the best education in the country, and, besides, we weren't banished to the sticks to rusticate. The "weekends at Yale and Princeton" may have been the answer to a maiden's dream for the Vassar girl, but we did not have to wait for ceremonial weekends for our entertainment, for there were those among the Harvard population who recognized our "merits."

It took more than a decade and the Second World War for these basic facts to sink in!

Radcliffe was still, in part, a commuter college; perhaps half my class came by subway or streetcar from Boston, the Newtons, Dorchester, or Cambridge. The rest lived in dormitories presided over by house mistresses and waited on at table by maids in white aprons and caps. The "hilarious joke" of the season was always, "Yes, you know she's Miss So-and-So, the Mistress of Bertram Hall!" — which gives an idea of the girlish humor of our undergraduate days.

My sisters and I enjoyed the best of both worlds, by living at home, in the shadow of the University but not subject to its parietal rules. We had only to put up with a mother who sometimes appeared in curlpapers at the head of the stairs, wondering aloud where we had been, "coming in at two o'clock in the morning," though she had learned to withdraw from the youthful scene after a decent interval, remarking, "My retiring is not always due to weariness but to a feeling that lovely and fascinating as I am, my years are against me, and boys prefer shallow youth to my profundities."

My mother's advice to my sister Wilma on entering Radcliffe had been, "Now, Wilma, get to know the odd ones. They'll be doing the really interesting things in life," the kind of stricture that was part and parcel with another injunction issued to my sister at an earlier time. Once when my mother made her wear "sensible" bloomers to school, and she objected, my mother said, "Don't pay any attention to what other children say. Be independent!" She went on to report ruefully about herself: "Wilma's sage reply was 'Being independent means doing as Mother wants!' " She never gave up, sending a flow of suggestions and advice to all her children throughout her life, no matter how far afield they may have strayed.

I do not recall whether my sister Wilma or the rest of us paid any attention to her advice on the subject of "the odd ones," but there was always a steady stream of classmates, eccentric or normal, coming and going through the house. At one point, Friday lunches were dedicated to any stray students or friends, or friends of friends who turned up, and Hortense, our long-suffering maid, would serve lunch and preside as surrogate hostess if none of the family was present. My mother recalls one such occasion: "We are full of soup and philosophy. Marian and Helen visited D. Meiklejohn's section in Philosophy and came back full of the relation of soul to matter and insisted on sharing it with the rest of us. David Griggs, a charming Junior Fellow working in geology on pressures within the earth, was here also and tried to stem the tide of argument up in the air to the solid foundation of the matter under our feet. In vain! Philosophy and the soul, combined with louder voices, won the day and vector mathematics sank into the sub soil!" Knowing my mother's predilections, I am sure her heart was all with vector mathematics.

We were rather hierarchical and snobbish in our judgment of our classmates. Concentrators in the sciences were thought to be rather "wet," and taking laboratory courses was something to be avoided, for it meant long hours of work in the late afternoon and a freezing walk back home or to one's dormitory in the winter's twilight. In our lighthearted approach to the whole subject of education, convenience rather than intellectual stimulus seemed to have been the basis for a good many course choices. Nine o'clocks were taboo, eleven o'clocks, desirable.

The aesthetes frequented the Fogg Museum, where Professor Sachs produced future platoons of museum directors in his museum course, and the intellectual elite concentrated in history and literature, where a remarkable group of tutors and young instructors like Perry Miller, F. O. Matthiessen, and Kenneth Murdoch created an atmosphere of intellectual and literary excitement for whole generations of students of American literature.

Sociology was a stepchild and psychology a minor pseudo-scientific discipline not much discussed in those days. History held a paramount place in the curriculum. Those of us who took Professor Sidney Fay's course in Modern European History emerged imbued with the idea that the Germans were not solely responsible for the First World War, a revolutionary thought that we digested with a certain amount of skepticism. But of one thing we were sure. There would never be another world war. The world simply could not afford it! So deeply was this concept instilled in us that in spite of Hitler's rise on the one hand and the Japanese invasion of China on the other, the Spanish Civil War, and the Italian invasion of Ethiopia, and all the other signs of international anarchy, when the Second World War finally broke out, it seemed absolutely inconceivable.

My mother once compared the academic interests of her years at Radcliffe with those of her daughters. "We were avid for science; the theory of evolution, the decline of outdated theology, the effects of new ideas on philosophy, were our concern thirty years ago. Now these girls are interested in world affairs, international relations, the natural result of a smaller world and the forced closeness to one another, etc. Science is so much a part of the air they breathe that they take it in stride, but must perfect themselves in these other human relations. The world *do* move!"

Harvard Square in the thirties, compared with its present incarnation, resembled a country crossroad. The streetcars still clanged along Massachusetts Avenue and the newsboys under the shelter of the kiosk leading into the subway sang out the list of newspapers, the *Boston Herald,* the *Boston Globe,* the *Post,* the *Evening American,* the *Evening Transcript* and the *Boston AD-VA-TISA,* like an incantation. At Christmastime the be-bonneted Salvation Army lasses stood in the snow ringing their bells or shaking their tambourines on the sidewalk in front of the bank. On the first warm day of spring there would be the usual "spring riot" on the part of high-spirited undergraduates throwing toilet-paper rolls out of their windows in the Yard or snake-dancing through the Square, or performing other high jinks — mild stuff by modern standards, but considered pretty far out for the times. The Cambridge cops looked on with a certain amount of benevolence and left the nabbing to the college cops. And late in the spring, during "the reading period," the Harvard Glee Club used to give concerts in the early evening on the steps of Widener while couples sat on the grass and held hands.

On fine days, the ladies of Cambridge would descend on the Square, their shopping bags over their arms, delighted to run into their friends in the peaceful atmosphere of Sage's, the meat market, Campbell and Sullivan, the fishmongers, Amee's, the paper store, or the post office next to Brattle Hall. Brattle Hall, which has passed through many metamorphoses since, was then the place where the budding hopefuls "came out" at Brattle Hall dances, a suitable spot for that rite, partaking as it did of that special genteel shabbiness and discomfort forever associated with Old Cambridge.

The favorite hangouts for the student population ranged from the all-night eateries like the Waldorf on "MassAve" to Gustie's in Brattle Square, where one could get a square meal for thirty-five cents and be waited on by the busty proprietress, who was apt to dictate what one ate. If one felt rich, nearby was St. Clair's, where the light was sepulchral on the "cocktail side," and where literary types like Kenneth Murdoch used to have their daily martinis and club sandwiches for lunch seated in the slippery, Naugahyde-upholstered, curved booths. Up the street, at the Brattle Inn, presided over by two maiden sisters, bright law students like Jim Rowe and Ed Retz (who went on to distinguished careers in the Roosevelt administration) and David Riesman, winding up their third year at the Harvard Law School under the tutelage of Felix Frankfurter, would argue cases over lunch in the ladylike atmosphere of the Inn's dining room. David Riesman, who, as I remember, was the intellectual pet and buzzing gadfly of his more worldly classmates (at least that is the way I think they saw themselves), would have a hundred ideas in one lunchtime, a good many falling flat but a few brilliant and penetrating. He seemed to be willing to try out anything and sometimes it worked!

My mother was forever pressing me to have "some of your nice classmates" around so that "we can have a good talk," a prospect that always seemed to me a bit embarrassing, and, even worse, boring. However, I would from time to time gather some of them together for dinner where my mother would challenge them with such topics as "Has Moral Indignation Gone Out?" and serious conversation would ensue, with apparently total participation by all those present. The atmosphere was always informal and any fool remark was accepted with respect. However, when one of the girls remarked, after an evening of talk about China at which a visiting missionary had spoken about her experiences in the Far East, "It was so interesting to hear her. Somehow I'd never thought of China before!" my mother wrote rather sardonically in a letter, "And poor old China, suffering and agonizing and sinning and perishing over there unnoted by our nice little well-bred girls." She encouraged the students to talk about what they looked forward to as careers, pointing out that "they must remember that the breadth of possibilities for them was the product of the work of pioneer women like Lucy Stone and the heroic suffragettes and that they must not be ungrateful." She was doing her best to break them out of their habitual patterns and apparently succeeded to an extent, for I was startled years later by some of my classmates who remembered those evenings given over to "great thoughts" as being one of the most stimulating and vivid memories of their college years.

chapter eleven

MY MOTHER, AS I THINK HAS ALREADY BEEN MADE CLEAR, ADORED travel, and her favorite reading was such books as Doughty's *Travels in Arabia Deserta* and the journeyings of Gertrude Bell and Richard Burton. I think it was this passion for travel that impelled her to send us girls off, at youthful ages, to various remote regions of the earth, partly because she believed that travel would broaden us and give us a sense of independence, partly because through us she could vicariously see the world. Today, with thousands of young people jetting around the globe, for whom no steppe is too remote nor any mountains too high, her aspirations for us must seem tame indeed. But as we were summarily despatched in the late twenties and early thirties, she was looked upon by some of her friends as an unfeeling mother, thrusting her fledglings willy-nilly into the world.

One of the first experimental animals was my sister Linda. A Radcliffe classmate of my mother's, Miss Adams, was head of the Women's College in Constantinople and having run into her at a Radcliffe reunion in the late twenties, my mother naturally thought: "Linda, seventeen, needs to get out from under mother's wing — Constantinople, why not?" So off my sister went, meekly, to an extraordinary year of foreign study in Turkey where she was the single American and the single blond in a bevy of black-haired Turkish, Rumanian, and Bulgarian adolescent girls. She picked up enough Turkish to baffle itinerant rug salesmen in later life and endeared herself to her black-eyed classmates by

Sketching in Foochow

playing the blue-eyed hero in all the school plays. However, my sister remembers that the long arm of my mother reached inexorably as far as the Dardanelles. The last letter that she received before she took the Orient Express to Paris on her way home, through "dangerous" Bulgaria and Yugoslavia, flatly stated, "Now Linda, remember, don't be pleasant to *anybody!*"

My mother was something of a xenophobe when it came to her daughters' romantic entanglements. We were rapidly recalled from foreign parts when anything like romance broke out. It was all part of the importance she attached to the emancipation of women and she was not about to have her daughters "get mixed up with foreign men, with their known contempt for women, who would dominate them and belittle them." Broad generalizations were the stuff of life to her. Having read Owen Wister's *The Virginian* at an impressionable age, she had a highly sentimental view of the American male as the quintessential romantic and gentleman, chivalrous and tender to women and strong in the crisis!

Perhaps with *The Virginian* in mind, my oldest sister Wilma was sent off to New Mexico in 1928 at the age of sixteen to study art and ride the sagebrush-covered mountains, though more likely it was the result of my mother's having fallen in love with the region from her researches for her children's books on Coronado and the Pueblo Indians. Since she could not go herself, she would send a surrogate! My younger sister Helen, the scholar of the family, had to take her year of foreign parts in the rather bland atmosphere of Stanford University, which, however, for a Cambridge-bound girl was quite a launch into the outside world. In fact, old Professor Peabody, the Harvard chaplain who was our neighbor, once stopped my mother on the street to remark on "how brave" she was to send her daughter "all the way to California." As for me, I was sent to China.

❧

When I had dutifully finished at Radcliffe College in 1934, the question arose: "What shall Marian *do* next?" My sister Wilma had married John K. Fairbank, budding China scholar, two years before, and they were living as students in Peking. Since I was always known to be "good at drawing and painting" and had a somewhat alarming appetite for the exotic ("where in Heaven's name did she acquire such tastes!"), what more logical step than a year in the Far East and exposure to Chinese culture? Besides which, since my father had been asked to lecture at the Peking Union Medical College in the spring, he and my mother were not far behind.

My brother-in-law was writing his thesis for Oxford on the history of the Chinese Maritime Customs Service. The Customs Service was a peculiar bureaucratic creation that came into being in 1854 when the Chinese government hired foreigners, mostly British and Americans, to appraise and administer duties on goods flowing in and out of Chinese ports. Many of these ports had been opened to foreigners after the defeat of the Chinese in the Opium War of 1839–1842, when a reluctant but powerless Chinese government had bowed to the demands, especially those of the British, that they should allow foreign traders on Chinese soil. These ports were known throughout most of the nineteenth and early twentieth centuries as Treaty Ports.

In quest of material, John Fairbank had arranged to spend two or three months traveling down through the Treaty Ports of the South China coast, from Shanghai to Canton, working on any documents in the British or American consulates still remaining after decades of termites, mold, and neglect. The plan was that I should join them in Shanghai, and my sister and I, dutiful hand-maidens, would serve as secretaries, copying out any relevant passages that he chose to record. It gave a virtuous raison d'être (there always had to be a good *reason* in my family for travel!) for an extraordinary voyage that began for me in the fall of 1934.

Travel to the Orient in 1934 was still something of an under-taking. The Dollar Line steamships took seventeen days from San Francisco to Shanghai on top of four and a half days on the train across the continent, "changing at Chicago."

They were great days for travel. "Being seen off" was a time-honored ceremony. Champagne in one's stateroom was what hap-pened in First Class; but in Tourist, a class we habitually occupied, there were special-delivery letters and telegrams, boxes of candy, baskets of fruit with cellophane wrappers and gaudy ribbons, and, if you were lucky, a cablegram at sea. The band played on the promenade deck, the little tugs tooted, and the great foghorns of the ship blasted off as the huge liner pulled away from her berth, snapping the colored paper streamers thrown over the railings to friends on the dockside, and headed through the Golden Gate. It was like a gigantic children's birthday party.

And so the voyage began; first the covert glances at one's cabin mate, with whom a good two and a half weeks of intimacy were to be shared, then the agony of seasickness overwhelming all other emotions followed by the ineffable joy of recovery, the nauseating smell of unaired saloons, the banality of shuffleboard, the endless games of bridge, the wonder of beautiful, unspoiled Honolulu after five storm-tossed days. There were the missionaries, the traveling salesmen, the marines returning to their China bases; the stunning storms at sea, with water smashing over the prow in great white bursts of spray; the casual purser, more casual and tipsier with every day that passed; and the returning Chinese, pleasant, discreet, and imperturbable among the rest of the passengers. Above all were the endless discussions of religion with my Southern Baptist missionary cabin mate. She was a scrawny, wiry little evangelist, twenty years old, who had received a "Call" to missionary work six years before. Her mission was at last to be fulfilled, and though she had never been outside her little Georgia town, she had set her plain but blissful face toward China in the sure faith that she was "going to save heathen souls for Christ." Not until many decades later did I once more see that beatific expression, this time on the face of a niece who had become a charismatic Christian.

In fact, missionaries were the most numerous group on the boat. Being a skeptical Unitarian and a youthful cynic, I was armed and prepared not only against their fundamentalism, but, having read Somerset Maugham's short story "Rain," I knew what the pitfalls were for young girls and amorous clerics on a slow boat to China. When a very amiable and attentive middle-aged Episcopal priest proposed that I would be a splendid bride for one of his sons, I felt sure there was more to the overture than met the eye. In fact, I began to enjoy the role in which I had cast myself of the siren with whom the frustrated, impassioned man of the cloth was helplessly infatuated. It was a blow to discover that the playful suggestion was genuine, though the son being offered up was only a junior at Yale (a further jar). Or was it? The father, a humorous and perceptive man, apparently remained undisturbed by what I thought to be my subtle wiles. Or did he? Perhaps he was signaling in some esoteric way, too rarefied for me to comprehend. I shall never know, but I hope that there was at least a flicker in his platonic heart.

❧

The S.S. *President Hoover* finally steamed up the Whangpoo River, after a seeming lifetime of shipboard existence, late on the seventeenth evening of the voyage, threading its way between the ghostly black junks and little sampans darting like dragonflies among the ships anchored in the blotchy waters. We lay off the Bund until morning, when my sister and brother-in-law came aboard, whisked me through customs and carried me off through the teeming streets to their "apartment." They believed in living cheap and their rooms in a scabrous old building on the corner of Shanghai's Broadway and Forty-second Street had all the appearance of my idea of an opium den. To add to the general feeling of proletarian living, the first guests who came to tea, bringing with them the atmosphere of conspiratorial paranoia and revolutionary zealotry, were the ineffable Agnes Smedley, and her friend Randall Gould, editor of the *Shanghai Evening Post and Mercury*. Since I had rather an exaggerated view of the "dedication" of Communist adherents, whose lives were supposedly devoted to "isms," it was something of a shock to discover that Miss Smedley's whole conversation was taken up with petty backbiting and radical gossip. In fact, it was no different from any other trivial gossip except for the damning of the Trotskyite "wreckers" and the virulence of the character assassination. The religious absolutes of my gentle, if relentless, fundamentalist missionary had nothing on the radical dogmatism of Miss Smedley. It was interesting that China should have been the country in which these two exemplars of fanaticism should have found such rich soil to till.

It was a memorable introduction to the "exotic East" but it was but one facet of the great and turbulent city. The riotous streets swarmed with rickshaw men, their rickshaws often overflowing with whole families, threading their way among clanging street-cars, buses, and the sleek limousines of wealthy Chinese and foreigners. Exquisite Chinese society women and cocottes, ablaze with their jade and diamond jewelry, thronged the lobby of the fashionable Cathay Hotel. The British Consulate General, the grandest building on the Shanghai Bund with its sober halls and offices where John Fairbank worked on consular documents, shone with polished brass railings and doorknobs and gleaming mahogany furniture, though the whole building was pervaded with the faint odor of mold, the proverbial bureaucratic smell of the Treaty Ports. In an elegant house in the French Concession where most of the foreigners resided, we had Thanksgiving dinner, our host a "simple" academic, obviously "living the good life," waited on by a retinue of amahs, bearers, and other servants. His Downstate U. was never like this! And one Sunday we were taken by Chinese friends to the house of an ancient Chinese scholar and gentleman whose Sunday morning relaxation was the painting of bamboo scrolls, an art of which he was the most famous prac-titioner in China.

Most poignant and horrifying was a visit to a silk filature factory in the poorest section of the Chinese city: two hundred women and children working in one room, lit only with the dimmest light coming through one door and a row of filthy windows, sorting out the silk cocoons and removing the outer skins. The enormous room looked like an obscene rat's nest writhing with humanity and smelling like a thousand unwashed feet. Some of the children were less than four years old and many of the women were nursing their babies while they worked. The hours were from four in the morning until six o'clock at night and the children earned about two cents a day. The women and children were patrolled by overseers with switches in their hands with which they struck recalcitrants. Upstairs, little girls stood all day in terrible steam, stirring the cocoons in boiling water, while the women led off the silk thread onto drying racks. Because they worked with their hands in the steaming water, their skin was white and macerated, in time eaten away. The wretchedness of the hellish scene was unimaginable and the expression of dumb resignation on the faces af six- and seven-year-old children unforgettable. Such scenes of industrial serfdom and exploitation were no doubt repeated over and over again behind the facade of the glittering metropolish, and the forces that foreshadowed the Maoist takeover where already at work, gaining strength from the abject misery of such enslaved men, women, and children.

❧

Our travels took us by boat from Shanghai to the remoter ports of the South China coast: Foochow, Amoy, Swatow, and on down to Hong Kong and Canton.

Sailing the China coast in those days had its hazards, as pirates still infested the waters between Shanghai and Foochow, our first port of call. Our boat, the *Chip Sing*, a raffish, rusting vessel, was found to contain a stack of rifles in the steerage that had been smuggled aboard by men carrying them under their clothes. I remember the screaming of the men and the violence of the Shanghai police as the offending passengers were removed, protesting all the while that they were bodyguards to a general returning to Foochow who naturally "needed an arsenal."

It was somewhat reassuring that heavy steel plates with peepholes to shoot through separated the bridge and the cabin passengers from the steerage. In addition, our little fortress was patrolled by a fierce-looking Sikh with huge mustaches, a turban, side arms, a scimitar, and a heavy rifle, though his musical-comedy appearance was not entirely convincing.

The steerage deck overflowed with passengers; women with nursing babies and bound feet (always a shocking sight to me), toddlers, and groups of men gambling, spitting, and fighting. It was a wonder that small children did not slip under the railings into the heaving, yellowish sea because of the press of bodies.

The noise was earsplitting, and the quacking and honking of ducks and geese bursting out of the raffia and reed baskets in which they were penned and the squealing of the shackled pigs added to the cacophony.

In the meantime, the five cabin passengers, including, besides ourselves, a missionary schoolteacher, and a young German Jewish art historian and collector of Chinese paintings, sat cozily in the tiny, airless cabin, drinking the inevitable strong India tea served wherever the British held dominion even in this land of exquisite teas. I have always wondered what happened to the art historian, who chose to wander through the remoter parts of China, discreetly picking up old paintings and scrolls. I feel sure he had the eye of a connoisseur and may today be the owner of a great collection. Or he may have returned to Hitler's Germany and been liquidated, though even in such a brief encounter one sensed in him the qualities of a survivor. I never knew his name.

On the afternoon of the second day, we entered the mouth of the Min River, surely one of the most beautiful rivers in the world, snaking between misty, craggy mountains, and after sailing past this awesome scenery for two or three hours, we finally dropped anchor in Foochow.

So many scenes come to mind from that far-distant time, memories of people and a kind of life that even then was becoming archaic. The once-thriving port of call for the British and American clipper ships of the China tea trade in the nineteenth century was now a pathetic backwater, its lofty old colonial mansions with their deep verandas and poinsettia hedges recalling its opulent past. They clustered together on the hills rising behind the port, and from the sand-strewn paths that meandered among the high-walled gardens, one could see stretching far into the distance the Chinese city and river below. A charming neo-Gothic Church of England chapel — built of the local stone, and musty with disuse — stood under an enormous camphor tree; and in the graveyard beside it were the pathetic headstones of sailing captains, youthful clerks, missionaries, women, and babies, dead of cholera or the plague, or perhaps of hearts broken by loneliness, poignant reminders of death in an alien land.

The oldest inhabitant was Mr. Brand, the tea taster, who ran 193 the seedy boardinghouse in which we stayed, and who was immortalized as one of Somerset Maugham's rumpled colonials in a short story published in *The Casuarina Tree*. He presided over his crumbling gray brick mansion like a grand seigneur, insisting on pointing out with pride and describing the provenance of every tortured knickknack, fat black Buddha, or carved Chinese pagoda with which his "salon" was choked.

At the end of the day he would regale us, his captive audience, with hour-long recitations. Like some Dickensian horror, his long, greasy, gray hair reaching to his shoulders, one hand on his expansive stomach and gesturing like a revivalist preacher with the other, he would intone "The Fireman's Marriage" or "The Death Scene from Henry VIII" by "W. Shakespeare." Both carried the same weight in his repertoire. In another age or in other circumstances he might have been a mediocre actor doing his turn in some provincial English music hall but instead he had come out as a clerk from the midlands forty years before to work for the trading firm of Jardine, Matheson. He had never gone back, nor had he, in those forty years, ever learned to speak a word of Chinese, communicating with the Chinese middlemen and servants in ugly pidgin English.

Mr. Brand's only other pleasure in life besides his histrionics was his aging English wife, a buxom, cheerful woman of strong personality, who, however, faithfully played the part of fragile simpering female that he had long since assigned to her. He used to lead me by the hand into their bedroom so that I could admire her, as she sat in her tatty dressing gown on the edge of their colossal bed, and brushed out her waist-long hair. Gray and faded though it was, he would exclaim, "Look at her hair, how long it is. How thick. Isn't it beautiful, beautiful!" and would go over and fondly spread out the hoary locks for me to see them better.

Together, he and she went each morning to his office in his huge tea godown (or warehouse), littered with bills and papers and with brass spittoons placed in strategic spots. A pallid young clerk, lately come out from some provincial English town, sitting on a high stool, wearing eyeshade, black paper cuffs, and elastics hiking up his shirt-sleeves, scratched away in a bulky account book with an old-fashioned steel pen. Shadowy figures of Chinese servants moved about in the background, as Mrs. Brand, her large bosom encased in an office apron, sat at a desk performing on an ancient clackety typewriter.

One morning, Mr. Brand introduced me into the mysteries of tea tasting. In a high room next to his office, lined from ceiling to floor with some two thousand canisters containing samples coming from hundreds of tea gardens "up-country," a Chinese aide poured out six different kinds of boiling hot tea, which were allowed to stand for a few minutes in their delicate porcelain cups. Then Mr. Brand, in his role as expert tea taster and irrepressible ham, with flourishes and pirouettes that would have done credit to a prima ballerina, raised each cup to his lips in succession, sloshing the tea around in his capacious mouth before spitting each mouthful into a battered tin basin. His false teeth did not fit very well and the clatter and rattle of dental hardware struck a homely note in this singular process. The tea leaves were then put on individual plates and examined for texture and color, after which Mr. Brand identified their source, categorized their quality, and with a ceremonial wave of his hand, dismissed the business of the day. From the tea-tasting room, he took me into the enormous godown, where hundreds of gaily painted tea boxes were piled one upon the other waiting for shipment. The smell of the interior was a pungent mix: the smoky scent of the tea, the faintly acrid exhalations from the dry bamboo slats and reeds of which the tea boxes were woven, and the ancient odor of mold, dust, and decay. The place must have looked and sounded exactly the same seventy-five years before, with the river running swiftly outside the great doors, with the hordes of gorgeously painted sampans and hulking junks, and the bustle and cries of the river people, a perpetual babble, as they lived out their lives from birth to death on these boats on the murky waters.

I remember the beauty of the river women of Fukien with their steel-black hair worn in elaborate coiffures secured with highly decorated, heavy silver barrettes and barbaric hairpins and with their feet *unbound*. They were still to be seen in those days, dressed in loose black pajamas and jerkins, swinging along the Bund under the ancient camphor trees, babies slung on their backs or flat baskets balanced on their handsome heads, with all the grace and pride of a race of Amazons.

The foreign community, as I remember, was a paradigm for all the tiny, inbred groups who huddled together in the largely by-passed ports of the South China coast. The social demarcations were rigid; Mr. Brand and his wife were strictly of a lower order when it came to the consuls, the bank manager, the Customs Commissioner; as for the missionaries, they lived a life apart, like oil and water, hardly ever mixing with the official community, and yet, in all, there were less than one hundred foreigners living in the city.

As I wrote in a letter home,

We dined with the American Consul. We dined with the British Consul, and enjoyed the mutual backbiting. We dined with the Customs Commissioner, and the head man of the Hong Kong Shanghai Bank, etc. [I had never met a banker before. How broadening travel can be!] All these are English and I was surprised to find them so friendly and outgoing. I guess their reputation for snobbishness has been exaggerated or maybe they are hard up for new faces. Wilma's and my reference to an interest in art and Chinese antiquities casts an aura about us. John's esoteric thesis subject and Oxford connections are absolutely devastating! And so we float happily along, passed from hand to hand. And then yesterday, we went across the river in a sampan, to have lunch with Mr. ———, a missionary who teaches at Fukien Christian University and got the other view. He is a great collector of Chinese pottery and the house was so full of shards there was hardly room to sit down. He is a manic collector and one feels that his poor beaten down wife and children have been denied new shoes and clothes so that he can feed his passion. And the Niagara of his talk gave me a whiff of how Sinologues react. At least the missionaries are in touch with the Chinese which is more than can be said about most of the other foreigners living in Foochow.

Almost every afternoon, my sister and I would set out with our paints and watercolor blocks to sketch. As I have already pointed out, sketching in "underdeveloped" countries can have its perils.

People are not hostile, just curious, and the Chinese were no different. They obviously found us irresistible, for not only were we "foreign devils" but women besides! It was hazardous to try to paint from the quays, as the crowds became so dense that we were in danger of being flung bodily into the water by the sheer pressure of five hundred kibitzers.

The Buddhist temples were safer, for they were somewhat removed from the crush of humanity, though the good-natured monks in their white robes, with shaven heads, were unabashed, giggling onlookers. The temples were gorgeous, with sweeping exaggeratedly curved roofs paved with brilliant yellow tiles and with blood-red plaster walls characteristic of the architecture of South China. From time to time the ringing of the deep-throated temple bells would break the stillness of the courtyard where we sat painting under some enormous ginkgo tree. The quiet of these beautiful old temples was almost deafening after the clang and clamor of daily Chinese life. I often wondered why the Chinese, who seemed to me a rather unmystical people, should produce so many monks, and came to the perhaps frivolous conclusion that the one way to escape the perpetual noise and overwhelming mass of humanity was to retire to a monastery. Monasteries and temples, perched as they were throughout China on remote and spectacular sites, offered the peace and tranquillity that elsewhere in that vast country were hard to come by.

Many of these monasteries clung to the sides of sacred mountains, which in the old days were objects of pilgrimages where the sick, the blind, the deformed, the sterile, and the mad climbed the winding trails in search of salvation. Mount Kushan, towering over the valley of the Min River, was one of these and my sister and I climbed it one day. Stone steps, worn by the footsteps of thousands upon thousands of pilgrims, twisted and turned for miles through sparse pine woods and we passed the derelicts of humanity along the way. No painting by Hieronymus Bosch could prepare one for the pitiful cripples, the horribly disfigured, and the pathetic old, dragging themselves like mindless ants to some dreamed-of deliverance. It was like Lourdes magnified a thousand times and a memory of China I have never forgotten.

After Christmas and New Year's in Amoy, the sleepy port of recent notoriety where we lived on a small island off the Fukien mainland and made our usual progress from Chinese fleabag to consular mansion, we arrived in Hong Kong.

Hong Kong in those days was still very much the outpost of Empire. Gentlemen in white flannels played cricket of an afternoon on perfectly manicured lawns, ladies dressed elaborately for tea in wide hats and gloves, and the "inscrutable Chinese" were no more than eerie shadows moving in the background, for all one had a sense of Hong Kong being their native turf. The capacity of the British to carry their culture with them wherever they went was never more evident.

We ran up against it in the form of British colonial officiousness a day or two after our arrival. We were summoned before some pompous British police sergeant for having failed to register within forty-eight hours of our arrival, confronted with our crime, and treated like case-hardened delinquents until wily John produced his impressive collection of letters of recommendation. Like so many other colonial types, the police sergeant, so firm, so immovable, so legalistic, was enough of a snob to let us off, though not without an insufferable lecture on "ignorance of the law" being "no excuse," as though we were a trio of reprobate schoolboys.

Our address, a seedy hostelry, was probably a source of some suspicion in the eyes of the Hong Kong police, for in our quest for cheap lodgings we had ended up in a Chinese hotel that turned out to be a brothel.

One afternoon the bellboy had knocked on the door of our room. "Velly much like the young leddy," said the bellboy, obviously the house pimp, who was representing his client, an eager Chinese counterpart of an American traveling salesman, standing on tiptoes behind him. My sister and I had been swishing through the corridors to the only bathroom in our bathrobes, which in those surroundings had obviously been considered as a come-on. We were both duly affronted, though I somewhat complacently felt that the young lady spoken for must be me. My brother-in-law rose to the occasion and with a remarkable display of trumped-up outrage and self-righteousness dispersed the pair, thereby causing them humiliating loss of face. The desk clerk must have thought we were pretty peculiar customers when John called up the management to complain in "horror"; after all, why all the fuss? Wasn't the gentleman traveling with his two concubines!

No sooner had we hit the bottom in the back alleys of the city than, like waifs transported by some fairy godmother with a magic wand, we were whisked up the funicular to the Peak. The usual process of being passed from hand to hand that seemed to operate throughout the Far East in those days was functioning again, and this time we attained to a state of grandeur well beyond our usual deserts, in the mansion of Tony Keswick, head of Jardine, Matheson Ltd., the oldest and largest British trading firm in China. Many of the documents with which my brother-in-law was concerned were those of Jardine, Matheson and Mr. Keswick, on hearing of his interest and our plight, generously invited us to stay with him in a huge house on one of the highest points of the island.

Of an afternoon, after a stint among the dusty archives, we would sit, if it were chilly, and have tea in the salon beside a coal fire while Keswick did needlepoint and gossiped with his friend Gerald York. York was a quasi journalist and a lanky "long drink of water," as the phrase used to be, a typical Oxonian of the thirties, with long greasy hair falling across his eyes and floppy gray flannels well spotted with samples of last week's menu. He was the master of one-upmanship and was forever at the scene of the latest event in China "when it happened" before "anyone else"! He had just appeared in "dear Peter's" (Fleming's) travel book *One's Company,* and there was much malicious gossip about Ian and Harold and Peter, to everyone's mutual satisfaction.

At other times, we would watch the sunset from the veranda, with its entrancing view of the harbor alive with junks, ferry boats crossing to Kowloon, sleek gray British gunboats, and British merchantmen with LONDON lettered on their sterns, standing at anchor or taking on cargo from lighters.

My memory went back to the signs on the warehouses along the London docks and the shiny brass plates on grimy office buildings in the City, announcing the names of trading companies and limited partnerships dealing in hemp from Calcutta, coconut oil from the South Seas, and tea from China. I was reminded of the English novels in which younger sons were forever going "out East" to seek their fortunes in Hong Kong or Singapore. Suddenly here was the reality, for it was from the trade carried on by generations of these ships in these distant roadsteads that so many of the fortunes were made that underlay Victorian prosperity and British self-satisfaction. But the deterioration of nineteenth-century British mercantilism was already far advanced as we had seen in the case of the aged Mr. Brand, the tea taster and tea exporter, in Foochow; and we had caught glimpses in Amoy and Swatow of the cushioned, privileged life of the British colonial soon to be in precipitate decline. In less than five years, the Second World War would have begun, administering the coup de grace to an outmoded, anachronistic way of life.

Looking back, it seems to me that we viewed it all like amateur anthropologists coming upon an exotic tribe of natives, which we had read about and felt lucky to have seen before its final extinction.

❧

It was at the start of the Chinese New Year when we took the train north from Shanghai, leaving behind the lush rice fields, the elaborate temples, the fantastic mountains of the South, as we crossed the sere North China plains on our approach to Peking. All along the way, blue-clad family groups stood outside their adobe-walled houses and waved as we passed. The children made spots of color in their holiday best, brightly flowered jackets and trousers, the little girls' hair braided with magenta ribbons and the baby boys with embroidered tiger caps and shoes, to ward off the evil spirits. Red paper cutouts were pasted on the doors, and an occasional gorgeous multicolored kite streaked the brilliant sunny blue sky. Otherwise all was dun brown: houses, rutted roads, frozen fields, leafless trees.

The year 1935 probably marked the beginning of the end of the old way of life in Peking. The Japanese, already occupying large territories in Manchuria, were preparing further incursions into China proper. That spring skirmishes took place only a few miles from the city and within two years the Sino-Japanese War, with all its ramifications and portents for the future of China, had broken out in earnest. So we were fortunate to see the old city in its tattered medieval splendor, with its people still living much as they had for hundreds of years. In fact, it seemed that all along the way in our travels, we had had the good luck to have glimpsed the ancient past, in Italy, in Spain, and in the Far East, before the onslaught of twentieth-century know-how, politics, economics, and wars had obliterated it forever.

The Fairbanks lived in a typical walled Chinese house in the east city built around two courtyards with its entrance door on a dusty *hutung*. A canopy of wisteria soon to be in extravagant bloom festooned a part of the main courtyard and early in the spring a whole garden of narcissus, brought in in shallow baskets on the shoulders of some passing street vendor, was created in the narrow beds that lined the pavement of the court on four sides. Cars were scarce; transportation was primarily by rickshaw or bicycle, and the air rang with the sounds of bicycle bells and the calls of street hawkers, water bearers, coal sellers, sweetmeats men, identifying themselves to the householders sequestered behind their high walls by their cries. The creak of the heavy two-wheeled carts piled with bags of millet or rice and drawn by scrawny horses was heard in the narrow lane and one morning I stepped out the front door and ran head-on into a large Siberian camel from the Western Hills, laden with baskets of coal for the Fairbanks' stoves.

Although my sister and brother-in-law were supposed to be poverty-stricken students, the full complement of the household servants consisted of Li, the head boy, a cook, and amah, and a small boy, a relative come in from some outlying village and

Peking

inserted into the household. The cook was a troublemaker and a petty tyrant, taking more than his usual increment of squeeze from every financial transaction, so that there was a good deal of wrangling from the kitchen court where these four and a virtual army of family hangers-on resided.

But in our courtyard all was peace and serenity. Each morning John, a tall blond figure sensibly garbed against the winter chill in his heavy padded Chinese blue gown, would retire to his study on one side of the courtyard, where, surrounded by Chinese texts and Chinese character cards and attended by his Chinese teacher, he attacked this impossible language. My sister, an art historian, worked on her restoration of T'ang rubbings in another cubbyhole. And I, in the dining room, again facing on the courtyard, took my morning painting lesson with the elegant Mr. Teng.

My vocabulary of a few well-chosen "haggling" words was all right for bargaining. Bargaining was the breath of life to all Chinese merchants, no matter how small the transaction, and I would have lost disastrous face if I had ever bought anything at the asking price. But it was not the idiom of art!

I soon discovered that the idiom of art demanded no words. Mr. Teng's gracious bowings and smiles were enough and we were soon on the best of terms. Each day he laid out his art materials, which he had brought carefully wrapped in a blue-gray cloth, on the dining room table as though he were setting it for an elaborate banquet; the six or seven brushes of different sizes were lined up in perfect order on one side, the ink stone and ink block arranged on the other; the rice paper in the middle, precisely squared with the brushes; and central to the geometric design, a copy of the classic Chinese text *The Mustard Seed Garden*, an ancient manual containing the entire vocabulary of strokes from which Chinese paintings are created.

With many smiles and many encouraging "hao's" (good), a few "boo hao's" (not good), and a lot of "hao boo hao's" (is that good?), we plunged along. He taught me how to hold the brush (always perpendicular to the paper), grind the ink (always clockwise), dip the brush, place it on the paper, and maintain a rigid order of strokes, ordained since time immemorial. No classical ballet was more stringently or precisely ordered, or seemed more effortless in its final effect, than the great Chinese landscape paintings and it was the basic rudiments of the philosophy and technique behind them that he sought to teach me. With me running fast to keep up, he took me over the threshold of this ancient art, taught me to draw plum blossoms, tree peonies in spring, mountains in a winter rain, gnarled pine trees, ginkgo trees, water running over rocks, bamboo in the wind, each having its own ordained vocabulary of strokes. It was like studying harmony and discovering the underlying elements on which concerti and symphonies are built. Forever after, though I remained an amateur of the art, I looked at Chinese paintings with a new eye; every stroke was meaningful, and the almost architectural planning and building of the great Sung scrolls and paintings, a source of wonder.

❧

The huge walls surrounding the city still stood as they had for hundreds of years, crenellated and pierced at intervals by enormous gates through which flowed the clamorous traffic of the metropolis. The present government saw fit to tear down these great bastions some years ago, thereby destroying one of the most awesome architectural relics of China's past. In those days, one could still walk along the footpath atop the wall and look down into hidden courtyards and temples and at certain axis points get an overview of the gridlike plan on which the city was laid out, at the center of which stood the Forbidden City with its fortresslike red walls and gold tiled roofs.

While the cold weather lasted, before the spring planting began, my sister and I used to ride our little Mongolian ponies across the frozen fields that began just beyond the sluggish moat that still surrounded the walls. We used to stop and exchange greetings with the villagers in their tiny hamlets, my sister in her fluent Mandarin, I in the always reliable language of smiles. We admired their babies, their pigs, and their geese, and wondered silently at the grotesque maiming of the women with their bound feet. Though the barbaric practice was against the law, the custom still prevailed among the peasants in their remote villages, where age-old traditions determining the destiny and fate of women were stronger than any government dictum.

Some years later, inspired by the memory of these intimate glimpses of village life, I wrote and illustrated a children's book, *San Bao*, about a small village boy who goes to the big city, Peking, and all the adventures that befall him. My children considered it something of a yawn, but I didn't care. It was really a vehicle for recording all the sights that I remembered so vividly: the street fairs with the jugglers and acrobats, the old gentlemen airing their caged songbirds, the wrestlers performing in the temple courtyards at New Year's time, the noodle sellers, the sword dancers, and the actors in the Chinese theater storming around the stage while attendants flung hot towels from the aisle to the patrons who sat noisily cracking sunflower seeds and spitting the shells out on the floor.

With our friends, we often packed up our bedrolls, wrapped up a few cans of food, beer, and evaporated milk, and set forth on expeditions. It was a great land for exploring, in such places as the lovely Buddhist temples in the Western Hills, the Ming Tombs (favorite tourist sights of the present-day guided tour), or the Great Wall. A rattletrap car might take us part of the way; then we might hire a tiny donkey or two to carry our baggage and proceed on foot. There was always a little teahouse along the way for refreshment and no matter how far afield we wandered there were always people.

One weekend, a party of us danced Scottish reels on the Great Wall, perhaps on the very site of Nixon's sanctified stroll, and laid out our bedrolls in one of the towers or out under the stars, forewarned to douse our campfire before we went to sleep lest it attract the attention of bandits. But inevitably, out of nowhere a couple of Chinese soldiers appeared and took up guard duty on our behalf, perhaps the very bandits against whom we had been warned, and next morning cheerfully accepted a tip and built us a fire for our morning tea. One thing was certain; in China, one was never alone!

In mid-April, my father, accompanied by my mother and my

younger sister Helen, arrived in Peking. He had been invited to give a series of lectures to the medical students at Peking Union Medical College for six weeks before my mother and he set off on tne Trans-Siberian Railway en route to the International Physiological Congress in Leningrad.

My mother, although quite sensible about most matters of health, had a phobia about appendicitis. As a result she bamboozled respectable Boston surgeons into removing the appendixes of her daughters Wilma and Helen before they ventured into the Far East. No acute appendicitis for them on the windy steppes! She held the strong conviction that "prevention was the better part of valor," even though the appendixes in both cases were splendid specimens of healthy organs. The possibilities of the logical extension of this train of thought were alarming. By moving fast, however, I seemed to have escaped the knife.

Things began to hop as far as the future rectification of the ancient problems of China were concerned with my mother's arrival. Her horror over bound feet was to be expected, but with her trained Minnesota eye, she noted the amount of land removed from cultivation as the result of the vast earth mounds marking graves sacred to the worship of ancestors. "Ridiculous, in a country starving for food!" Later, no doubt infected by the pleasant lassitude that eventually overcame most foreigners in Peking, she humorously admitted, "I have definitely and finally abandoned the problem of the graves that use up so much arable land. It's hopeless and must be left to a larger organization than I can offer." Later, Chairman Mao finally turned the trick. And in the process, the armies of diggers putting these grave sites back into cultivation inadvertently discovered undreamed-of archaeological treasures.

My mother even wanted to organize the Boy Scouts "of which this city seems to be full" to weed the roofs of the Forbidden City of grasses growing "like thin hairs on an old man's head" before they destroyed "those gleaming roofs."

She, who had been brought up in the self-help school of thought, took some time to adjust to the life of leisure and service to which her daughters had accustomed themselves with such

206 ease. Rickshaws presented a problem. She finally concluded after "nearly wearing out my abdominal muscles helping push the rickshaw" that the best thing was to give in and let "poor Jen do the work," resigning herself to what she felt was a "heartless performance to let these men work like animals."

On the domestic scene she, too, soon succumbed with grace to the privileged life. "We are the most pampered creatures you ever saw. When we ask any question as to how such and such a thing can be done, Wilma and John say 'Ring the bell,' which we do, and the boy appears, equal to any emergency. Wilma has improved on the conditioned reflex and now insists that her father let his gastric juices run, and *then* ring the bell, a far more perfect way to be hungry than Pavlov's."

My father quickly established the routine of his academic life, much to the disgust of my mother, who remarked, "Father might just as well be in Cambridge, for except for his rickshaw ride every morning to PUMC and the weekends in the country he sees only rheostats and smoked drums and the insides of cats." However, the members of the department presented him with a robe of imperial blue silk, a black silk cap, and shoes, and so enchanted by his costume was he that he took to wearing it out to official dinners and looked most dignified and Chinese in it.

My mother's response to stimuli was as usual pragmatic and humorous. She thought the *kang*, the heated platform on which the peasants slept at night, so sensible: "Doesn't a central furnace seem a wicked waste of nature's resources by comparison?" She noted that "in this country, no animal is ever left alone. Even pigs have chaperones when they go out to rummage in the outer world" and after having been caught in one of the dust storms that often blew up in the spring over Peking, remarked, "I feel as though I had been to the Gobi and I am certainly a 'part of all that I have seen.'" She loved to sit in the garden and listen to the sweet sound of pigeons with whistles attached to their backs as they swooped over the city, forgetting for the moment such crucial questions calling for her reforming zeal as birth control, beggars, female infanticide, bound feet, grave mounds, rickshaw men, and the grass growing out of the roofs of the Forbidden City.

On an expedition into the countryside one day, we stopped off in a little village to see a theatrical group sing and perform in the open air. My mother wrote, "The troupe was hired for four days by the villagers, and those four days were the Wagner Festival at Bayreuth for this little huddle of houses. We almost cut out the troupe with the fascinating appearance that we presented. They all wanted to know how old I was, and I told them, as I always do now, for I find that I acquire merit thereby, that I was eighty years old." A hush of wonder fell over the crowd at the thought of her great age and since exaggeration was the breath of life to her a little stretching of the truth seemed quite appropriate. The fact of the matter was that having one's ancient parents along on any outing in China was like having children in tow in Italy; in both cases their presence opened doors, evoked murmurs of approval, and generally created an atmosphere of warmth and fellowship.

chapter twelve

EARLY IN JULY, MY FATHER AND MOTHER SET OFF ON THE LONG
journey from Vladivostok to Moscow by the Trans-Siberian Railway. It was characteristic of my mother that she should have
approached her Russian trip with a mind she hoped she had been
able to wipe clean of prejudice. She was genuinely ready to
receive a positive and optimistic impression of the Communist
experiment in spite of misgivings. Her letters are a mix of glowing
response and increasing dismay, as the evidence of the human
toll resulting from the system was borne in upon her.

They were traveling as guests of the government since my
father had been asked by Pavlov to give the opening address at
the International Physiological Congress in Leningrad. Pavlov
was of course revered as one of the scientific treasures of the
USSR, so that nothing was too good for his chosen colleague and
his wife. And indeed nothing seemed to be too good for them!

The first-class wagon-lit described in the enthusiastic Intourist
brochures as the height of luxury boiled down to one dirty toilet
with accompanying washbowl for the entire car, and no screens on
the windows, so that when they were opened in order to relieve
the 95–degree heat, cinders blew in and begrimed everything and
everyone. "Our waiter already looks like a coal heaver and in
desperation we have decided that we do not care whether we are
dirty or clean for the next ten days." In true Russian fashion,
there was a samovar at one end of the car corridor where the
passengers slaked their thirst and avoided dysentery with a steady

The Kremlin, Moscow

stream of tea. "It would have gagged me once," my mother wrote, "but now it is the elixir of life to my parched lips."

The standard gripes about Russian ways of doing things and Russian sense of time were soon being voiced. The train and the meals were all being run on Moscow time "though we were twelve days away" and the usual two-hour wait for every meal in the dining car reduced my father to two meals and my mother to one "at 4 P.M. by nobody's time and never even on that time."

Even her usual equanimity in the face of the filth and slovenliness of their "de luxe" accommodations collapsed after eight or nine days and she confessed that "plain living and high thinking never seemed to me drab before but I have seen nothing suggesting anything else in Russia so far." And being a fanatic about flies, not only at home but abroad, she continued to kill the flies that flew in the windows, along with the cinders, across the length and breadth of the Siberian steppes.

"However," she wrote, "we have just passed the Trans-Siberian going to Vladivostok and I feel ashamed of my carping criticism of our accommodations when I see what is offered to the heroic citizenry of this country packed like sardines into wooden shelves. It is interesting to see how they live on this trip. They rush out at every station with their tea pots or cans and get hot water at the spigot which sticks out from a heater of what looks like cement. They form in a line in front of a little window and buy black bread, good, too, a bit sour as the Russian bread is, but tasty. With these basics they have the fundamentals for existence."

My mother's attempts to buy berries at one of the little stations with an American dollar were unavailing and she recognized her naiveté in having tried. "Everyone was wary and said it was no good. The strawberries were there, lovely little wild ones, hulled, but the women shook their heads as they saw Washington's benignant face on the paper. No one was going to take a chance on Washington's head and lose her own."

On the same station platform, the first bit of drama of the trip took place. There was a sudden outcry from a fellow traveler, an attractive Polish woman, who had helped my parents by interpreting for them. "There has been a robbery, your husband has been robbed!" It apparently was a small town where murderers and thieves were sent into exile and one had brushed up against my father and deftly relieved him of his gold watch. The two train guards who had been watching my parents with some trepidation as they wandered heedlessly in the crowd saw the deed and immediately apprehended the culprit, who was quickly surrounded by military bigwigs traveling on the same train. "Our Polish friend said that the thief would be severely beaten: 'sometimes they beat them to death,' which was cold comfort to us as you can imagine." They were warned on all sides against pickpockets and especially if they were robbed, "not to make an outcry for either the robber or his accomplice might cut our faces or stab us if we attempt to stop them."

As the Siberian countryside unrolled day after day, it reminded my mother of her native Minnesota with its gentle hills and birch trees and an occasional hut with women and children inhabiting it and pigs rooting in the barnyards. Even the meadows were gay with familiar flowers, white daisies, fireweed, daylilies, and clover, and she was thrilled to see, for the first time since leaving home, cattle pastured knee-deep in grass. "Except for the few isolated farms, some lumber camps and a few potato fields, the land is waiting for its settlers," she observed. "I imagine that the country looks much as it did before the Revolution, but there is certainly a new spirit abroad, new buildings going up, attempts at beautification, etc., people thinking and taking part in a new civilization. Its effect cannot be less than that of suffrage on American women and probably immensely more. The filth and poverty is nothing new and probably seems to many of these dwellers in remote regions, life itself."

My mother's attempts to keep an open mind about the great Communist experiment were always being challenged by what she saw with her sharp eyes and deduced with her good sense. "We may have used Chinese coolies to build our railways, but these people use their criminals. The fact that some of these criminals are cultivated people called counterrevolutionaries does not alter the matter from their point of view. . . . The need for workers on these large projects is so great that no doubt there is enormous pressure to arrest 'counterrevolutionaries' or, if possible, create them. We have just passed a group building a bridge with men with fine faces not like the roughs we have been seeing and I have been wondering if they are some of the old intelligentsia." She remarked that the cattle cars they passed on the sidings were full of "criminals," two filled with women, and "the face of one, so utterly despairing, haunts me." With growing dismay, she watched another string of cattle cars full of convicts as they passed Lake Baikal and could not help wondering if the call had gone forth: "I want 1000 more men and 200 women in the railway doubling beyond Chita." On one of the station platforms where they had a half-hour's wait, she saw in the sea of peasant faces that of a man, dressed in a gray peasant smock, of unmistakable quality. "He looked at us as if to speak to us and we at him in the same way recognizing each other as kin through all the differences of race but we both hesitated and the moment was lost. I was left with the strange feeling as if someone had signaled us from a desert island and we had passed the signal by. I shall not soon forget him."

At every station she noted whole families of immigrants patiently waiting for trains, sitting on their bags and surrounded by bundles, children stunned with weariness, and the glassy stare in the eyes of the parents, people resigned like dumb animals. It reminded her of the Union Station in St. Paul when she was a child: the immigrants from all over the world, passing through; family knots huddling together, often exhausted and bewildered, but there, at least, willing travelers.

She was bemused watching a little Japanese fellow traveler, a student in the diplomatic service, on his way to Lisbon to study Portuguese. "He is clean and dainty in all the dirt in which we move. I wonder what he thinks, elaborate, conventional, politely giggling little man as he looks at the officers of the Red Army traveling 'soft' with us, big roughnecks, red-faced, vulgar, untidy, yet high in the ranks, commanders, next to the top. I have seen their hairy chests and dark blue undershirts in which they spend most of the day, and thought I would not want to fight them, but

perhaps the Japanese comforts himself that brains, not brawn, 213
win modern wars."

On arriving in Sverdlovsk, my father was typically concerned about making himself known to Professor L. A. Andreyev, a student of Pavlov's, who was to meet the train. He need not have worried. An avalanche of commissars, the mayor of the city, the head of the Trades Union, the head of the Board of Education, the head of Hygiene, and a lady physiologist with a funereal spray of flowers for my mother were waiting on the platform. As my mother remarked deprecatingly, "Our fellow travelers watched the scene with bulging eyes. They had not realized what great ones were in their midst, any more than we had."

After an orgy of welcoming speeches by the officials, most of them young and zealous, my parents were whisked off to the hotel, the usual grim Stalinist tenement, already beginning to crumble though it was only two years old. The city was described by my mother as looking like a boneyard, torn apart as it was by the exigencies of pulling down the old and putting up the new buildings. But so proud were the guides of their booming city and so enchanted was she by their energy and enthusiasm that she readily entered into the spirit of the place.

She was taken at her request to day-care centers, birth control centers, abortoriums, divorce courts, marriage courts, and, at a children's camp, the younger children started her out as a Pioneer with a red handkerchief around her neck secured by a Soviet button clip. One of the boys speaking excellent English dedicated a poem to her, the general gist of which was "we will be ready to fight the capitalists when that glorious day comes." "Good English but quaint selection," was my mother's wry comment. They even took my mother and father to the theater, one dedicated exclusively to musical comedy, the current offering being a bowdlerized Russian version of a tatty French musical. All American musicals were considered too bourgeois: except, oddly, *Rose Marie!* When my mother insouciantly asked whether they ever did Gilbert and Sullivan, the director answered chillily that they did not. Having been thoroughly snubbed, she concluded, "Even though G. and S. make fun of kings and princes, perhaps their tone is altogether too light for a proletarian audience, seriously bent on making over the world." In fact, after a series of what she deemed to be innocuous questions on a variety of subjects to the attendant officials that met with like rebuffs, my mother finally decided, "In this country I feel much like Alice through the Looking Glass. The animals are always being offended by my most innocent questions."

However, she was charmed by the common people that she met in her various excursions. "I have not tried 'Scratch a Russian and find a Tartar,' but by dint of not scratching I have found the dearest and the kindest people. The rank and file are certainly at work trying to build a better world and they long, like children, for praise. [I am sure she gave it to them.] I tell you, with all the tragedy of the past there is something about this Russian experiment that gets to you. In the face of these nice young enthusiasts, I begin to feel my critical faculties blur." But not for long!

For one day she was arrested by the GPU, the Russian secret military police. She had taken a stroll by herself to photograph some of the old log houses with their highly carved and decorated window frames and lintels and had come on the square where the house stood in which Czar Nicholas and Czarina Alexandra and their children had been incarcerated and murdered. She had wandered into the weedy garden that surrounded the moldering building and stood "sentimentalizing a bit about the poor Romanoffs and the ruin they brought to their people and themselves" and had taken some pictures of the yard to remember it by. A young man suddenly emerged from the house shouting and making violent gestures and through an interpreter my mother learned that she had committed a heinous crime by her picture-taking and all protestations of innocence of any intent to disobey the law proved vain. When her "captors" demanded to see her passport, she realized that she had set forth without it, an unthinkable thing in the USSR of the 1930s (as no doubt today) and her case seemed to arouse even deeper and more serious suspicions. On the desk of her interrogators she happened to see a pile of newspapers of that day in which, she recalled, there was a story about my father and mother having visited the inevitable factory the day before. She suggested to her captors that they look through the paper and find the item, which they did. "I am sure that that alone saved me from languishing days in a prison cell, infested with cockroaches, rats and all the orthodox fixings of a prison." Even so, two military officers who had been summoned escorted her into the street and there she was put into a police car that was waiting for her. "It looked like a tumbril to me though the doors had the old, familiar, and difficult Ford method of opening."

She was taken to the Central Military Police Station and further interrogated in a room lined with pictures of lynchings of Negroes on the walls, after which she was transferred to another car, where she sat between two hatchet-faced women police officers while a high official sat in the front seat with the driver. This time, she was driven to what she discovered later was the headquarters of the dread GPU. There she was again cross-examined by two more high-ranking officers through an interpreter "as to how long I had been in the USSR, what I was doing here, where I had come from, how long I had been in Sverdlovsk, how I liked it (which I thought a quaint question under the circumstances) and what evidence I could offer that I was the wife of Dr. Cannon. 'I know who Dr. Cannon is, of course,' said the officer. 'Everyone does, but I do not know Mrs. Cannon.' " She suggested perusal of the day's paper, "where you will see my picture with my husband's, but this sprightly remark seemed to fall on stony soil." She was finally released after her film was confiscated and conducted back to her hotel by the two GPU officers and one of the grim-faced policewomen, who accompanied her to her room, evidently to see whether she had told the truth. My mother made light of the episode in order to spare the feelings of Professor Andreyev, who was upset enough, but she reflected later, "I have lived over in my imagination the sufferings of the thousands of innocent persecuted persons who have lived in this country . . . what an example of the suspicion and official stupidity which mars and poisons the really fine things this country is trying to do."

When my parents later reached Leningrad, the Soviet Commissar of Health, Kaminski, having been apprised by the distressed

216 Professor Andreyev of her misadventure and arrest in Sverdlovsk, personally offered my mother the apologies of the government of the USSR. She responded that no apology was necessary, and that no harm was done to her, but, in typical fashion, not willing to pass up such a golden opportunity to set things right in the USSR, she told him in no uncertain terms "that the only tragedy in my mind was the revelation of the unhealthy mental attitude of the governing forces of the country." Kaminski's response was not recorded.

The last day of their stay in Sverdlovsk, they were called upon by three Americans, an architect and two engineers in the employ of the USSR. "They told us tales of the side we do not see, the sufferings of the old intelligentsia, the brutalities exercised against them, now, today and every day, the atmosphere of fear everywhere and the deprivation of the people in general. 'Who are in the prisons here in Sverdlovsk?' I asked, thinking of my possible companions. 'The finest people in the city,' answered the engineer with conviction. Yet both engineers thought there was much that was admirable, a great idea behind it although the performance was horrifying to a civilized person. The architect observed, 'What I cannot understand is how anyone had the colossal nerve to try it!' "

From Sverdlovsk, my parents flew over the Ural Mountains and "on to the great farming region beyond, with its wheat fields alternating with extensive forests. We flew over villages with no churches — some of the little communities showed signs of a liquidated church with a great cross of uncultivated land where the church had been. I felt as I looked down from the sky that without the church steeple pointing upwards, the villages looked like a collection of dog kennels. This is probably bourgeois sentimentality and to be discounted." My mother was really exercising her observational faculties more than her usual wont and noted that "as we draw nearer Moscow, we begin to see more use of lipstick and cosmetics of every kind. The Intourist Agent in Kazan, a man, even had his finger nails reddened."

From Kazan they took a boat:

clean and comfortable, the best conveyance we have seen yet in the USSR and followed our peaceful way up the Volga to Gorki. The river life was what the Mississippi must have been in Mark Twain's day. Peasants were getting in and getting out at every stop . . . shabby, pushing, eager, laden with bark baskets of berries, babies, and huge bundles. The first class passengers from the upper deck watched them indifferently as it seemed to me they might have watched cattle being loaded. But the people on the upper deck were indeed a superior group of human beings. Many were students, boys and girls together on their way back from a holiday, quiet and well behaved. There were also distinguished looking older people, in the same simple clothes that everyone wears but clean and worn with an air that suggested silk and satin. Dr. Andreyev looked for traces of his childhood home on the Volga, but it was gone, liquidated as a possession of a bourgeois. He felt very sad about it. . . . It is forlorn to realize that nowhere are there evidences of gracious living. The Soviet levels down everywhere and produces an ugly equality. . . . One can hardly object to having fine old houses put to social uses, but one hates to think that there is so little fine in personal living to serve as an example and to inspire imitation.

In Moscow, my mother's pendulum, which had momentarily come to rest on her peaceful boat trip on the Volga, began to swing ever more hectically. On the one hand, she visited the Children's City where she was impressed by the large numbers of children being beautifully cared for while their mothers worked. The day-care center idea, whose time has come only in the last few years in this country, was far advanced by this time in the USSR. She visited the Bolshevo Criminal Commune, where 7500 criminals ran the commune themselves, certainly a new idea in penology. But she could not help observing, "If they were half as humane to their political prisoners as they are to their murderers this would be a happier country." On the other hand, the tale of the mindless harassment and imprisonment of a distinguished doctor, a connection of Russian friends of my parents, sickened her. "Why will this government degrade its humanitarian program with such action? The same old savagery as under the czars exists and towards people who are doing their daily work of serving the

sick and the suffering." After several more tales of brutal de-
structiveness of innocent lives, my mother's pendulum really
stuck. "I am beginning to think that nothing is precious except
liberty, and I am going back to America more determined than
ever that what I can do to give the Communists and others the
freedom they deny to their fellow men, I shall do. One thing you
cannot imprison is the free spirit of man. You may cow it as they
do here, put the shackles of silence upon it, destroy what is best
in human nature, but you cannot change that mind."

Her Alice-through-the-Looking-Glass perplexity continued.
After visiting the House of the Red Army, an elegant headquarters for the army brass, she remarked that though she passed
through room after room of flags, pictures, statues, and mementos
extolling the marvels of the Red Army, there was not a word or a
sign of Trotsky, or a suggestion that he ever existed. "I thought it
was the most amazing achievement yet, as true to History as
talking about our Revolution and deleting George Washington;
Trotsky, the creator of the Red Army without whom there might
never have been one or the USSR either."

Her sense of the absurd was forever being piqued. "We have
just discovered that we cannot visit Lenin's tomb as it is closed
pending the body's annual renovation! And this in a land that has
repudiated the bones of the saints. It is certainly quaint." And
she thought it doubly quaint that a whole session of the Congress
should have been devoted to a report on the details of the preservation of Lenin's body for the edification of the physiologists,
though Egyptologists might have found it more fascinating.

At the Leningrad station my parents were met by Intourist men,
couriers of all kinds, and then "dear old-young Prof. Pavlov and
his son." As with so many men of science, there had for many
years been a deep bond of common interest transcending the
barriers of politics and language between my father and Pavlov,
based on their mutual study of the digestive process and the
changes brought about in it by nervous and emotional factors.
They had exchanged scientific papers and corresponded for years
before they met. In 1917 my father had received alarming reports
that Pavlov was suffering from hunger and deprivation during the

chaotic days of the Revolution and he had promptly appealed to the American physiologists for help. In a brief time he was able to send $2000 in the care of a Finnish colleague to be given to Pavlov in any way that seemed best. He later learned that Pavlov had characteristically used the money for his laboratory instead of spending it to protect himself against the rigors of life under the Soviets.

In 1923, when Pavlov, at the age of seventy-four, visited this country for the first time, under the auspices of the Rockefeller Institute, he and his son were held up in New York and robbed at gunpoint of all their money, $1500, as they were boarding a train for New Haven and Boston. Penniless, they had to turn back and seek friends. They returned to the Rockefeller Institute and explained what had happened. As my father wrote, "Professor Pavlov was as much affected by the indignity he had suffered as by the loss of his money. When asked what he would like to do, he said that he wanted to go to Boston and after that pay a short visit to the Woods Hole Biological Laboratory. That done, he wished to return to Russia where he would be safe!" He visited the physiological laboratory at the Harvard Medical School and stayed at our house in Cambridge. "In the cool house we spent the hot July afternoon in reading and conversation," my father continued. "When evening came, we set forth for the Harvard Yard. Since my family was in New Hampshire the house was empty when we left it. As I closed the door behind me Pavlov inquired, 'Where is the watchman?' I explained that there was no watchman. Seeing my old Ford car in the yard, he remarked, 'Someone will steal your fine automobile.' When I assured him there was no danger of that, he threw up his hands and exclaimed, "What a profound, what an abysmal difference there is between the morality of New York and the morality of Cambridge!"

After lunching with the elder Pavlovs in their apartment looking over the Neva, my mother wrote of them, "They are lovely, so simple and genuine, he with the vigorous motions of a young man and the active interest and enthusiasm of his youth; she sweet, deeply religious with pictures of the Virgin and Child, an old icon, by her bed. I asked her whether she could go to church and she shook her head as she remarked sadly that the aspirations for a higher life were left out of the planned life of today and that mankind would sink and not climb without it."

My mother reported that "part of the respect and consideration given him [Pavlov] is probably due to Lenin's remark on his death bed, 'Take care of Pavlov!' The dying Bolshevik recognized the selfless devotion to his science of the great Russian physiologist; and also probably his importance to the reputation of the future of Soviet science. Probably Lenin, a brave man himself, also admired him for his courage before the threat of Lenin's own ruthless methods." She goes on to tell the story of Pavlov's having been summoned to be examined by a Bolshevik committee on heretical remarks he had been reported to have made in his classroom. "He came to the meeting, made a few remarks, answered a few questions, then looked at his watch and said, 'I cannot stay any longer, gentlemen. I have to lecture in ten minutes,' and promptly walked out of the room, leaving the committee aghast at such an affront to their dread authority."

On another occasion my mother told of a long talk with Pavlov's daughter, an aide in a psychiatric clinic where many hysterical and nervous victims of the Revolution came to be treated. They were not the intelligentsia (who were not welcome) but peasant and worker types who had been uprooted by the Revolution from their former ways of doing and thinking. Most of them were from eighteen to thirty years old and had hardly in this time of disruption known what a home was. They had been asked to learn a new way of life, to adapt themselves to it, to work extremely hard in factories unfamiliar to them, and they had broken under it. Miss Pavlov's "description of it," my mother wrote, "was pitiful and she felt that the people of a country paid high for revolution, physically and nervously as well as materially and that evolution was to be desired every time."

When my mother asked if she did not think that possibly the men that ordered these exiles and imprisonments were not themselves, like the patients in the hospitals, victims of the Revolution, Miss Pavlov agreed with her absolutely. "Only so could their conduct be explained," she said and went on to wonder if the top men realized what was going on in the GPU, "for it was all so staggeringly stupid, produced hatred of the regime, roused needless antagonism in other countries and damned the fair cause into which they were putting all their brains and effort."

On August 10, my parents were driven to the Uritski Palace, the magnificent building in which the Duma met, where Kerenski addressed the constituent assembly and whence he fled from the oncoming Bolsheviks. They later discovered that the car in which they rode had once belonged to Kirov, whose assassination the winter before had brought a train of brutal reprisals among party members. My mother was moved to remark, "It gave me a bizarre sensation when added to the experience of being arrested in Sverdlovsk."

The great auditorium was packed with two thousand people and Pavlov, "looking like a beautiful old saint, presided, flanked by Professor Hill of England and Professor Lapique of Paris. . . . Pavlov spoke, his speech a stirring indictment of war, which they all dread and expect; then the Commissar of Health of the USSR, Kaminski, said a few words touching on Lenin, the wonderful Stalin and all the other gods of this world, and, after the Commissar, the head of the Leningrad Soviets," wrote my mother, adding with irrepressible esprit, "He was the true Communist type, head close shaven, a phrenologist's delight, but also different because his face was close shaven and he wore a necktie." My mother's concern with appearances and apparel was something new for her, which must have meant that the slovenliness was of an extreme order.

After a few further remarks by the president of the All Union Academy of Sciences, a white-haired, feeble old man of ninety-five, Pavlov briskly handed the meeting over to my father "without a word of eulogy," wrote my mother, "which I thought in excellent taste." In his opening address, among other things, my father emphasized the international unity of science and spoke bluntly of the importance of absolute intellectual freedom in the pursuit of scientific truth. He further stated that in the face of growing nationalism and antagonism between various ideologies and political systems it must be remembered that "the scientific triumphs of the past have not been achieved by workers of a single nation, nor representatives of a single racial group. These triumphs of science have resulted from a generous interchange of information concerning methods and results. In like manner, the significant problems which remain are not limited or national. They are large human problems, the solution of which will be facilitated by free intellectual intercourse without respect for national boundaries."

He went on to quote Pavlov's words of 1923 as reinforcement of the responsibilities of science: "Only science, exact science about human nature itself, and the most sincere approach to it by the aid of the omnipotent scientific nature, will deliver man from the existing darkness and will purge him from his shame in the sphere of inter-human relations."

As my mother wrote, "The address, wrought in a quiet study in Cambridge, took on a momentous quality in that assembly of people coming from countries in the turmoil of uncertainties, on the verge of war and poisoned by race hatred and intolerance."

In the atmosphere of the times, it was a resounding speech and many colleagues from Germany, Italy, and Spain congratulated him on his "courageous speech" though my mother pointed out that "to speak your mind is no great venture for an American and that it is easier [for my father] to pour out his burning convictions than to be internally consumed by them." She went on to observe that among the European physiologists "the Germans thought that he referred to the Russians, the Italians thought that he referred to the Germans, the Russians thought that he referred to Western Europe and only the French took it to themselves and said that they would translate it and give it publicity in the hope of a change of heart on the part of the government."

The final banquet of the congress was held in the sumptuously carved and gilded throne room of the Palace of Catherine the Great. Elaborate tables loaded with food "tortured into shapes and forms of temples, swans, flowers, etc., the kind of display which would have been appropriate to an oriental potentate, but not to a proletarian country" struck my mother as another puzzling challenge to her purist view of what proletarian behavior should be like. She was further startled when the banquet turned into an "orgy" with the starchy wives of the English and American physiologists being assaulted by their husbands' drunken and amorous Russian colleagues, somewhat the worse for a Niagara-like flow of wine and champagne.

I do not think my mother was ever able to rid herself of her Alice-through-the-Looking-Glass perplexity in the face of the contradictions she saw at every turn. She finally threw up her hands at one of the scientific meetings where the Russians insisted on stressing the difference between bourgeois and proletarian physiology — "a mysterious distinction no one else is keen enough to see" — and again after a demonstration by a Russian doctor when he stated categorically, " 'Now this is an absolutely true fact!' We wondered what the rest had been." In total frustration she flatly concluded, "the contradictions are too much for me!" while my father, after some wild scientific claim by a "proletarian" scientist, concluded in his turn that Russian science, like its art, is vivid with imagination!

And so, in a state of continuing astonishment and bemusement at all that they had seen and learned, with abiding affection for the people they had met and horror at the mindless cruelty and bestiality of the system and of many of the men in power, my mother and father passed over the border into Finland, heaving the well-known sigh of relief as they came out into the fresh air of that democratic country.

chapter thirteen

After the Chinese adventure, my sister Helen and I sailed across the Pacific and eventually arrived back in Cambridge, there to meet our parents coming around the other way. My sister returned to her last year at Radcliffe, while I, having experienced the wider world and finding it to my taste, set forth to make the obligatory assault on New York, which all self-respecting "career" girls in those days felt must be the next stop.

Some, to be sure, went to Washington to work in the Roosevelt New Deal, but more felt the pull of the big city; a job at Macy's was considered glamorous; but even more challenging was the much-coveted role of girl researcher for *Time*. However, having lost my heart to China, I wanted a job that would have connections with the Far East. I was lucky enough to find a position as a research assistant in the Institute of Pacific Relations, in its rabbit-warren–like headquarters on East Fifty-second Street where I worked for two years in the mid-thirties. When, as it turned out, three weeks after I arrived at the IPR, I was consulted, though a twenty-two-year-old tyro, as an "expert on China" by one of those "exotic" girl researchers for *Time*, any thought of joining the Luce publications as a female slavey evaporated.

The atmosphere of the IPR was strictly egalitarian. There were perpetual staff meetings at which all employees from the lowliest secretary (as a matter of fact, no one was lowly!) to executives, visiting Oriental scholars, wandering students, and fresh-faced

The old farmhouse, Franklin, New Hampshire

researchers were soberly consulted on all policy decisions, no matter how trivial or how weighty. In a peculiar way, all the characteristics of the sixties were manifest. The big-happy-family, all-proletarians-together, approach was emphasized to a self-conscious degree; everyone was immediately on a first-name basis and the position of women was equal, if not superior, to that of the male. In fact, the IPR was populated by powerful women, and the patrician figure of Frederick Vanderbilt Field, rich and radical, the executive director of the American Council, was like that of some classical youth surrounded by a troupe of Amazons.

We wrote articles, helped edit the *Far Eastern Survey*, read *The New York Times* and the *New York Herald Tribune* at our desks, held earnest talks on the telephone in answer to equally earnest queries, worked up statistics from the Japan Year Book, apparently our sole source book, and yawned a good deal at the fecklessness of much of our labor. Considering the fact that during the McCarthy era the IPR was accused of being the devious institution that corrupted a generation of China experts and of being instrumental in "losing China" (that ridiculous concept), I often reflect that the chief emotion many of the staff felt during my years was that of *futility*. We used to complain loudly that no one ever paid any attention to the blameless articles we wrote or helped to edit in the *Far Eastern Survey* and *Pacific Affairs!*

❧

It was the depth of the Depression and the height of the Popular Front and there was a political fever in the air that was a new experience for me. It was palpable as one walked the streets, went to the movies, ate in restaurants, a kind of desperation which one felt in the hard-pressed counter boys, harried waitresses, street beggars, and men and women shivering in the frigid streets of mid-winter in Manhattan. Many of the staff of the IPR were political activists, and I tagged along with them, attending dinners for Earl Browder and fund-raisers for the United Mine Workers and the CIO. Hardly an evening passed without some member rushing off into the night to a conference or meeting devoted to left-wing causes. The Trotskyites and the Stalinists were excoriating each other and one was always finding oneself at some party or gathering where furious political controversy was taking place.

I remember attending a rehearsal of the left-wing revue *Pins and Needles*, put on by members of the ILGWU, in a loft down in the garment district, and feeling enlivened by the energy, brashness, and spirit of the performance and delighted by the music of Harold Rome, though doubtful about the simplistic political message. I recall sitting in the balcony of the Fourteenth Street Playhouse, listening to the hortatory words of Clifford Odets's *Waiting for Lefty* and *Awake and Sing* and not being quite able to enter into the welter of emotional fervor and identification that the rest of the audience exulted in. It was exhilarating, but at the same time seemed faintly ludicrous. I was still the little Cambridge girl loose in the big city. The skepticism of my upbringing would not be downed. The isms and absolutes as well as the sentimentality of the fellow travelers and the faithful party liners seemed somehow unrealistic, dehumanized, and phony. I could never get used to the way "the people" so often came out as abstractions or statistics to be manipulated for political purposes.

On the other hand, I remember seeing Clare Boothe's *The Women*, which seemed to me extremely daring and sophisticated, and, above all, Lillian Hellman's *The Children's Hour*, which I thought the most brilliant play I had ever seen. It was supposed to be about lesbianism, I was told. I was pretty vague about what "lesbianism" meant, but there were certainly tensions and overtones in the play that even I could not miss. It was the days when *The Well of Loneliness* was one of the great underground books, and after seeing the play we sought it out for further illumination.

In the meantime, my roommate and I lived a kind of subterranean life in a cockroach-ridden, one-room apartment a block off Washington Square. It seemed to consist of one long hall with two grubby windows giving out on an air shaft, a sordid kitchenette in a closet, and a daybed that opened up into two hard pallets; first one to bed got the one with the springs. It was a typical disastrous choice of two neophytes; but it was cheap and we did not know any better. We were fair game for all our visiting friends who strung along the hall, head to foot, when they spent the night. An especially tall Australian, six feet six, once monopolized the total space from the front door to the so-called living room area and for a whole week I had to stumble over him to go to work, as Australians appeared to be nerveless, heavy sleepers. I was forever rescuing my roommate from the clutches of unwanted boyfriends that she seemed to attract on her forays uptown on the IRT subway to the Juilliard School where she was supposedly studying voice. They would come to the door or call on the phone and I would deny any knowledge of anyone by that name, an exercise in white-lying that I must say, no doubt because of the rigor of my upbringing in which lying was looked upon as a cardinal sin, I never got very good at. Once when she had unguardedly agreed to go out to dinner with one pathetic specimen, I rushed to the restaurant by prearrangement and announced in hushed, tense tones that "a long-distance call has come through, your father is deathly ill, and you are called home immediately" — a transparent performance and a sad little subterfuge all around. But we thought ourselves very clever. We were, no doubt, like hundreds of other scared, homesick young things isolated in a strange city having come from the sheltered, ordered, existence of a settled home. Besides which, we had never learned to say *no*. Youth would scoff at such naiveté and diffidence today.

My roommate did not last long, but I seemed to have been made of sterner stuff, for I stayed on to live in various exotic haunts, including a small room at the back of a children's theater in the East Thirties, where I had to stumble through the spooky drops and scenery for *Hansel and Gretel* to reach my tiny bedroom. It was not a setting to inspire confidence, but I took it as a challenge, feeling that if I could beat down my fears of papier-mâché hobgoblins, I would be armed against the world.

❧

In the summer of 1936, I attended, with other members of the New York office, the International Conference of the IPR at Yosemite. Delegations from the United States, Japan, China, the Netherlands, the USSR, England, and France, as well as others with interests in the Pacific, gathered under the great spruces of the valley floor for round-table discussions, while low-level functionaries such as myself and other members of the staff acted as recorders, secretaries, and errand-runners for the great and the near-great.

Our bird's-eye view was informative. The British were always earnestly caucusing "in committee" while the French delegates seemed to take their duties rather lightheartedly, spending a good deal of time playing bridge in their elegant suite in the Ahwanee Hotel, no doubt in an attempt to re-create the Parisian atmosphere in the face of "all that nature." There was a good deal of drama and tension in the course of the two-week conference, for not only did the Spanish Civil War erupt in the middle, but the Moscow Trials got under way. There was a dramatic moment when Vladimir Romm, the correspondent for *Izvestia* in the United States and a member of the Soviet delegation, was called back to Moscow, to what he must have known would be his fate, for he was one of those who stood trial and was later liquidated. The Japanese were represented by the military and by "officials" (read "military"!) of the South Manchurian Railway, as well as by some members of the government that in a few months launched the all-out Sino-Japanese War.

I wrote to my mother: "It is curious how electric the air gets when the Japanese are even indirectly concerned in the discussion. They are in a terrifically touchy state of mind, and apparently incapable of approaching the problem of their place in the affairs of the Pacific in an objective light. . . . There are four or five unidentified Japanese thugs that hang around that I am sure are spies!"

I remember a scrub baseball game gotten together between the Japanese and American delegates and secretariat, a typically goofy, informal contest, in which the contrast between the Japanese and the American players was remarkable. The Japanese were intensely serious and determined to win, while the Americans fooled around, perfectly willing to give the Japanese a break when they lagged behind, lest their loss precipitate an international incident. In a way, it was the beginning of the end of innocence, for the roles played by most of the participants of the conference in a very few years suffered cataclysmic changes and the issues and questions that were so earnestly discussed had long since become academic.

Over the years, the old farmhouse in Franklin became more and more the refuge of my parents where they spent long summers and fall and spring weekends as we children grew up and began to live our independent lives. But it drew us, too, like a lodestone, and we would return as often as we could to the scene of our carefree childhood.

The modern world had had its way with the simple country life. The candlesticks and kerosene lamps by which we used to read Edgar Wallace and Conan Doyle detective stories were forever banished when electricity was finally installed, my mother's rationalization at such extravagance being that "the simplicity of life is not wholly the possession of inconveniences." We rather missed the smell of broiling moths and beetles that pervaded the night air as whole regiments of insects used to attack our wavering candle flames. The outhouse was abandoned for more modern plumbing and a genuine shower bath with hot and cold running water replaced the tin watering can that used to hang suspended from a hook in the ceiling of the "bath house."

Some of the old farms around us had been bought by Polish immigrants who had been brought over to work in the textile mills after the First World War. Most of the women spoke only broken English, went barefoot in summer, wore babushkas over their heads, and worked long hours in their gardens, producing wonderful vegetables out of the rocky soil, while their husbands worked in the mills. My mother loved to visit them in their spotless houses, buying their vegetables and their delicious cottage cheese with chives, and as time went on, she helped some of their ambitious children to go on to the state university after they finished high school. She wrote about them: "It is too interesting to see these Polish people repeating history. They are taking the beautiful New England farms, neglected and run down, and beginning again as our ancestors did, clearing out the stones, cutting down the trees, fertilizing the soil and making good farms out of willing, but abused nature's bounty." She wrote her second novel, *Heirs*, about the impact of these vital energetic Poles on the exhausted, gone-to-seed native Yankees.

A continual stream of visitors came and went, climbing the dusty hillside road and from time to time special requests were sent out for guests of a certain size and shape, at one point my mother asking for a "tall guest, for I have just begun painting my room and the ceiling is none too easy to reach." There was an influx of foreign visitors, especially as the circle of my parents' friends widened through the years and became more international. After a weekend of Chinese visitors who had been sent with a letter of introduction from the Fairbanks in Peking, my mother wrote rather ruefully to report to them on the visit, ". . . the Chinese gentleman departed on Monday, after having suffered the anguish of being called by me at different times Mr. Dung, Dr. Teng, and Mr. Tong . . . etc.; I think he concluded that I was a flighty nitwit and tried to forgive though I doubt whether he could forget." One thing that could be said for my mother was that she always *tried*.

The amount of activity my mother generated — mostly because she hated to see people "idling," a restful habit she never acquired — such as cutting down trees, picking blueberries, or burning brush, was hard on the more inert visitors. My brother-in-law John Fairbank, after a rigorous weekend, once wrote a wicked bread-and-butter letter to my mother in the imaginative form of a whimsical letter home by an exhausted Chinese visitor: ". . . and then we helped our host and hostess cut some of the wood they burn in the winter. I suppose that with week-end guests every week in summer, it is possible to arrange for the winter quite comfortably, a very provident idea! Our host said that we cut about $4 worth of wood, so it is plain that heavier guests, say Russians or Germans, could be easily worth $50 a weekend." After describing an exhausting game of badminton into which the "sedentary Chinese scholar" had been "drafted," the letter continues: "We had no sooner got ourselves into a lather of exhaustion and perspiration this way, than we all jumped in an auto to go on a 'picnic.' In this case I noted carefully we left a hill covered sparsely with green trees and after dashing madly through the dust for the distance of a two day walk, shouting at each other meanwhile, we reached another place with almost the same kind of trees, except not so many on one side. We had timed our arrival for the hottest sun of the day and immediately built a fire and all stood around it. This is the same principle as vaccination that fixes you so that nothing can hurt you any more.

"It is also interesting to observe the family relationships. Apparently the matriarchal system is followed and sons-in-law marry into their wives' family, although they keep their own name. We could not discover whether one of the men was a son-in-law. When we asked, our host said that he was a boy friend, but I cannot find it in the dictionary."

The general conclusion seemed to be that, "as Mencius says, among barbarians, it is best to act like a barbarian especially if they have you in their power."

❧

Our summer neighbors came year after year, and summer life took on a certain pattern. Not only did the Yerkeses live up the hill, but also a family of musicians and an entomologist, and across the valley in my Aunt Ida's house, Miss Louisa Eyre, a sculptress from Philadelphia. Professor George Pierce and his wife built a summer house on the site of the "chalet," which had finally collapsed from old age and inexpert carpentry.

As time went on, the back roads became infested with scientists, biologists, zoologists, and a chemist or two, one a Nobel prizewinner, buying up old deserted farms, no doubt inspired by my parents' original purchase of their farm. Alas, the humanities were sadly underrepresented, but my mother tried to make up for it in her one-woman crusades!

At one point, having either exhausted the repertoire of the Greek and English theater of Euripides and Shakespeare or simply run out of exploitable or tractable children, my mother drafted Miss Eyre to start an art class in our barn. It turned out to be a great success.

The local farmers' children not only earned untold riches and numerous Hershey bars by posing, but some of them became pupils, and one at least became a gifted sculptress. Of the other children that used to attend, one became a well-known architect, and another an art critic, while all four of us sisters continued to sketch and paint through the years. My sister Wilma became an art historian, and I, in apparent emulation of my great-grand-father, became a portrait painter. So the influence of this informal art academy seems to have been strong.

My father, who had never held a sculpting tool before, took up modeling. My mother, who once described my father as "having that driven" look because he wasn't *doing* anything, had re-marked, "Give your conscience a vacation. I suggest it needs it as much as any of your other faculties," and in pursuance of that end she had handed him some clay and a pair of calipers. He attacked the problem with his usual care and intelligence, as my mother said, "hovering over his busts and reliefs like Phidias over his masterpieces." He was thrilled when at one point he took first prize at the Doctors' Art Exhibition in Boston for a bust of my sister Helen. In a letter describing the event, my mother wrote rather facetiously, "He gets a Blue Ribbon just like a prize bull or rooster. The only other one he ever got was when at the age of 18 in competition with 26 women he took first prize at the Minnesota State Fair as breadmaker. Now he is dilated with pride and plea-sure. What is the adrenal gland and its activities by comparison."

Mr. Wilson Eyre, Miss Eyre's architect brother, used to visit her from time to time, bringing with him the atmosphere of gen-teel Philadelphians, many of whose huge houses on the Main Line he had designed. We used to take him off on sketching trips around the countryside, where he was often observed perched on a large granite boulder, sketchbook in hand, dressed in gray spats, well-creased pinstripe pants, silk monogrammed shirt, polka-dot bow tie, pince-nez glasses on a long black silk ribbon, and a black wide-brimmed hat, an exotic figure to be found in a New Hampshire cow pasture. With his habit of looking down his nose through his wobbly spectacles, he was the essence of Whistleresque superciliousness, although he seemed to enjoy his

234 yearly slumming among the simple folk. It was years later that I discovered that he was the architect for the Detroit mansion of Mr. Freer, who gave the Freer Gallery of Art in Washington in which Whistler's Peacock Room was originally installed. So the connection was not far off.

For many years, on Sunday evenings throughout the summer, the summer folk used to gather with their picnic suppers on various hilltops or front lawns and hear a talk by one of their group or by some visiting worthy. Before ennui set in after a period of years, and before a general desire not to be informed or uplifted finally overwhelmed the participants, the scope of subject matter of the evening talks ranged from "The History of Apes," and "Social Work among the Rural Poor" to "Life in New Hampshire in the Early Nineteenth Century" and "Supersonic Bugs." This latter subject grew out of the fact that Professor Pierce, who was a pioneer in radio physics and engineering and had made important contributions to the development of sonar listening devices, used to amuse himself in the summer by studying the sounds of insects, some of which were ultrasonic and out of the hearing range of the normal human ear.

Wearing an ancient fishing hat, his short plump form encased in an old shirt and stained army riding breeches, which hung loose below his knees, he cut a droll figure as he strolled over the new-mown hayfields with his butterfly net and collecting bottle in pursuit of grasshoppers and crickets, so that their supersonic calls could be recorded. Many of the visiting young people were drafted for "bug hunting," a peculiar kind of child labor well remembered by one of my friends years later, as well as the other projects of the irrepressible Uncle George, of whom one of the clerks in the hardware store "downstreet" once remarked, "He sure is a comfortable fellah!"

He was always full of projects, the more complicated the better; transplanting large trees that inevitably died; damming the stream for a swimming pool and then stocking it with trout, which were always fished out by the local small boys before he arrived for the summer; or creating a plumbing system so individual and intricate that none of the local plumbers could comprehend it. In fact, he liked to have the plumbing done badly so he could keep fixing it. Once when he had invested in a new lawn mower, my mother wrote, "Uncle George is looking for work and has asked to borrow our badminton court for his lawn mower," and when he and my father decided to dig a well under the russet apple tree on the way to the chalet she further observed, "not that we need a well, but to do a useless piece of work in this utilitarian world seems so worthwhile."

There seemed always to be a theme to the books that were read and passed around from house to house each summer. One summer, I remember, was given over to reading the life and works of Mary Baker Eddy, but a few years later a more sprightly topic enlivened the season when the reading consisted of a volume of *The Letters of D. H. Lawrence,* as well as Mabel Dodge Luhan's *Lorenzo in Taos* and Dorothy Brett's equally fantastic tale of Lawrence's sojourn in Taos, *Lawrence and Brett.* So much joy did these volumes bring into everyone's life that at the end of the season there was a Stunt Party in which Aunt Florence (Pierce), being the only member thin enough to play Lawrence, performed in an orange beard made out of knitting wool; Miss Eyre herself, slightly deaf and given to using an ear trumpet as a joke, took the part of Dorothy Brett, who in real life was stone-deaf and used an ear trumpet; my mother was a bossy Mabel Dodge Luhan; and my father, in a shawl and braids, mumbling imprecations, played the part of Tony Luhan, "Lo the poor Indian," who had been shanghaied out of the Taos pueblo by Mabel. Uncle George, who was something of a Puritan, from Texas, was scandalized by D. H. Lawrence and all his works, thinking him an "indecent old thing," and protested the "idea of such a book [his volume of letters] having a circulation when at one point not a single copy of Archimedes' book could be sold in the U.S." All men to their tastes!

The end of the thirties saw the erosion of our lively family life in the old house in Cambridge behind the Busch-Reisinger Museum and by 1939 the last members of the family had finally moved out, leaving it to the tender mercies of the bureaucracy of the University. My sister Linda married a young geologist, my sister Helen, a young psychiatrist, and my brother by now had become a full-fledged surgeon in Boston. My Aunt Ida, at last, had her own apartment, though I think she always missed the general turmoil of family life. My Aunt Bernice bought one of the oldest houses in Cambridge and restored it, turning it into a little gem with her pretty antiques and her exquisite taste; her children's store, Miss Cannon's Shop, was already an institution in Harvard Square, and my mother used to tease her about its success: "Bernice is driven to death by business and is really quite plaintive about the way people WILL insist on buying from her."

My mother's letters (the source throughout this book for all my inspiration) took on an unwonted note of softness, not to say namby-pambyness, as she tactfully tried to avoid offending in-laws. We children used to make fun of her tendency to describe "how wonderful, how gifted, how humane," all newly acquired relatives seemed to be, and longed for the pithy, sometimes outrageous, letters of the old days. Even so, her letters were always awaited with anticipation, though often those unlucky enough to receive the last carbon had to employ sophisticated techniques of code-breaking in order to read it. She maintained an elaborate correspondence with her distant children and her sisters in St. Paul, as she had with her mother before she died, transmitting the news and weaving a web firmly binding her family close. In an almost Oriental way, she believed in the importance of family loyalty and affection. Suffocating as it may sound, it somehow was not, as her remarks and admonitions were always leavened with humor and good sense. In answer to a turndown of one of her bits of advice to my sister in Peking, she wrote, "Don't worry about my being 'upset' at your refusal to fall in with" some suggestion that she had made. "I shall simply have a dozen more suggestions to take its place. The acceptance of my wild ideas never worries me. All I ask is to retain the freedom to *make* them."

My mother once wrote, "An invitation to dinner at the

Whiteheads has just come. I told Mrs. Whitehead that an invitation from them was like a *royal command,* of course one accepted." Whether this was the dinner described in Lucien Price's
Dialogues of Alfred North Whitehead, I do not know, but he gives
a rather charming picture of my parents in the mid-thirties. "The
other guests were . . . Dr. Walter B. Cannon and his wife Cornelia. He is a rugged, ruddy Midwesterner with a hearty voice,
simple, direct, and no nonsense. An authority in his subject, he
is freighted with honors which he wears invisibly. His wife is a
good deal like him, full of humour and kindness, learned, clever,
witty, but sees no reason for putting on side. There was no need to
waste time over social preliminaries."

International politics permeated the air in the last years of the
thirties, and my father's involvement in medical aid to the victims
of the Spanish Civil War was a constant theme throughout my
mother's letters. Because of his espousal of the Loyalist cause, he
was the object of scurrilous attacks not only by local and federal
authorities but by conservative members of his own profession, a
state of affairs that prompted his friend Professor Ralph Perry to
remark to my mother, "the kind of people who excoriate him for
his advocacy of Loyalist Spain makes me sure that he is right!"
Being a sensitive and idealistic man, he was often deeply depressed when his motives and character were impugned. However, he had fought the good fight for things he believed in
throughout his life and did not withdraw from the battle when
things got hot or unpleasant. When the Japanese invasion of
China exploded, he took up the cudgels again, working for aid to
the beleaguered Chinese. He was instrumental in finding jobs in
this country for some of his distinguished Jewish physiological
colleagues fleeing from Hitler's purges and once wrote a most
moving letter describing the extraordinary contributions of the
Jews to medicine. It said in part:

The advancing front of medical science owes no debt to narrow pa-
triotism. . . . In the appallingly unjust and cruel measures which Ger-

many and Italy have taken against the Jews, there is utter disregard of the great benefactions to all mankind which have come through Jewish contributions to medical science and art. Is a Hitlerite bleeding to death and desperately dependent on a blood transfusion? His life is saved by methods revealed by Landsteiner, a Jewish Nobel Laureate who showed how to avoid the fatal mixing of incompatible bloods. Does the Italian doctor wish to know whether a patient has typhoid fever? He applied observations first made by Widel, a Jew. Is one of our children in danger of diphtheria? Her resistance to that infection is tested by a process invented by Schick, a Jew — a process which, wisely utilized, could wholly eradicate that once terrifying disease. The tens of thousands of victims of syphilis in countries where antisemitism is rife must rest their hopes for relief on a diagnostic method fundamentally devised by Wasserman, a Jew, and on a curative method discovered by Ehrlich, another Jew chosen as a Nobel Laureate for his beneficent services to mankind. Warburg, Willstatter, Meyerhoff, Friedlander, Schiff, Magnus . . . [and many more] all have advanced medical science and art in such important ways that each is associated with one or more significant contributions. And a host of other Jewish physicians and investigators could be listed who have helped the structure of modern medicine. Throughout medical history the Jewish people have sustained a most illustrious tradition of bringing great gifts to the relief of man's estate. . . . We should all remember that it is the habit of savage mobs to crucify their savior and "know not what they do."

In May 1940, when there was fear that the United States might be drawn into the Second World War, my father was asked to became chairman of a Committee on Shock and Transfusion of the National Research Council, working once again, after a hiatus of twenty-five years, on the problems of wound shock first studied by him and others in France in World War I.

He was, at this time, the single American who was not only a member of the National Academy of Sciences of the United States, but also of the Royal Society of Great Britain and the Academy of Sciences of the USSR and in the latter capacity served as liaison with Soviet scientists during the war. But his health was failing, and in October 1945, he finally succumbed after a long battle with leukemia, indubitably the result of his exposure to radiation in his early experiments with the newly discovered X ray some forty years before.

All his children, except his daughter Wilma, who was in Chungking, China, serving as cultural attaché with the American Embassy, gathered with the rest of the family in the old house in Franklin where he had died to "celebrate" his life, which had ended. "Celebrate" really was the word, for though we mourned his death, there was a kind of exaltation in recalling the richness of that life and the quality of his person; his humor, his kindliness, his fairness, his fresh imagination that never seemed to dry up, his intellectual rigor, and the uncomplaining courage with which he bore the almost intolerable pain of his last years.

❧

My mother lived on for twenty-five years after my father's death. I think she momentarily lost her nerve after he died, for under her high-spirited exterior she was a deeply emotional person, and the security of his affection was the wellspring of her being. For a brief moment, one caught a glimpse of those private dreads and thoughts that were usually rigorously controlled out of her strong sense of pride and self-discipline.

She believed that turning in on one's self was "self-indulgence," showed lack of backbone, and threatened the secret core that was not to be revealed. She hated what she thought was the "scab-picking" of psychiatry. But she was fortunate to have been throughout her life surrounded with an atmosphere of love and approval, and with that sense of security she could move mountains. Without it she might have had to face down a lot of things that she had no doubt sublimated; she would have "wasted a lot of time" in the matter of self-examination; and who would know whether she or the rest of us would have been any happier? She never probed her children's psyches, granting us the blessedness of privacy.

And who am I to say that she did not have the unexamined heart? She was a highly intelligent woman and I know that in the anguished turmoil after my father's death, she reflected long and hard on her life, regretting what she felt had been her acts of omission in her relationship with him. She got her nerve back eventually, but there was a change in her nature, a deepening of it, I think, which her wrestling with the darks of her sorrow, in all probability, produced.

She did not repine, but took up her life again, with all its old vigor. Although she was as uncompromising in her values for herself as ever, and lived serenely with them, she showed a remarkable ability to adjust herself to new mores, although I am glad that she did not live long enough to be exposed to the so-called sexual revolution. That, I fear, would have been too much for her. She was a great favorite with her grandchildren. One of her grandsons was badly crippled with polio and had to spend several months at a rehabilitation center outside of Boston. She used to go out every week to help him with his algebra; she was determined to overcome adversity in herself and help other people to overcome it too. Although she had forgotten everything she once knew about algebra, she did not think that she was beyond learning at the age of seventy-two, and he learned algebra by teaching her.

Her passion for travel at last found full expression. At the age of seventy-four she traveled around the world by herself, and off the beaten track. No packaged tours for her. Although a baby girl was named for her in a remote headhunters' village in the wilds of the Philippines, it did not stop her from preaching birth control along the way, in India, in Turkey, and in Greece.

In 1959, when she was eighty-two, she went back to Russia, this time on a conducted tour. She was the perfect traveler, even at her advanced age, who could eat anything and sleep anywhere. When the plane in which the group was traveling was grounded in some small city in the Caucasus because of some mechanical breakdown, she refused to leave the plane to spend the night in a hotel, saying she was "sick of hotels" and "wanted to sleep in the plane." Nothing that the Intourist guide, the airline employees, or the pilot said could move her. And so, being sensible people, not half as rigid or hidebound as one might have thought, and faced with an irresistible force in the shape of an indomitable old lady, they let her stay and she curled up in her seat and slept undisturbed. On another occasion on the trip when the group was traveling by bus, she had looked forward to seeing the pass by which Tamburlaine had crossed the mountains of the Caucasus. The pass was off the route and also out of bounds because of security, but she insisted, and the bus driver finally capitulated and remarked, "How did you know about that!" How indeed! She was a voracious reader of travel books, diaries, memoirs, journals, and chronicles and had no doubt picked up this item of information along the way and stored it for future reference.

The next year, on a trip to Italy and Yugoslavia with my sister Linda, she returned to the Eremo Franciscano, thirty years later. My sister described the hilarious journey on muleback up the rocky mountainside:

One mule was available and the saddle the muleteer used was naturally for goods not bodies. So mother had to mount a pack saddle with its hard straight board sides softened only by a thin blanket. I walked behind the mule hoisting mother to the left or right as I saw her tipping in one direction or the other. Getting on was as hard as staying on and required the mule to be taken to a lower level in the alley so that Mother could jump on rather than climb. The whole manoeuvre was an engineering feat. Once she was there she was fearful of falling and kept calling back to me to save her. A shooting spree in the olive orchard required some loud yelling by me in English and the driver in Italian to insure mother not getting shot from her steed.

We arrived and mother unwound, hardly able to walk and we virtually lifted her into the dark interior of the abbey. One by one the familiar figures of the past came out from their rooms where they had retired. They lit candles under the saints in the niches in the corridors, and brought tea and cheese and olives for us to eat. Finally, out of the dark came a figure large and decrepit braced by two sturdy nuns on each side holding her up. It was the Mother Superior, Sorella Maria. It was the first time she had been out of her room or her bed for months. She and mother sat at the table holding hands, embracing, patting each other as mother accommodated herself to the thoroughly-expressed Italian ways. Meanwhile, the English-speaking sister asked me all about the grandchildren which she seemed to know in name and in deed. I finally asked her how she knew so much. It seems that mother had been corresponding with them for thirty years!

After about an hour during which they urged us to stay, mother said to me, "I've got to go. I can't keep up this excess of emotion much longer." And so we departed, after ardent, if shaky embraces, and with mutual assurances "of their next meeting being in Heaven!"

When she was eighty-nine and planning a trip to Guatemala, she amused one of her daughters in a letter by lively comments on her decrepitude: "I only hope we escape a revolution in Guatemala, for Central America is pretty well stirred up by Castro. I do not want to be captured for ransom. If I am, don't pay it. I'd rather die. 'Old lady with fresh dental plates, useless knees and incurable disease of old age and approaching senility.' Not worth $.30 so refuse to pay!"

A year or two later, when sitting in the car waiting for my sister, who was buying apples in an orchard farm near Franklin, my mother suddenly called out to her, "I'm dying, Linda. We must go home. This is such an undignified place to die!" When my sister exclaimed, "Mother, how do you know you're dying?" she said, "How *can* I know, I've never died before." Not your usual death scene!

She would have liked to have believed in some sort of life after death, I think, for she would have loved to have met my father again, who forever remained the center of her life. But she was a liver of life, and would have found it intellectually impossible to believe in a Heaven or to have any illusions about the finality of death.

She was forever an unreconstructed agnostic, but also a person full of wonder at the mysteries of the universe. She wrote when she was eighty-six years old, "Why do we bother to dress up the commonplace life with second-rate, so-called miracles when the whole universe is so magnificent that all our imaginings are paltry beside its wonders of reality. With Margaret Fuller, I accept the universe, marvelling and admiring as I do so, but not grovelling before its majesty nor worshipping at its triumphs nor humbling myself before a creator whom I create to explain in my terms what is inexplicable. Give me the world and a chance at its experience and I am satisfied. Margaret Fuller accepted the Universe, but there is no word of her enjoying it. It seems that to be part of the universe is the greatest gift given to one. To know something of its mysteries, to know its true and accidental or native miracles, is to have lived, to have felt the full sense of being."

❧

In 1965, she received, with two others, one of the first Founders Awards from Radcliffe College. After listing her accomplishments as a writer, citizen, and as a spokesman and worker for causes that concerned her, the citation summed up: "A woman who knows how to live life to the fullest, enjoying a family which includes twenty grandchildren, neighbors, books, and travel, and is always eager to work in a realistic and courageous way for human welfare, you represent an ideal of womanhood and service that will always endure no matter how customs change."

A few years before her death at the age of ninety-three, she was interviewed by Alice Albright, a reporter for the *Harvard Crimson*, who wrote a charming profile of her: "A captivating little lady with the face of a Leonardo drawing, Mrs. Walter B. Cannon is a very extraordinary person whom Harvard could proudly name its matriarch. She has been attached to the community for 82 years, as daughter of a Harvard alumnus, Radcliffe undergraduate, wife of a medical school professor, mother of three Radcliffe daughters and one Harvard son, grandmother of two Harvard freshmen and one Radcliffe sophomore, and great-grandmother-to-be of a potential Harvard or Radcliffe student."

One can almost hear her pronouncing her final words, no doubt spoken in her brisk, faintly provocative voice, calculated to enliven the closing moments of the interview: "I am a very ordinary person who has been fortunate enough to live a very privileged life!"